D0848397

ISLAM
and
DEMOCRATIZATION
IN ASIA

ISLAM

and

DEMOCRATIZATION IN ASIA

EDITED BY
Shiping Hua

CAMBRIA PRESS

Amherst, New York

Requests for permission should be directed to:
permissions@cambriapress.com, or mailed to:
Cambria Press
20 Northpointe Parkway, Suite 188
Amherst, NY 14228

Library of Congress Cataloging-in-Publication Data

Hua, Shiping, 1956–
    Islam and democratization in Asia / Shiping Hua.
        p. cm.
    Includes bibliographical references and index.
    ISBN 978-1-60497-632-8 (alk. paper)
1. Democratization—Asia. 2. Islam and world politics—Asia. 3. Islam and
culture—Asia. 4. Asia—Politics and government. 5. Asia—Religious life and
customs. 6. Asia—Social conditions. I. Title.

    JQ24.H83 2010
    320.95—dc22

2009038075

TABLE OF CONTENTS

LIST OF FIGURE AND TABLES

ACKNOWLEDGMENTS

Most of the essays in this collection were developed from papers delivered at the workshop, "Islam and Democracy in Asia," held on March 13–14, 2008, at the University of Louisville, Louisville, Kentucky, in the United States of America. As the local host, the Center for Asian Democracy at the University of Louisville provided funds to ensure the success of the workshop. My assistants, Stacey A. Schoen and Christy L. Rhodes, provided valuable support for both the workshop and the book. I am also indebted to the anonymous referees whose most valuable comments were extremely helpful for the successful completion of the book.

ISLAM
and
DEMOCRATIZATION IN ASIA

INTRODUCTION

Shiping Hua

More than a century ago, the French aristocrat Alexis de Tocqueville remarked that Islam was not compatible with democracy and therefore, the conflicts between Islamic nations and the West were inevitable.[1] This viewpoint was certainly not shared by all.[2] The September 11, 2001, terrorist attack on the World Trade Center in New York City intensified the debate. With the rapid economic developments in Asia in recent decades, another important topic of debate has increasingly attracted people's attention: the compatibility of the so-called "Asian values" with democratic ideals.[3] The debate has become even more intense with the combination of Islamic and Asian values vis-à-vis democratization. Asia contains the most populous Islamic country in the world: Indonesia. Is Islam compatible with democratization in the context of Asian cultures?

To address these important issues, a series of books have been published. Most of them deal with the relationship between Islam, Muslims, and democratization within a subregion in Asia, such as Islam and democracy in Central Asia,[4] Islam and Muslims in South Asia,[5] and Islam and democracy in Southeast Asia.[6] Some deal with the same issue with a focus in the future.[7] However, a book that focuses on the relationship between Islam, Muslims, and democratization within the context of Asian cultures from the perspectives of theory and empirical country studies in South, Southeast, and Central Asia does not exist. The current book fills the vacuum.

The Center for Asian Democracy at the University of Louisville hosted the "Islam and Democracy in Asia" workshop in Louisville, Kentucky, the United States, on March 13–14, 2008. The workshop was designed to explore the relationship between Islam and democratization within the context of Asian cultures and institutions. The ten essays included in this volume were selected from over 120 received from scholars all over the world. Presenters at the conference included not only scholars, but also practitioners such as diplomats. Although most presenters were from scholarly institutions in North America and Europe, over half of them have their ethnic origins in Asia. This diverse group of essays also represents a variety of viewpoints: some believe that Islam is compatible with democracy; others have doubts about it. Topics of the papers presented vary. Some are about theories that explore the relationship between Islam and democracy. Others are empirical studies that deal with the subject matter from the regional perspectives of South Asia, Southeast Asia, and Central Asia.

In chapter 1, "Islamic Governance and the Democratic Process," Muqtedar Khan articulates, from an Islamist perspective, what constitutes the modern notion of Islamic governance. He examined Islamic sources for ethical governance guidelines and the notion of an Islamic constitution. He developed a model of Islamic governance and then argued that neither of these can be achieved without a systematic democratization of society and the application of democratic processes in the system of governance. He thus argues that Islam and democracy are not just compatible, but that democracy is an essential and necessary ingredient of Islamic governance.

Khan points out that Islamists have resisted and even rejected this line of argument on the grounds that it privileges modernity and democracy a priori and then evaluates Islam using modernity as a standard. However, when he starts with the Islamist premise, using Islam as the standard measure of the necessity of democratic processes, he also comes to the conclusion that democracy is necessary. He believes that this line of argumentation will have a greater impact on convincing traditional and political Muslims of the need for democratization and also allay their perceived fears that democracy is a threat to Islam.

In chapter 2, "Islam and Democracy: An Examination of Liberal Muslims' Political Culture," Moataz A. Fattah points out that most literature on democratization suggests that the image of democracy has never been more favorable. However, it has been suggested that predominantly Muslim countries are markedly more authoritarian than non-Muslim societies. In other words, while Latin America, Africa, Eastern Europe, and South and East Asia experienced significant gains for democracy and freedom over the last twenty years, the Islamic world experienced an equally significant increase in the number of repressive regimes.

To test this thesis, Fattah examines a set of related questions that tackle the issue of Muslim culture and democracy based largely on survey research. Do the attitudes of ordinary Muslims stand as an obstacle toward the adoption of democracy? Why do Muslims not bark for democracy when the evidence suggests that all the world does? Can people who have been fed a steady diet of authoritarian-government-controlled information and ideas maintain democratic attitudes? It is important to note, however, that since these governments rarely permit the conduct of independent survey research regarding politically "sensitive" issues, no one really knows how successfully they indoctrinate their citizens.

In chapter 3, "Islam and Democracy in Asia: What Can We Learn from the Underdog Strategy?" Laure Paquette argues that whether Muslims are in the minority in a particular country or are in the majority, elements of extremism can be identified. She analyzes these two types of government using the model of underdog thinking. This model is new to the study of Islam and democracy in Asia, but has previously been applied to a wide-ranging series of case studies at the state and international level in East Asia. Founded on the premise that the weak do not think like the strong, and that their use of strategic thinking in political situations is also different, the model provides a method of analysis to understand underdogs, and for underdogs themselves to improve the effectiveness of their actions.

Paquette presents some of the uses of this model for these two types of government, using several examples and a case study. First, she explores the characteristics of underdog thinking and examines examples of Muslim minorities and the Muslim weak state using underdog strategic thinking. Then, she explores how Muslims could be encouraged to participate in democracy. Of key interest here, for example, is whether underdog strategic thinking can be helpful in identifying who are the key actors, the political movers and shakers. In addition, the chapter explores how the strategic thinking of the underdog will guide the behavior of the Muslim minority in a period of democratization, either to improve that minority's political effectiveness, or to help the government predict and manage that minority. Finally, it also explores how the underdog's strategic thinking will guide the behavior of the weak or failed state with a Muslim majority when that state is also in a period of democratization, and how this framework may help greater powers understand and manage the behavior of that state.

The following three chapters deal with Islam and democracy in the context of South Asia. In chapter 4, "Islam and Pakistan," Ambassador Touqir Hussain argues that Islam has provided a legitimate cause for Islamic activism in Pakistan. Since the birth of the nation had a weak national identity, Pakistanis have historically looked for a surrogate identity, and have often found it in religion. After all, the country was created in the name of religion. But religious activism turned on itself as Pakistanis also defined their identity in opposition to India, thus creating an administrative military state and a nexus between the military and the mosque that went on to foster religious extremism. Years of authoritarian rule, degraded rule of law, social injustice, and weak institutional architecture had its own consequence: encouraging the public tendency to resort to extremist solutions. In this somber mood, Islam served as an anchor of stability.

The spectrum of extremism has thus widened with the interplay of religion with a failed social and political order. War on terrorism, global Islamic revival, and tensions with the West expanded the influence of Islam. Many Islamic thinkers are engaged in an intellectual effort to bring Islamic values to the center of the debate in the Islamic world, as a means of renewing their societies that are under siege from Western cultural and political assault. There is thus a new wave of predominantly religion-based revisionism in which religion has become a medium of expression of social discontent, economic dissatisfaction, political activism, and personal unhappiness. The Islamists are riding this wave.

In chapter 5, "Bangladesh: The New Front-Line State in the Struggle between Aspiring Pluralist Democracy and Expanding Political Islam," Ambassador Tariq Karim remarks that Bangladesh, with its more than 147 million people who are hostage to widespread poverty, presents itself as a most interesting case study: a third-world nation struggling to establish, preserve, and consolidate democracy against the grain of a legacy of deep-rooted political schizophrenia that is apparently embedded in its identity and history. The country's bloody birth itself was indelibly framed within the larger contestation that then defined the Cold War paradigm. At its independence in 1971, Bangladesh emerged as a uniquely homogenous nation in South Asia, with its population comprised of 98 percent ethnic Bengalis. Despite 88 percent of its people being Sunni Muslims, it had rejected political Islam as the defining logic for state-foundation and consolidation, and proclaimed secularism along with democracy, nationalism, and social justice as the core pillars of the state.

Bangladesh was considered until recently as a possible role model for developing Muslim nations because of its inherited secular tradition, its democratic aspirations, and inclusive world vision. It has a long history of struggle against authoritarianism for democratic rights, and is a democracy in which voting gives each individual a say in electing leaders of their choice and in governance issues. However, the progressive abdication of the pluralist vision of democracy and good governance by successive political parties elected to government, whose indulgence of a zero-sum politics relentlessly undermined and corrupted the core

institutions upon which any democratic nation must rely, has been concomitant with creeping inroads made by Islamist extremism. Thirty-
seven years after its independence, the nation's political fabric revealed
a deeply divided people, pitting Bengalis against Bengalis, and described
by some hyperbolically as pushing the nation to the perilous edge of
civil war. Only intervention by the army and the installment of an army-
backed government in January 2007, marking a disturbing return of the
military to the political arena after a hiatus of fifteen years, prevented
that scenario from becoming reality.

In chapter 6, "Muslim Experience of Indian Democracy," Omar Khalidi remarks that with Muslims representing fully 12 percent of India's
population, the Indian Muslim population exceeds most Middle Eastern countries' Muslim populations, and is rivaled only by Indonesia
and Pakistan. India is also the world's largest democracy. Despite all its
shortcomings, Indian democracy is sharply contrasted with its absence
in its immediate neighborhoods to the east (Bangladesh, Myanmar) and
the west (Pakistan and beyond). India is also officially a secular country,
again in contrast to the neighboring countries of the Middle East. For all
of the reasons outlined here, a study of the Indian Muslim experience
with democracy is critical to any discussion on Islam and democracy in
Asia and elsewhere.

Khalidi's study explores three interrelated themes. First, it considers
the Indian Muslim elite's perception of the British-style parliamentary
democracy in the nineteenth century, and why they thought it would be
injurious to their interests in a multireligious society in which they are a
minority. Instead, the Indian Muslim elite sought and gained an electoral
system—Separate Electorates—perceived to be in their interests. Second, it examines Indian nationalist (mainly Hindu) critique of the system
of Separate Electorates, and its abolition in the 1950 constitution. Third,
it examines the implications of Muslims' poor numbers in parliament
and state assemblies on power-sharing, as seen through cabinet appointments, allocation of state resources for development, and the protection
of lives and property during the riots and pogroms that are part of contemporary Indian life.

The following two chapters deal with Islam and democracy in the context of Southeast Asia. Chapter 7, "Challenging Democracy? The Role
of Political Islam in Post-Suharto Indonesia," by Felix Heiduk, shares
some insights on the impact Islamists have and the role they play in
a Muslim-majority democracy like post-Suharto Indonesia. With Muslims making up more than 80 percent of its population of more than 200
million people, Indonesia is the biggest Muslim-majority nation in the
world. Since 1998, Indonesia has also made a significant transition to
democracy. Indonesia's transition to democracy has been challenged by
various problems such as a large-scale economic crisis, the pauperiza-
tion of large parts of its population, various legacies of the Suharto-era
like corruption and nepotism, armed separatism, intra-communal conflicts between Muslims and Christians, and Islamist terrorism.

Yet the country stayed on its course toward democracy. A majority
of the population as well as the country's political elite regard the idea
of turning Indonesia into an Islamic state as counterproductive to the
democratization process of the country. Thus, if Indonesia's democratization remains stable and working, the country could become a role
model for the compatibility of Islam and democracy for the Muslim
world. Therefore, insights from Indonesia might help to enhance the promotion of democracy and its policies in other parts of the Muslim world.
Within this framework, the study seeks to analyze the role Islamists have
played and continue to play in the context of Indonesia's democratization process.

In chapter 8, "Islam and Democracy in Malaysia: The Ambiguities of
Islamic(ate) Politics," Naveed S. Sheikh points out that Islam in Malaysia has been used both as a top-down strategy of legitimization by the
state, and a bottom-up strategy of delegitimization by partisans seeking
to challenge, and ultimately capture, state power. Islam has also been
used horizontally, as social capital, to bind together a racial (in)group
vis-à-vis minority (out)groups in the pursuit of distributive privileges. In
addition, Islam has been used as a civic resource for nation and institution
building. Although ubiquitous, the constructs of 'Islam,' 'Islamic,' and
'Muslim' have nonetheless historically been almost infinitely malleable.

Sheikh argues that Islam is bound to remain a permanent, if contested, feature in the Malaysian political landscape for the foreseeable future. The presence of the Islamic discourse alone also bears no predictable correlation with either preference formation or policy choices. Above all, God remains transcendent in Malaysia.

The last two chapters focus on Central Asia. In chapter 9, "Taliban and Al Qaeda Suicide Bombers in Afghanistan: Tracing the Emergence of a Terror Tactic," Brian Williams reports on his field research, completed in the spring of 2007, from when he was hired by a U.S. government agency to travel to Afghanistan and provide a firsthand account of the Taliban's much-touted spring offensive. In this mission, he was asked to focus on the mysterious rise of suicide bombing in the country. His job was to find out who the bombers were, where they were getting their inspiration, and what their overall strategy was.

The results of his intensive fieldwork—which took him from the dangerous Pashtun tribal areas along the Pakistani border through the Hindu Kush mountains of central Afghanistan to Herat on the Iranian border—were most unexpected and have changed the way we view the war in Afghanistan. Most importantly, they have pointed the finger at Iraq, and have shown that the uniquely vicious form of terrorism emanating from the Iraqi theater of operations has radicalized the Taliban insurgency. While the U.S. military is reluctant to admit that the Iraqi terrorism (which has included unprecedented use of beheadings and suicide bombings) has anything more than a demonstrative effect on Afghanistan, his research points to direct ties between Iraqi and Afghan insurgents. This is perhaps the first indicator of what scholars have long feared, the emergence of the "Iraq effect" in other parts of Islamic Eurasia. Through interviews with Afghan National Directorate of Security officials, Afghan National Army, Afghan National Police, Afghan government, Northern Alliance warlords, off-record U.S. military, and Pashtun tribesmen he has collected considerable evidence of Taliban insurgents traveling to the Sunni triangle for terrorism training. Williams also uncovered irrefutable evidence of Iraqis and other Arabs coming from Iraq to Afghanistan to train their Taliban counterparts. Most importantly, his work shows that the Iraqis succeeded in convincing the Pashtun-Taliban, who previously had strong taboos on suicide of any sort, that "martyrdom operations" were sanctioned by Islam.

In chapter 10, "China and Central Asia: Developing Relations and Impact on Democracy," Morris Rossabi argues that since the collapse of the Soviet Union, China has increasingly played a role in the five Central Asian countries, a development that surely will have an influence on both democracy and Islam in the region. Economic relations between China and Central Asia have accelerated over the past decade. China has constructed a pipeline from Kazakhstan to Xinjiang and has built a road to Tajikistan, among other projects that have created links between it and its neighbors. Trade has increased dramatically, and Chinese products are readily found throughout Central Asia.

Rossabi also explores the political ramifications of these developing economic links for both Central Asia and Xinjiang. Will China's economic leverage in the region translate into political leverage? How will China's role in this region affect any attempt to move to more democratic institutions in Central Asia? What will be the impact of China's role in Central Asia in general?

With these insightful essays, it is the aim of this volume to cast some much-needed light on the relationship between Islam and democratization within the context of Asian cultures and institutions.

ENDNOTES

1. Alexis de Tocqueville, *Democracy in America* (New York: Penguin Putnam, 2001).
2. Abdulaziz Sachedina, *The Islamic Roots of Democratic Pluralism* (New York: Oxford University Press, 2001).
3. Samuel P. Huntington, *The Clash of Civilizations and the Remaking of World Order* (New York: Simon & Schuster, 1998).
4. Adeeb Khalid, *Islam after Communism: Religion and Politics in Central Asia* (Berkeley: University of California Press, 2007). Also, Karen Dawisha, Bruce Parrott, eds., *Conflict, Cleavage, and Change in Central Asia and the Caucasus (Democratization and Authoritarianism in Post-Communist Societies)* (New York: Cambridge University Press, 1997).
5. Francis Robinson, *Islam and Muslim History in South Asia* (New York: Oxford University Press, 2004).
6. Laskar Jihad, *Political Islam in Southeast Asia—Moderates, Radicals, and Terrorists* (London: Routledge, 2003); Noorhaidi Hasan, *Islam, Militancy, and the Quest for Identity in Post-New Order Indonesia* (Ithaca, NY: Cornell University Press, 2006); Donald Porter, *Managing Politics and Islam in Indonesia* (London: Routledge Curzon, 2002).
7. John L. Esposito, John Voll, Osman Bakar, eds., *Asian Islam in the 21st Century* (New York: Oxford University Press, 2007).

PART I

THEORIES OF THE RELATIONS BETWEEN ISLAM AND DEMOCRATIZATION

CHAPTER 1

ISLAMIC GOVERNANCE AND DEMOCRACY

M. A. Muqtedar Khan

In 2005 it seemed as if democracy had finally arrived in the Middle East. Iraqis and Afghans had voted in large numbers, providing hope that democratic regimes introduced by the American occupation forces would take root. Elections had returned to Saudi Arabia after nearly four decades. Large pro-democracy rallies in Beirut were raising the vision of an Eastern European–style democratic wave in the Middle East. There were constitutional changes taking place in the Gulf and for a brief historical moment it appeared that the American policy of externally stimulated democratic change might actually work.

But subsequent events have underscored that things are never so simple in the Middle East. Political realities in the region come in multiple layers of complexity. The subsequent retreat of democracy across the Middle East and the reemergence of the trio of authoritarian regimes—Egypt, Jordan, and Saudi Arabia—in the form of "allies of stability" have once again brought the region to a pre–September 11, 2001, political equilibrium where the United States seeks to maintain a temporary stability in collaboration with states in the face of pressing demands for change from the masses.

America's post–September 11 foreign policy had one fundamentally new idea—that democracy was an antidote to terrorism. This idea basically emerged from the reluctant recognition that one reason why terrorism thrived in the Middle East was the proliferation of undemocratic authoritarian regimes that promised much but delivered little on the economic front (Jordan and Egypt, for example) and repressed their masses and obstructed any political reform in the face of insistent demands for change. But now, however, through some really bizarre logic, the U.S. administration has concluded that America's failure in Iraq and the electoral successes of Islamists, especially those of Hamas and Hezbollah, make the democracy-promotion policy highly undesirable. The abandonment of the democracy-promotion policy is illogical since it has succeeded to some extent; both Hamas and Hezbollah have since been busy with the machinations of democracy and have indulged in very little terrorism. Hamas' goal at the moment appears to be "how to get EU aid without recognizing Israel," rather than "what can we do today to destroy the Zionist entity." Nevertheless, Washington curiously prefers an authoritarian Middle East with terrorism, rather than a democratic Middle East with Islamists in power.

The United States government will be making a big mistake by not supporting democracy in the region out of fear that it would lead to Islamization. Democracy clearly has a moderating influence on Islamists. The struggle of Hamas to adjust its agenda from ideological to a more pragmatic one by accepting a power-sharing arrangement with the opposition in order to pursue a larger, less partisan good despite winning it all is a positive sign that Islamists will persist on the democratic pathway. The emergence of an Islamist AKP (Justice and Development Party) in Turkey is another example of how democratic participation moderates Islamism. Second, people's expectations are already rising and they will continue to press for more political reform. If Washington returns to the pro-stability posture and once again aligns openly and firmly with authoritarian regimes as Secretary Rice suggested, then it will find itself not only battling terrorism by jihadists but also pro-democracy activism by Islamists.

GOING BEYOND THE ISLAM AND DEMOCRACY DEBATE

While democracy is globalizing, having already established itself as the most legitimate form of governance, in vogue in most of the world, it continues to face a huge deficit in the Arab world. The democracy deficit in the Muslim world, however, has been mitigated by some stabilizing and some fledgling efforts at democratization in Indonesia, Malaysia, Pakistan, Bangladesh, Turkey, and Iran. Most commentators in the West, especially in the United States, are inclined to dismiss Iran as a totalitarian regime run by clerics, but they ignore the fact that in spite of its many aberrations and limits, the current Iranian system has proven to be quite durable and is indeed more democratic than most regimes in the region, and certainly more than the pro-West, pro-United States Iran under the Shah. Nevertheless, democracy is glaringly absent from most of the Arab world, and with the rise of political Islam and Islamic politics in the region, the compatibility of Islam and democracy has become an important global issue.[1]

There are commentators in the West and in the Muslim world who share common interests in asserting that Islam and democracy are incompatible. Some Western scholars argue that Islam is incompatible with modernity, and in particular democracy, and insist that Muslims must either abandon Islam or reform Islam in order to join the "modern world."[2] Some Muslim scholars and militants reject democracy, arguing that it is contrary to the way of God (the Islamic *shariah*), and in their eagerness to reject Western domination they also reject democracy, falsely believing that democracy is something uniquely Western.[3] Fortunately, these arguments have been soundly rebutted both in theory and in practice. The compatibility of Islam and democracy is not in question anymore. Muslim theorists have systematically demonstrated that

Islam can co-exist with the democratic process, and by highlighting the presence of democracy in several Muslim countries and the presence of Muslims in the West and in other places like India where democracy is well-established, have drawn attention to the fact that Islam and Muslims can thrive in democratic societies.[4]

The challenge is not to argue that Islam and democracy are compatible—that debate is settled, although its conclusions are not widely acknowledged. The challenge for Muslim theorists is to go a step further and show how an Islamic democracy may be conceived and what its constitutive principles and architectural features will be. In this brief chapter, I will seek to approach democracy from within the Islamic context and describe the broad principles of Islamic democracy. In the debate on the compatibility of Islam and democracy, the idea of democracy has often been taken for granted and treated as a stable and uncontested idea; it is Islam that is approached from *outside-in* with a view to interrogate it to ascertain its ability to confirm to democratic principles. In this essay I shall adopt an *inside-out* approach. I will simply articulate what I believe should be the Islamic structure of governance and readers will be able to recognize its fundamentally democratic nature.

THE MYTH OF SECULARISM AND THE NEED FOR THE ISLAMIC STATE

Political theory inspired and influenced by European enlightenment has taken secularism as a necessary and uncontested condition for good governance. Even though this may or may not be empirically true, most Western ideologues assert the secular nature of Western polities while simultaneously taking the virtues of secularism for granted. As a Muslim intellectual living in the West, researching and teaching political theory and political philosophy, I have always marveled at the durability of the idea of secularism. For a civilization that boasts considerable sophistication in most areas, to assume that politics and religion constitute two separate realms or that the two can be separated is uncharacteristically naïve. This belief, not in separation of Church and State, but in the *separability of Church and State*, in my opinion is one of the enduring myths of modernity. This myth rests on the false assumptions of *pure politics* and *pure religion*; neither exists in real life.[5]

All core issues are not only normative in nature but also impinge on individual and collective identities. Neither the conception of the individual self nor the construction of the collective self is free from political or religious considerations. Christianity played a significant role in the collapse of communism in Eastern Europe, and Islamists found a way to come to power in secular fundamentalist Turkey. The place of religious symbols in the public sphere, whether it is *hijaab* (Muslim headscarf) in French public schools or the Ten Commandments in American courts, remains contested primarily because there is no consensus on the exclusion of religion from the public sphere anywhere.

Not only does religion play a role in politics, but politicization of religion is also a common occurrence. The use of the gay marriage issue by Republicans in the 2004 presidential election underscores the continuing political salience of religion in the modern West. I have noticed that often, American politicians try to couch their religious motivations in secular terms while advocating specific policies. A very good example is the unyielding support for Israel and Israel's occupation of the West Bank and Gaza among certain Republican politicians with Christian Evangelical connections. While they support the occupation for biblical reasons, they justify it by arguing that Israel is the "only democracy in the Middle East." I often wonder if their support for Israel would stop if Israel became less democratic, or if it could be shown that millions of people within Israel's borders do not enjoy basic democratic rights.

In the Muslim world, on the contrary, legitimacy comes from Islam and therefore many politicians justify material motivations using Islamic cover. While religious politicians in the West often use secular discourse for legitimacy, Muslim politicians deliberately Islamize mundane issues for the same reason. Religion in the West lacks legitimacy in the public sphere and must therefore be concealed; in the Muslim world, all legitimacy derives from Islam, hence Islam is used as a justification for politics.

There are two reasons why religion and politics are intertwined.[6] The first is the increasing use of complex discourses for the purpose of legitimization. Today all politicians seem to follow the Machiavellian dictum—it is not important to be just, it is important to be *seen to be just*—and therefore politicians and political parties and regimes produce discourses to legitimize their goals and strategies. It is in the production of these discourses that religion either underpins political logic or camouflages politic motivations, depending upon the cultural context.

The second, and perhaps the most important, reason why religion will always play a role in crucial issues is the important role that religion plays in identity formation. All important political issues eventually affect individual and collective identity and in the process trigger religious sentiments. As long as religion plays a role in people's identities, it will play a role in politics. The contemporary European experience of and obsession with secularism is a tiny departure from the course of human history. Moreover, European distaste for religion in politics does not derive from religion *sui generis*, but from its experience with a particular manifestation of religion—the Catholic Church.

On the contrary, Islam for Muslims and for many non-Muslim chroniclers has contributed to the development of pluralism, religious tolerance, and communal harmony. The golden age of *Andalus* and the period of the Mughal Empire in India are two widely cited examples of how Islam is potentially capable of providing the infrastructure for a society where pluralism and tolerance triumph. Even the discourse of the "war on terror" acknowledges that liberal Islam, with its emphasis on enlightenment, peace, and tolerance, is the antidote to the rise of terrorism and sectarian violence in some Muslim societies today.[7]

Thus, concluding that (a) secularism as a necessary condition for good governance is a Eurocentric myth and (b) that Islam has historically demonstrated its capability to underpin social harmony and pluralism, I shall now make the case for the Islamic state. Most contemporary Islamists argue that an Islamic state is necessary to provide Muslims with the mechanism necessary for social engineering and moral and cultural reform. They envision the Islamic state as a political unit that will provide Muslims independence from Western domination and autonomy to practice Islam and institutionalize Islamic norms. For many Muslims, the Islamic state is a vehicle for Muslim self-determination.

I believe that Muslims can approach the issue of defining and creating a virtuous republic either on the basis of universal norms or through a parochial paradigm based on Islamic values. The end product in my mind is the same, since there is not much disparity between universal norms and Islamic values. The difference is in politics. If Muslims use contemporary universal language to seek self-determination and good governance, then their political activism may be received with less hostility from the rest of the world, but may have more difficulty in gaining legitimacy at home. But if they use Islamic language for seeking self-determination and good governance then they will enjoy instant legitimacy at home but will inspire insecurity and even opposition abroad, since non-Muslims worldwide have developed a fear and dislike for Islamist governments primarily because of the world's experience with the Taliban in Afghanistan and the mullahs in Iran and Saudi Arabia.[8]

Muslim theorists of the state argue that the Quranic principle of *Amr bil marouf wa nahy anil munkar*—meaning "command good and forbid evil"—is the Islamic justification for the creation of an ideological state that is geared toward establishing the Islamic *shariah*. This principle is essentially drawn from the Quran:

> Let there arise out of you a band of people inviting to all that is good, enjoining what is right, and forbidding what is wrong [Quran 3:104]

> You are the best of the nations raised up for (the benefit of) humanity; you enjoin what is right and forbid the wrong [Quran 3:110]

> The Believers, men and women, are protectors one of another: they enjoin what is just, and forbid what is evil [Quran 9:71]

And since what is good and what is evil is articulated in the *shariah*, in order for Muslims to invite people to the good and forbid evil, Muslims must "establish the Islamic *shariah*." This is the standard justification for the Islamic state and was essentially articulated by Ibn Taymiyyah.[9] While one can always dispute whether the text of the Quran necessitates the creation of a state, we cannot deny that social norms have become so intertwined with the policies of the modern state today as to make the good and the political inseparable.

The question, then, that becomes paramount for Muslim political theorists concerns the nature and consequences of the Islamic state. Will this state created to institute good and penalize bad become a tyranny of those who claim to know what the *shariah* is, or will it become a collective human endeavor in pursuit of the virtuous republic that will facilitate the good life. I am convinced that Muslim political theorists can design an Islamic system of governance that will encourage good and forbid evil, but will also foster a culture of tolerance and compassion for different and even multiple understandings of what that good might be.

The Key Features of Islamic Governance

The key features of Islamic governance are constitution, consent, consultation, and protection of religious freedom. While these principles need to be explored and articulated in the specific socio-cultural context of different Muslim societies, it is important to understand how they are significant and derived from within Islamic sources.

The Constitution

The compact of Medina that Prophet Muhammad (pbuh) became a party to provides a very important occasion for the development of Islamic political theory. After Prophet Muhammad migrated from Mecca to Medina in 622 CE, he established the first Islamic state. For ten years Prophet Muhammad was not only the leader of the emerging Muslim community in Arabia but also the political head of the state of Medina. As the leader of Medina, Prophet Muhammad exercised jurisdiction over Muslims as well as non-Muslims within the city. The legitimacy of his sovereignty over Medina was based on his status as the Prophet of Islam as well as on the basis of the compact of Medina.

As Prophet of God he had sovereignty over all Muslims by divine decree. But Muhammad did not rule over the non-Muslims of Medina because he was the messenger of Allah. He ruled over them by virtue of the tripartite compact that was signed by the Muhajirun (Muslim immigrants from Mecca), the Ansar (indigenous Muslims of Medina), and the Yahud (Jews). It is interesting to note that Jews were constitutional partners in the making of the first Islamic state.[10]

The compact of Medina provides an excellent historical example of two theoretical constructs—a social contract and a constitution. A social contract, an idea developed by Hobbes, Locke, and Rousseau, is an imaginary agreement between people in the state of nature that leads to the establishment of a community or a state. In the state of nature people are free and are not obliged to follow any rules or laws. They are essentially sovereign individuals. But through the social contract they surrender their individual sovereignty to the collective and create the community or the state.

The second idea that the compact of Medina manifests is that of a constitution. In many ways the constitution is the document that enshrines the conditions of the social contract upon which any society is founded. The compact of Medina clearly served a constitutional function since it was the constitutive document for the first Islamic state. Thus we can argue that the compact of Medina serves the dual function of a social contract and a constitution. Clearly the compact of Medina by itself cannot serve as a modern constitution. It would be quite inadequate since it is a historically specific document and quite limited in its scope. However, it can serve as a guiding principle to be emulated rather than a manual to be duplicated.

In simple terms, the first Islamic state established in Medina was based on a social contract, was constitutional in character, and the ruler ruled with the explicit written consent of all the citizens of the state. Today Muslims worldwide can emulate Prophet Muhammad and draw up their own constitutions, historically and temporally specific to their conditions. Following the precedent of Prophet Muhammad any polity claiming to be an Islamic system of governance must have a constitution that is pluralistic in its character and does not differentiate between people on the basis of their religion or ethnicity. The compact of Medina indeed considered all those who were party to it as people who constituted one nation.[11]

Consent

An important principle of the constitution of Medina was that Prophet Muhammad governed the city-state of Medina by virtue of the consent of its citizens. He was invited to govern and his authority to govern was enshrined in the social contract.[12] The constitution of Medina established the importance of consent and cooperation for governance. According to this compact, Muslims and non-Muslims are equal citizens of the Islamic state, with identical rights and duties. Communities with different religious orientations enjoy religious autonomy. This idea is essentially wider in scope than the modern idea of religious freedom. The constitution of Medina established a pluralistic state—a community of communities. It promised equal security to all and all were equal in the eyes of the law. The principles of equality, consensual governance, and pluralism are beautifully enmeshed in the compact of Medina.

The process of *bayah*, or the pledging of allegiance, was an important institution that sought to formalize the consent of the governed. In those days, when a ruler failed to gain the consent of the ruled through a formal and direct process of pledging of allegiance, the ruler's authority was not fully legitimized.[13] This was an Arab custom that predates Islam but like many Arab customs was incorporated within Islamic traditions. The early Caliphs practiced the process of *bayah* after rudimentary forms of electoral colleges had elected the Caliph, in order to legitimize the authority of the Caliph. One does not need to stretch one's imagination too far to recognize that in polities that have millions rather than hundreds of citizens, the process of nomination followed by elections can serve as a necessary modernization of the process of *bayah*. Replacing *bayah* with ballots makes the process of pledging allegiance simple and universal. Elections therefore are neither a departure from Islamic principles and traditions nor inherently un-Islamic in any form.

The Quran also recognizes the authority of those who have been chosen as leaders and in a sense deputizes these consensual rulers.

> O you who believe! Obey Allah and obey the Messenger and those in authority from among you. (Quran 4:59)
>
> ...and consult them in affairs (of moment). Then, when thou hast taken a decision put thy trust in Allah. (Quran 3:159)
>
> ...those who [conduct] their affairs through [shura baynahum] mutual Consultation. (Quran 42:38)

Many of those who claim that Islam contains democratic principles have singled out the principle of *shura* to illustrate their point.[14] *Shura* is basically a decision-making process—consultative decision making— that is considered either obligatory or desirable by Islamic scholars. Those scholars who choose to emphasize the Quranic verse: "...and consult with them on the matter" (3:159), consider *shura* as obligatory, but those scholars who emphasize the verse wherein "those who conduct their affairs by counsel" (43:38) are praised, consider *shura* as desirable.[15] Remember the first verse directly addressed a particular decision of the Prophet and spoke to him directly, but the second verse is more in the form of a general principle. Perhaps this is the reason why traditional Islamic scholars have never considered consultation as a necessary and legitimizing element of decision making.

Thus we remain in limbo. There is no doubt that *shura* is the Islamic way of making decisions. But is it necessary and obligatory? Will an organization or a government that does not implement a consultative process become illegitimate? We do not have a decisive answer to that issue. One thing is clear, though—more and more Muslim intellectuals are agreeing that consultative and consensual governance is the best way to govern. Jurists, however, remain either conservative or ambivalent on the topic. Many of them depend on non-consultative bodies for their livelihood and even their religious prestige and they are in no hurry to deprive themselves of the privileges that non-consultative governments extend to them. Thus, in a way they are implicated in the delay in public recognition that governments in Muslim societies must consult to retain their legitimacy.

But assuming that *shura* becomes the norm for Islamic institutions, movements, and governments; does that automatically imply that democratization will follow? I am hopeful but skeptical. I do not believe that *shura* and democracy are the same kinds of institutions. It is my sense that *shura* and democracy differ in three basic ways:

1. Unlike *shura*, democracy allows modification of foundational texts. You can amend the constitution but not the Quran or the Sunnah. On the face of it, this does not seem like a problem since Muslims are by definition supposed to accept the primary sources of Islam. In practice, however, one is not dealing with the sources themselves but rather the medieval interpretations of these sources, and *shura* is for all purposes subordinated to the past understanding of Islamic texts.

2. *Shura* remains nonbinding while democratic process and laws are binding and can only be reversed through a democratic process and not by unilateral and oligopolistic processes.

3. The way *shura* is discussed in Islamic discourses, it seems to me that it is something that the leader/ruler initiates and is expected to do. *Shura* is the leader consulting some people; it is not clear whom—scholars, relatives, or the entire adult Ummah. Will women be consulted, too? How about gays and lesbians and non-Muslims? In a democracy, on the other hand, people consult among themselves about who will govern and how. Notice how *shura* is top-down and democracy bottom-up.

Finally, I would like to say that *shura*, like democracy, is a deeply contested notion. It is the successful and just practice and institutionalization of these ideas that counts rather than theoretical finessing. Unfortunately, we do not reflect on these issues seriously. Moreover, we must include more and more Muslims in the process, in order to make this theoretical reflection itself a shuratic process. We must, however, be careful not to use the debate between the similarities and dissimilarities of *shura* and democracy as a surrogate for concluding whether democracy and Islam are compatible. There is more in Islam than *shura* when it comes to reflecting over the nature of good governance and best polities.

CONCLUSION

There is much in Islamic sources and Islamic tradition that is favorable to making democracy the vehicle for delivering the products of Islamic governance, such as social justice, economic welfare, and religious freedoms. There is, however, a need for more rigorous, intimidation-free and widespread discussions and debates within Muslim communities on the need for and nature of good self-governance. The barriers to democracy in the Muslim world are not limited to narrow interpretations of Islam or the fascist tendencies of some of the contemporary Islamic movements. Existing social-political conditions, failure of states, and the negative role of foreign powers have also contributed to an environment that does not encourage democracy. I am convinced that Islam is not a barrier to but a facilitator of democracy, justice, and tolerance in the Muslim world. But for that to happen, Muslims must revisit their sources and re-understand them in the light of contemporary realities and complexities.

ENDNOTES

1. See Noah Feldman, *After Jihad: America and the Struggle for Islamic Democracy* (New York: Farrar, Straus & Giroux, 2003).
2. See for example, Bernard Lewis, "Islam and Liberal Democracy," *Atlantic Monthly* 27.2 (1993), p. 89.
3. See Abdulwahab El-Affendi, "Democracy and its Muslim Critics: An Islamic alternative to Democracy?" In *Islamic Democratic Discourse: Theory, Debates and Philosophical Perspectives*, ed. M. A. Muqtedar Khan (Lanham, MD: Lexington Books, 2006), pp. 227–56.
4. For this line of reasoning, see Mumtaz Ahmad, "Islam and Democracy: The Emerging Consensus," Islamonline.net (May 6, 2002). On the World Wide Web: http://www.islamonline.net/english/Contemporary/2002/05/Article15.shtml. Also see the collection of essays in Khaled Abou El Fadl, Joshua Cohen, and Deborah Chasman, eds., *Islam and the Challenge of Democracy* (Princeton, NJ: Princeton University Press, 2004), and in M. A. Muqtedar Khan, ed., *Islamic Democratic Discourse: Theory, Debates and Philosophical Perspectives* (Lanham, MD: Lexington Books, 2006).
5. I have discussed this phenomenon in greater detail in M. A. Muqtedar Khan, "The Myth of Secularism," in *One Electorate under God? A Dialogue on Religion and American Politics*, eds. E. J. Dionne Jr., Jean Bethke Elshtain, and Kayla M. Drogosz (Washington, DC: Brookings Institution Press, 2004), pp. 134–39.
6. A similar argument is made by D. B. Billings and Shaunna L. Scott, "Religion and Political Legitimation," *Annual Review of Sociology* 20 (1994), pp. 173–202.
7. M. A. Muqtedar Khan, "Radical Islam, Liberal Islam," *Current History* 102:668 (December 2003): 417–421.
8. An excellent classical example of the universal approach is the work of Ibn Khaldun in his *Muqaddima*, and an example of the Islamic approach is in al-Mawardi in his work *Ahkam Alsultaniyah*. In contemporary times, the works of the Iranian philosopher Abdolkarim Soroush are a good example of the universalist approach and the works of the late Maulana Maududi of Pakistan represent the Islamic approach.
9. See M. A. Muqtedar Khan, "The Islamic States," in *Routledge Encyclopedia of Political Science*, eds. M. Hawkesworth and M. Kogan (London: Routledge Press, 2003).

10. For a similar analysis of the Compact of Medina, see Ali Bulac, "The Medina Document," in *Liberal Islam: A Source Book*, ed. Charles Kurzman (New York: Oxford University Press, 1998). For the entire text of the Compact of Medina, see M. H. Haykal, *The Life of Muhammad*, trans. Ismael R. Al Faruqi (Indianapolis: NAIT, 1988), 180–183.

11. See M. H. Haykal, *The Life of Muhammad*, 180.

12. Representatives of the tribes of Medina had already pledged their allegiance to Muhammad and invited him to come and be their leader, in what is referred to by historians as the pledge of *Aqabah*. See A. H. Siddiqui, *The Life of Muhammad* (Des Plaines, IL: Library of Islam, 1991), 117–132.

13. See Khaled Abou El Fadl et al., *Islam and the Challenge of Democracy*, 11.

14. See for example John L. Esposito and John O. Voll, *Islam and Democracy* (New York: Oxford University Press, 1996).

15. For a more comprehensive discussion of this see Muhammad S. El-Awa, *On the Political System of the Islamic State* (Indianapolis: American Trust Publications, 1980), 89–90.

CHAPTER 2

ISLAM AND DEMOCRACY

AN EXAMINATION OF LIBERAL MUSLIMS' POLITICAL CULTURE

Moataz A. Fattah

Most literature on democratization suggests that the image of democracy has never been more favorable. Inglehart, along with others,[1] concludes that "democracy has become virtually the only model with global appeal."[2] However, it has been suggested that predominantly Muslim countries "are markedly more authoritarian than non-Muslim societies, even when one controls for other potentially influential factors."[3]

In other words, while the countries of Latin America, Africa, East Central Europe, and South and East Asia experienced significant gains for democracy and freedom over the last twenty years, the Islamic world experienced an equally significant increase in the number of repressive regimes.[4]

It has been a tradition in the West to attribute this deficit of democracy in the Muslim world to the infertile culture and the lack/weakness of the social agents of democracy.[5]

Interestingly, President George W. Bush, one of the most unpopular names in the Muslim world, has refuted the use of culture as an explanation for the deficit of democracy in the Muslim world:

> Some skeptics of democracy assert that the traditions of Islam are inhospitable to the representative government. This "cultural condescension," as Ronald Reagan termed it, has a long history. After the Japanese surrender in 1945, a so-called Japan expert asserted that democracy in that former empire would "never work." It should be clear to all that Islam—the faith of one-fifth of humanity—is consistent with democratic rule.[6]

This chapter's task is to examine a set of related questions that tackle the issue of Muslim culture and democracy. Foremost among these questions will be: do the attitudes of ordinary Muslims stand as an obstacle toward the adoption of democracy? In other words, following Sherlock Holmes, why do not Muslims bark for democracy when the evidence suggests that the entire world does? Or do they? Can people who have been fed a steady diet of authoritarian-government-controlled information and ideas maintain democratic attitudes? Since these governments rarely permit the conduct of independent survey research regarding politically "sensitive" issues, no one really knows how successfully they indoctrinate their citizens.

RESEARCH DESIGN AND THE SURVEY METHODOLOGY

This chapter uses as a laboratory the attitudes of the educated elite in thirty-three Muslim societies around the globe, including Muslim minorities in four countries, as a means to investigate whether their cultural infrastructure is conducive to democratization. To do so, I use firsthand survey data collected from a probabilistic/cluster written survey of college students and graduates. This data is verified and complemented by a non-probabilistic (network/stratified) Web-based survey of educated

Muslims in general.[7] The data was collected by a group of researchers headed by the author and funded mainly by the Middle East Research Council in Beirut, Lebanon, during the period from March 1, 2002, to August 29, 2002. This survey is a preliminary step to build a barometer of attitudes toward democracy in the Muslim world. The survey will be called hereafter the Muslim Culture Barometer (MCB).

One should be careful when handling the data of this survey. The study population is only a group of Muslims with two specific characteristics. First they are "elite" in the socioeconomic sense of the word. By going to college and/or having access to the Internet (either through owning computers or using them in the workplace, schools, or Internet cafés) one is led to believe that they are definitely educated and non-poor (yet not necessarily rich). Thus, no claim is made about the universality of this study. It reflects the attitudes of this group of people, who can easily be described as the most educated in Muslim countries. As appendix D shows, the literacy rate and college education attainment dramatically varies from society to society. Also, since about twelve of the Muslim societies have been surveyed only through the Web-based version, then the access to the Internet is going to limit our findings in these countries to the middle/upper classes.

Second, the respondents to this survey are also "alert" in two senses. The respondents are attentive to politics and vocal about their concerns regarding the future of their polities. This was clear from the passion one finds in their answers to the open-ended questions and during the focus group discussions that followed the written surveys. Being elite and alert makes them a unique but highly influential segment of the population.[8]

While no pretense is made at representing all Muslims, the non-representation of illiterate Muslims in this study, though it may be a major flaw when trying to predict election results, should barely be seen as an insurmountable defect for two reasons.[9] First, previous empirical research shows that the educated function as mediators of ideas and information to the non-educated. In other words, they are the attentive, influential opinion leaders[10] who lead and influence the non-educated.[11] Second, all government leaders and opposition figures are drawn from that attentive, educated group. In other words, they represent the attentive, influential citizens and future elite.[12] In a different context, they are characterized as the "subset of citizens who are likely to be cognitively engaged in the affairs of politics and therefore likely to exert influence upon them."[13]

In summary, the limitation should be acknowledged that all the findings in this article are restricted to this "alert elite" that have the aforementioned characteristics. Considering the percentages of Muslims who had the chance to gain postsecondary schooling (as provided by the UNESCO) and the average GDP per capita in the sample and as provided by world development reports (as provided by the Human Development Report of the World Bank), one infers that the pooled data speaks for about one-fifth of Muslims, given the fact that all the respondents are older than eighteen and younger than fifty-five (see appendix D).

CONCEPTUALIZATION AND MEASUREMENT

As stated earlier, this article examines the cultural requisites for democracy among Muslim educated elite using their aggregate[14] political attitudes. In other words, it examines the democratizability of Muslim culture and not the prospects of democratization in Muslim polities. Though related, the process of democratization is a function of many other actors and factors and not only of the dominant culture. As will be shown in this chapter, the political cultures of Egyptians, Tunisians, and Moroccans are conducive to democracy yet the dominant elites are very reluctant to adopt the necessary democratic constitutional and political reforms.

To be more specific, the democratizability of political culture in this context means the willingness of Muslims to accept democratic institutions and processes (democratic hardware) and democratic values and norms (democratic software). The MCB survey, World Values Surveys (1995–2008)[15] and Pew's Religion and Politics surveys[16] show that most individuals, including those of the very few Muslims countries that would allow these kinds of surveys, give lip service to democracy. However, most of these surveys do not clearly address the most important issues in Muslim societies, such as the political rights of women, non-Muslims, Muslims from other sects, secularists, and Islamists. In other words, this survey tries to go beyond the attitude toward the word "democracy" to understand the attitudes toward, as Sartori put it, the thing "democracy."[17]

The MCB survey gave Muslims the chance to determine their attitudes toward institutions and processes such as parliaments, political parties, periodic elections, and voting. Hereafter, I will use "democratic hardware" to refer to the attitudes toward these institutions and processes of competition and representation. Likewise, the respondents to the surveys had the chance to express their attitudes toward democratic values and norms such as sociopolitical equality and religious tolerance and trust toward Muslims from other sects, non-Muslims, and women. Hereafter, I will use "democratic software" to indicate this sense of political equality and tolerance. Using the analogy of computer hardware and software reflects the interdependence between the core values and institutions of democracy.[18]

Building a scale to measure the democratic software in the thirty-three Muslim societies surveyed, I used factor analysis (as reproduced in appendix B), which shows that the responses to four questions (among the nine questions that were developed to measure the democratic software) were found to fall into one dimension, forming a reliable and internally consistent measure of support for sociopolitical and religious tolerance (Cronbach's estimate of reliability and internal consistency $\alpha = .763$). As shown in appendix B, the four questions examine the attitude of Muslims toward the political rights of Christians, Jews, other non-Muslim minorities, Muslim minorities, and women. These questions were meant to measure political tolerance and sense of equality. The democratic software dimension was standardized and scaled to 100 points, for ease of interpretation, where higher scores represent the highest level of tolerance, trust, and sense of equality.

Three questions were found to score the highest factor loadings in gauging the democratic hardware with a decent level of reliability and internal consistency (Cronbach's estimate of reliability and internal consistency $\alpha = .875$). After recoding, the scale was standardized to 100 points, for ease of interpretation, where higher scores represent the strongest support for the democratic hardware. Taken together, the hardware and software measurements would help to produce a cultural map of Muslims' aggregate relative attitudes toward democracy as produced in figure 1.

FINDINGS AND ANALYSIS

The first and most obvious finding of this study is that though Muslims belong to the same religion, they are heterogeneous enough to make a grand theory of Islam and democracy overly simplistic. This result is depicted in figure 1, a map of the attitudes of literate Muslims in thirty-three societies of the world.

FIGURE 1. Cultural map of Muslims' attitudes toward democratic hardware and software (Web and written survey data).

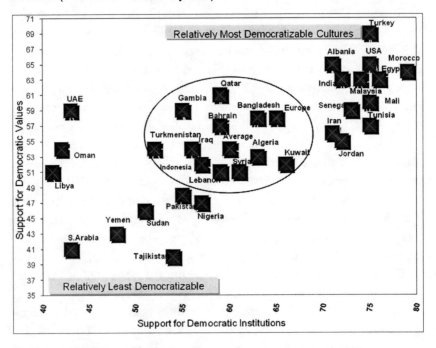

Source. Muslim Culture Barometer 2002.
Note. Countries with representative samples of upper-class, educated Muslims only.

On the horizontal axis, attitudes of Muslims toward democratic institutions and procedures (democratic hardware) are depicted in a 100-point scale. On the vertical axis, a 100-point scale of political tolerance (democratic software) is presented. The pooled sample indicates a significant diversity of opinions.

From Muslims of Turkey, Morocco, and Egypt on the upper right corner to those in Saudi Arabia, Yemen, and Libya, the idea that Muslims have one unique vision regarding democracy is not supported. The first observation regarding the map is that if one judges by the crude number of sampled societies that have 50 points or more in terms of support for democratic hardware and software (countries above the horizontal line and to the right of the vertical dotted line), one can infer that most Muslim societies do not prefer autocracy over democracy. This finding, in general, is consistent with Norris and Inglehart's findings.[19]

The second most obvious finding is that the Muslim societies fall into four broad categories as demonstrated in table 1.

TABLE 1. Categorization of Muslim cultures.

		Democratic Hardware		
		Low	Moderate	High
	Low	Nigeria	Algeria	Albania
		Pakistan	Bahrain	Egypt
		Saudi Arabia	Bangladesh	India
		Sudan	Europe	Iran
		Tajikistan	Gambia	Jordan
		Yemen	Indonesia	Malaysia
			Kuwait	Mali
Democratic Software			Lebanon	Mali
			Qatar	Morocco
			Syria	Senegal
			Turkmenistan	Tunisia
				USA
	High	Libya		
		Oman		
		UAE		

Each one of these categories will be discussed in more detail.

A. High Software and Low Hardware Category

The first category of Muslim culture is best exemplified by the UAE, Oman, and Libya. In terms of sociopolitical tolerance and equality (democratic software), Libya, Oman, and the UAE score 51, 54, and 59 points respectively, but with relatively low support for democratic institutions, around 41–43 points. Based on the interviews with Libyans, the real discriminatory attitudes of Libyans is not toward their fellow Libyans but toward non-Libyans such as the half million Africans (around 10% of the population) who live and work there. A similar observation can be made about the relatively low political status of women in the minds of Libyan men. However, literate Libyan females are reported to be less parochial. Thus, they enjoy a higher level of self-esteem and sense of political efficacy compared to a decade ago.[20] About 64 percent of literate Libyan women think that women should be equally enfranchised and that they have the capacity to assume top executive positions. This result is almost identical to another survey conducted in Libya in which 63 percent of Libyan women thought that they could hold positions that may involve authority over men.[21] However, tribal traditions as a source of the low status of women in the minds of men, even if literate, are a factor that cannot be overlooked in understanding the Libyan political culture.[22] Literate Emirati women are even more self-confident, with around 73 percent of them defending their rights as political actors, including 25 percent accepting that women should hold top executive positions. Unlike Libyan men, the majority of the UAE literate men (around 60%) accept that women should participate in politics as legislative representatives, although only 7 percent give them the right to hold top executive positions.

Women in Oman are both self-perceived and perceived by men in general to be of relatively higher status compared to their peers in Libya and the UAE. In the pooled sample, around 33 percent of Omanis (men and women) would agree to give women top legislative and executive positions; however, this percentage goes down to 26 percent in the case of Libya and 10 percent in the case of the UAE.

The three countries' poor support for democratic institutions deserves some scrutiny, too. The three countries together can be held as exemplars of semi-rentier states where "no taxation, no representation" seems to work fine.[23] Libyans, for one, despite their relatively moderate level of sociopolitical tolerance, display a very low level of support for democratic institutions. This discrepancy can be understood by the bizarre system of government that al-Qaddhaffi of Libya has established.[24] In the survey conducted in the course of this research, when Libyans were asked about how satisfied they are with the performance of the system, only 20 percent showed a notable level of satisfaction. The rest were either unsatisfied or not sure. Muslims of the UAE and Oman are stronger advocates of their incumbents in both the written survey (in the case of the UAE) and the Web-based surveys, albeit at the expense of their support for democratic institutions. Around 80 percent of Emiratis show satisfaction with their political system while around 52 percent of Omanis have the same attitude. These two scores are the highest in the whole sample. Among all the interviewees in the UAE, there was not one single supporter of copying Western democratic institutions in the country. According to Sa'eed, one of the interviewees in the UAE, who lived in Britain for two years, "democracy is a good system of government that we do not need in the UAE." Analogously, it is a solution to a problem or a medicine to a disease from which they do not suffer. In summary, the three countries represent comparatively high levels of sociopolitical and religious tolerance (democratic software), with relatively low level of support for the procedures and institutions of political participation and competition (democratic hardware). This characterization makes these countries the closest to stable non-democracies.

The classification of the rest of the thirty cases into three categories reveals fewer discrepancies and more symmetry between support for democratic hardware and software.

B. Low Hardware and Low Software Category
Saudi Arabia, Yemen, Tajikistan, the Sudan (and possibly Pakistan and Nigeria) form what can be labeled the relatively least democratizable

cultures, given the attitudes of their citizens toward democratic institutions of participation and competition and sociopolitical tolerance and trust. These countries occupy the lower left corner of figure 1, which puts them in the same category, albeit for different reasons. Saudis' feeble support of democratic institutions can be understood by the legacy of this kingdom that has never experienced publicly elected government of any sort since its modern inception in 1932 (or even possibly since the early years of Islam, 1,400 years ago). Besides, Saudi officials rarely if ever use, abuse, or misuse the word *democracy* or any of its connotations in any of their public speeches or allow it to sneak into public school curricula. Additionally, opposition in Saudi Arabia has always been seen to be equal to dissent; and having political parties leads to *fitnah* (internal divisions).[25] Around 74 percent of the Saudi respondents to the survey strongly disagreed with the compatibility of democratic institutions and procedures such as political parties, parliament, and elections with Islamic *sharia* (Islamic legislation) as they understand it. Even though Saudi Arabia has a fully-appointed Shura Council, Saudis do not think that it is of any use because of its powerlessness. Ordinary Saudis, according to a Saudi engineer, call this council "manshaffa," which means towel. When the royal family wants to make unpopular decisions, it sends them to the council just to give them a flavor of legitimacy. In other words, if the council is fully appointed by the king, then he is its constituency. A Saudi journalist who received a degree in journalism from the United States said:

> It is highly destabilizing to allow political parties in the [Saudi] Kingdom. Tribal and familial cleavages will spontaneously convert into party competition and political campaigns with a lot of agony and prejudice. In a country that is named after one family, other unsatisfied families are not going to be controllable.

As for sociopolitical tolerance and a sense of equality, women's position and the negative image that Shiites have in their minds of Sunnis, and vice versa, do not facilitate treating all Saudis as morally and politically equal regardless of belief, gender, and religion. Around 40 percent of the

Saudi respondents believe that women should not be enfranchised and 34 percent prefer to limit their participation to voting if Saudi Arabia adopts some type of elections. A Saudi businesswoman blames ordinary Saudis for not being open-minded, not because the government prevents them from interacting (learning) with non-Saudis, but because "this is the nature of the Saudi people who are not ready for learning or interacting with others. Saudis are peculiar people [in this regard]."[26]

Women in Saudi Arabia are not considered full citizens in the legal, social, and financial senses because of their "inferiority to men rationally and psychologically. That is why a woman is always in need of man's custody."[27] The pooled data shows that around 35 percent of literate Saudi women would not think of themselves as political actors at any level and 33 percent would limit this participation to voting, without being able to represent themselves in elected councils or assuming executive positions. Considering that the data depicts only the attitudes of literate Muslims, this result raises questions about the type of education they get. The answer comes from a Saudi intellectual and political scientist who states that most of the Islamic values that students get in Saudi Arabia come from *salafi* (traditionalist) teachers who do not train their students in critical thinking, but rather in memorizing and blindly believing in sayings that would not serve pluralism, tolerance, or relative thinking.[28] What is worse is that they are socialized to believe that the authentic and (only) true Islam is the (traditionalist) Islam of Saudi Arabia. This notion means that other Muslim (let alone non-Muslim) societies are corrupt and thus should be avoided rather than studied and examined. With around 50 percent of Saudis currently under the age of eighteen and thus still being influenced by what they learn in school, the forces of reform in Saudi Arabia should speed up the process of reviewing this educational material.

Given the peculiarity of Saudi Arabia as a country without non-Muslim citizens, it is meaningless to expect political tolerance toward non-Muslims. However, the attitudes toward the remaining non-Muslims in Arabia (not necessarily within the boundaries of Saudi Arabia) and Shiites are clear from the Islamic rhetoric adopted by some sheikhs (religious scholars) who fully reject Shiites since they are people of *bed'a* (man-made innovation) who curse the first great caliphs of Islam and attack the mother of the believers, 'Aisha, as a Saudi scholar put it. In a sermon given by Sheikh Abdulrahman al-Hozzeffi under the title, "Wipe out the Jews, Christians and Shiite from Arabia,"[29] one finds complete support for this type of intolerance.

Though Yemenis, Sudanese, and Tajiks show remarkable religious tolerance toward non-Muslims (especially Christians and Jews) in terms of their rights to build their houses of worship (over 75% agree or strongly agree), this tolerance fades away when it comes to the issue of political rights. Only 4 to 7 percent of the Yemenis, 2 to 12 percent of Sudanese, and 7 to 11 percent of Tajiks agree to give non-Muslims or Muslims from other sects the right to fully participate in elections, assuming top legislative and executive responsibilities.

The misuse of democratic techniques and procedures to create phony images of legitimate rule has caused a lot of harm to the perception of democracy in the minds of the Muslims of Yemen, the Sudan, and Tajikistan. Four Sudanese students, whom I interviewed in Khartoum and Um Durman, the Sudan, differentiated between a "democracy," referring to their own country's system of government, and real democracies. The pooled data show that Yemen's excessive tribalism, despite the claims that it is weakening,[30] and highly conservative attitudes toward women and Muslims from other sects are responsible for the weak support for democratic software. Sudanese and Tajikistani civil wars may help explain the relatively low level of sociopolitical tolerance.

However, the puzzle remains in the feeble level of support for democratic institutions. Unfortunately, the confusion between real and phony meanings of public elections and elected bodies in most of these countries accounts for the lack of respect for democratic procedures and institutions. Only 10 percent of the Sudanese and 12 percent of the Tajiks think that elections and referenda, respectively, are free and fair. Sudanese interviewees were very critical of the phenomenon of putting all major opposition figures in jail or in exile and holding free elections afterwards; a phenomenon that is very common in most Muslim countries.

The civil war, along with the four abrupt military coups, and the tension among the political and intellectual elites drove down the hope of real democratization in the Sudan. The Sudanese people chose to punish the government by boycotting both legislative and presidential elections, which ended up with empty ballot boxes in most of the counties; yet still the "elected" president Omar al-Bashir claimed landslide victory in the 2000 elections, which encouraged the ruling party to propose a change to the constitution allowing the president to be reelected an unlimited number of times to guarantee the stability of the country.[31]

Pakistanis and Nigerians have a problematic position in the cultural map of Muslims' attitudes toward democracy. Given their support for democratic institutions and procedures (democratic hardware), they do not belong to the same category as Saudi Arabia, Yemen, and the UAE. Yet given their relatively weak level of tolerance, it is easy to include them with the previous cases. For further explication, as figure 1 shows, they have relatively moderate support for democratic institutions and procedures (around 55 points), which is relatively higher than all previous cultures and as good as Indonesia and the Gambia. Conversely, the two cultures do not show equivalent levels of sociopolitical tolerance. By examining the individual responses of the two cultures, it is clear that there is a lack of trust among the Nigerian and Pakistani Muslims and non-Muslims in their respective countries. Furthermore, Pakistani Sunni, Shiite, and Ahmadi do not hide their negative attitudes toward each other, with 73 percent of them refusing intersectarian marriages among themselves. Yet, as expected with most minorities, the Shiite and Ahmadi minorities tend to have more tolerant attitudes toward the Sunni majority. The data suggests that the tension among different Pakistani ethnic groups such as the Punjabi, the Sindhi, and the Pashtun, among others, seems to be of secondary importance or has no significance unless concurrent with religious cleavages among different sects of Muslims and non-Muslims (Sunni 77%, Shiite and Ahmadi 20%, Christian, Hindu, and others 3%). This result actually confirms other readings of the unstable social fabric of Pakistan.[32] Similarly, in Nigeria, the overlapping religious and ethnic cleavages can explain the lack of sociopolitical tolerance.[33] Though around 75 percent of Nigerians agree or strongly agree to the right of Christians and Jews to build their own houses of worship (a right that was actually given to the people of the book by Islam), percent of the respondents believe that Christians and Jews should be disenfranchised and 32 percent think that their participation should be limited to voting and nothing more.

This finding suggests that Nigeria's public culture among Muslims (50% of the population) poses a problem not only to the country's prospects of a sustainable democracy, but more fundamentally to the unity of the country in general. Though the survey did not capture the specifics of the possible ethnic hostilities in Nigeria, a quick look at Nigeria's electoral disputes that were coupled with ethnic violence and military coups from the 1960s on reveals the problems of nation building that the country has to face.[34]

Women in Pakistan are not seen as necessarily politically incompetent or unequal to men, particularly when compared to the previous cases. In Pakistan, almost 68 percent of the respondents have no problem with women's participation in politics as ministers (33%) or members of parliament (35%), let alone voting. However, according to the Pew survey, only 52 percent of Pakistanis think that women should decide for themselves on the issue of veiling.[35] This result does not contradict with the previous finding about women's participation in politics since the *hijab* (head scarf) for both traditionalist and modernist Islamists is considered part of *sharia* rather than a personal preference. (Actually, to have this large of a percentage of Pakistanis giving women the right to decide on this issue is quite surprising.) In summary, the deficit in Pakistan's democratic software can be attributed mainly to non-gender, religious issues.

Unlike Pakistan, the gender gap is a real problem in Nigeria, with around 17 percent of the respondents refusing to participate in politics in general and 57 percent limiting women's participation to voting, with only 2 percent trusting women to hold top executive positions such as minister. Once again, Pew's survey confirms this attitude toward women from a different perspective by showing that 53 percent of Nigerians (the highest among the surveyed Muslim countries in their sample) clearly disagree with allowing women to decide on veiling.[36]

Regarding the attitudes toward democratic hardware, the negative experiences of military interventions and high levels of corruption and manipulation of elections in both countries have impacted the attitudes of ordinary Muslims toward the visibility of elections and democratic procedures.[37] Only 20 percent of the pooled respondents from Nigeria and Pakistan showed some satisfaction with the performance of political parties and elected officials. A fifty-seven-year-old Pakistani respondent commented on the Web-based version of the survey by saying:

> The survey overlooked the role of the military...I never voted for a government without being overthrown by a coup...There is no need for elections if the officers see themselves [as] better politicians.

A Nigerian respondent described elections as "an arena for bribery and corruption" that makes it absolutely undemocratic and un-Islamic. Another Nigerian and four Pakistani respondents made similar comments. This criticism of democratic institutions is very common in both countries. Moreover, around 70 percent of the respondents in both countries chose "not sure" regarding whether democratic institutions such as parliaments and elections are against Islamic *sharia*.

The Sudan, Pakistan, Yemen, and Nigeria in particular are examples of countries that have periodic elections that in and of themselves are causing more problems to both the democratic hardware and software. These fraudulent and risk-free elections make individuals increasingly less trustful of their value, which deeply harms the democratic hardware in the minds of the public. In addition, in deeply divided societies the easiest way for political competitors to win votes is by appealing to ethnic, tribal, and religious constituencies, which is very destructive of the social fabric of society and thus worsens the public attitudes toward democratic software.

Based on this reading of the political cultures in these countries, one can partially explain why these countries have not seen mass-initiated or mass-supported democratic transitions. In three of the seven cases where elections are common, the turnout in most of the elections was around 35 to 41 percent in the last legislative and presidential elections according to the usually exaggerated official sources.[38] This reading of these cultures indicates that unless major cultural shifts occur, any elite-led democratic transitions, if they happen at all, will need to address the issue of intolerance toward women (as in Saudi Arabia, Yemen, Nigeria, and Libya), other sects of Muslims (Saudi Arabia, Yemen, Pakistan, and the UAE), and non-Muslims (Pakistan, Nigeria, and Yemen). Holding other non-cultural factors constant, one may anticipate that even if the ruling elite decide to administer a genuine democratic transition, or if international pressures try to tilt these countries into democracy, most likely they will find themselves forced to adopt one of two strategies:

1.   To adopt, at least for the short-run, some form of exclusionary democracy (i.e., excluding given sects of society)—analogous to most Western democracies that disenfranchised women or other minorities for quite some time—until there is a higher level of support for the normative aspects of democracy (such as senses of equality and trust) among those who are already enfranchised.

2.   To adopt the quota system by allocating a certain number of seats to women and other minorities. It is highly possible that these seats can be less than the actual ratio of women and other minorities for the total population to appease the illiberal majority in the short run.

These two strategies may help countries shirk the possibility of unsuccessful transitions that may lead to domestic tension (e.g., civil war), if it is not already there.

These strategies assume that well-crafted democratic hardware can coexist with poor democratic software. The support for this assumption comes from some established democracies that have managed to survive even with relatively low levels of democratic software. Israel is a case in point. According to a survey conducted by the Israel Democracy

Institute, 57 percent of the Jewish citizens of Israel support forcing the Arab citizens of Israel (their de jure fellow citizens) to depart Israel, while 53 percent of them object to giving Arabs full citizenship rights. Additionally, 77 percent believe that Arabs should not take part in any "vital decisions."[39] Taking these indicators together, one would put Israelis' support for democratic software, as operationalized in this project, not far from the Sudan and Tajikistan.

Building upon the experience of Israel, a good policy recommendation for democracy builders in the preceding Muslim countries is to proceed with cautious and gradual democratic hardware reforms without upsetting the fragile social fabric of society due to low levels of tolerance, sense of equality, and trust.

C. Moderate Software and Moderate Hardware Category

The prospects for democratization increase the more one moves rightward in figure 1, since the support for democratic hardware increases. The circle in the middle of figure 1 denotes cultures that are less resistant to sociopolitical differences and more accommodating of democratic institutions and procedures. These cultures include eleven groups of Muslims (including the ninety-one Iraqis who responded from Arab countries) and, most notably, two minorities: Lebanese Muslims and Muslims of European countries. Turkmenistan is in a problematic position mainly because of the low level of support there for democratic institutions and procedures. Except for Iraq, all Muslims of these countries were exposed to the initial steps of democratic transition (such as the Gambia, Indonesia, and Bangladesh) or at least some liberalization process (such as Kuwait, Qatar, Bahrain, and Turkmenistan) in the past twenty years. Unlike cultures of the first group that are relatively less supportive of democracy either on institutional/procedural or sociopolitical tolerance/trust bases, Muslims of the middle circle of cultures seem to be more ready to enter the democratic era, as long as it is not fictitious or part of a self-survival mechanism on the regimes' part.

Most of these cases, with the exception of Muslims in the European Union countries, are products of the third wave of democratization and they are embodiments of Huntington's saying, "A general tendency seems to exist for third-wave democracies to become other than fully democratic."[40] All these cultures currently have some sort of public elections. Some of them are new to elections, such as Qatar and Bahrain, while others, such as Syria and Iraq, have never witnessed competitive multiparty elections. A third group has had bloody experiences with elections, including Lebanon and Algeria. Kuwait stands alone as the country that fully disenfranchises women, which makes it the opposite of Indonesia and Bangladesh, with their female heads of governments.

The Gambia is constitutionally a presidential republic, yet despite democratic institutions there is no fair chance for the opposition to check and balance the government. Turkmenistan is a country under dictatorial rule with the lowest support for democratic hardware in this group of countries (53 points). With the exception of Muslims of Turkmenistan and of Europe, approximately 40 to 46 percent of the Muslims of other countries in this group characterize their current political system as exactly in the middle between fully free and a full dictatorship, which reflects their tendency to see the pros and the cons of the status quo and to compare it with what real democracy looks like. An Algerian professor of sociology commented on this, saying that

> most of the people in these countries, with the exception of Iraq, Syria and Turkmenistan, can opine and talk freely yet they are not politically effective. They are like one-eyed men. They cannot say that they cannot see but they cannot say they see well like normal people either.

Surprisingly, the data suggests that Qatar has the highest level of support for democratic software in this group of cultures (around 62 points). Actually Qatar, along with Bahrain, is often quoted as a good example of modernizing liberal elites that are ahead of their own people. The semi-city-state of Qatar has made the best use of its coherent social fabric and small population by putting the locus of attention on women's issues since the assumption of the government of Hamad Bin Khalifa al-Thani in 1995. The number of Qatari women joining universities is higher than Qatari men with full political rights.[41] Around 49 percent of Qatari respondents, the highest ratio in all gulf states, think that Qatari women can be voted in to the parliament and assume ministerial positions. This finding on its own merit is a possible answer to a question raised in the *New Yorker* in 2002. Under the title of "Democracy by Decree," the reporter asked: "Can one man propel a country in the future?"[42] The answer seems to be yes. Though there is no data available about the Qataris' attitudes toward democratic aspects before 1995, Qatar's political culture puts it in the highest rank compared to all other gulf states in terms of its support for democratic software, and second to Kuwait in terms of support for democratic hardware.

Kuwait, on the other hand, lacks support for women's enfranchisement, with around 45 percent refusing to support women's right to participate in politics at all. Lebanon, Indonesia, and Syria's relatively clear deficit in software is hardly attributable to the public's attitude toward women. Only 5 percent in Indonesia, 7 percent in Lebanon, and 13 percent in Syria think that women should not be entitled to vote in public elections. In a clear sign of respect for women, the Pew project showed that 86 percent of Muslims in Indonesia and 90 percent of Muslims in Lebanon endorse women's right to decide on wearing *hijab*; an attitude that, generally speaking, can be described as modernist or liberal. However, in the three countries there is a high level of intolerance and lack of trust toward non-Muslims and toward different sects of Islam (especially in Lebanon). The effect of the Lebanese civil war on Muslims' low level of tolerance toward Lebanese non-Muslims is clear, but it is still high compared to other countries that experienced similar tragedies such as Tajikistan, Nigeria, and Pakistan. Moderately less tolerant than Indonesians, 33 percent of the Muslims of Lebanon who responded to the survey consider it right to disenfranchise all non-Muslims, and only 5 percent favor the right of non-Muslims to assume top executive offices such as ministers. The shadows of the civil war are still around in Lebanon even during basketball games, where one hears slogans of racial and religious bigotry. In a recent basketball game, the fans of al-Riady (the "Sportive"), mostly Muslims, shouted "Syria...Syria" in reference to their support of the Syrian army that empowers Lebanese Muslims. In response, the fans of al-Hikma (the "Wisdom"), mainly Christians, shouted "USA" and "Hakim…Hakim" in reference to the Christian leader of the so-called Lebanese forces who was famous for killing his Muslim opponents during the civil war.[43]

Not taking other factors into account, mass-led democratic transition is a possibility in these countries that occupy the middle circle of figure 1; yet it is not highly likely given the moderate level of support for democratic hardware. This does not mean that there are no political demands for economic or social reasons. But these demands are most likely to fall short of demands for real democratic transition.

However, elite-led democratic transition would not meet much resistance at the mass level, provided that appropriate institutional design strategies are followed since the level of tolerance is not that high, either.[44] The case of Iraq is significant in this regard. The ninety-one Iraqis (mostly living in other Arab countries) who responded to this survey showed a relatively acceptable level of tolerance and trust toward each other (53 points), which is actually higher than Indonesia, Syria, Algeria, Lebanon, and Kuwait. There is nothing in the current data that shows Iraqis to be exceptionally antidemocratic. However, as mentioned earlier, the countries in the middle circle do not have the level of tolerance that would make a quick resort to elections a smart move. Besides, it indicates that the U.S. effort to democratize the Middle East could have started by putting pressures on other countries that have more democratic software and hardware than Iraq such as Egypt, Morocco, and Tunisia. An Iraqi liberal warned against early elections in Iraq: "Iraqis have to move toward democracy cautiously and gradually…Though, the odds of a democratic Iraq are high, democracy needs training."[45]

The circle in the middle contains the average of all Muslims as well. The average Muslim, regardless of his/her respective country, is relatively but not highly tolerant toward women, non-Muslims, and Muslims of other sects, with a score of 54 points. In other words, average Muslims are not as necessarily and inherently intolerant as the stereotype suggests. An average Muslim scores around 60 points of support for democratic institutions and procedures as long as they are real and genuine.

D. High Hardware and High Software Category

The symmetry between support for democratic hardware and software continues with the group of cases in the upper right corner of the graph labeled as the relatively most democratizable cultures. These countries are relatively the most democratizable given their high level of tolerance and trust and support for democratic institutions and procedures.

That is why when it comes to explaining why some of these countries have not already achieved stable democracies, the data suggest that one should search for non-cultural explanations. For instance, Moroccans have the highest level of support for democratic institutions and a relatively high level of tolerance, yet it is not a constitutional monarchy following the Westminster model. The monarch still plays a crucial rule that makes the political parties, in effect, administrative parties.[46] This finding actually can be explained by the fact that the independence was achieved mainly by the efforts of the al-Istiqlal/Independence Party founded in 1944 and through a lot of negotiations and coalitions inside an elected parliament. In addition, in a rare exception in Muslim countries, starting from 1962 the Moroccan constitution emphasized a representative government, elected parliament, and multiparty system under a strong monarchy. One can argue that the lack of a stable democratic system in Morocco cannot be attributed to the individuals' attitudes, as the pooled data suggest, but to the role played by the king.[47]

Turkey, on the other hand, has the highest level of sociopolitical tolerance in terms of culture and very high support for democratic institutions. However, military interventions to protect and safeguard the secular system along with a somewhat illiberal constitution pose a great obstacle toward full democratization. Based upon both the survey data and interviews, Turkey has a publicly tolerant culture that does not reflect on the practices of its government, especially of its military arm. One should recall that the public already voted a woman with *hijab* into the parliament. It was the secular government, induced and supported by the military, that disqualified her, not the Turkish people.[48] Even the Kurdish issue does not seem to be the battle of Turkish citizens but of the military inducing successive governments since 1924.[49]

Muslims in the United States seem to be more supportive of democracy than any other Muslim minority, even when compared to India and Europe (and definitely Lebanon). For instance, 57 percent of American Muslims believe that women should be given all political rights without reservations. This ratio goes down to 51 percent in the case of EU Muslims and 41 percent in the case of Indian Muslims.

With the exception of Iran, almost all other societies in this group have (semi-) secularist constitutions and governmental platforms. This finding supports the arguments made by some secularists that secularism, once introduced to Muslim societies, will increase the level of tolerance and peaceful coexistence among religions and sects.[50] Additional support for this claim is the position of Iran in figure 1 in terms of its democratic software. Only Jordan scores below Iran in this group of countries. Surveyed Iranians score around 55 points on the scale of democratic software, not because Iranians are intolerant, but because "they do not go in terms of their tolerance to the level of infringing upon the roots of their religion" as an anonymous Iranian reformist lawyer commented. This analysis finds support in the pooled data. In the questions regarding the political rights of Christians, Jews, and other non-Muslims; women; and Muslims from other sects the mode was to allow all of them only to vote and to become members of the parliament. Yet the second most supported option was to give them full political rights including becoming top executives, which suggests that Iranians in general are tolerant, but cautious.

The relative deficit in Jordan's democratic software is attributed mainly to the clear polar skewing regarding the political rights of women, where 33 percent of the respondents refuse to give women any political rights and 42 percent want to give women full political rights. Another factor that seems to be responsible for the relative deficit of democratic software in Jordan is the attitude toward Muslims from different sects and tribes, with 55 percent of the respondents refusing to give others any political rights. As one of the respondents commented, this may be because of the fear of the effect of tribalism and sectarianism on the unity of the country rather than because of prejudice or bigotry.

Toward an Aggregate Explanation

In the previous section, it has been demonstrated that Muslim societies are not uniform or invariant regarding democratic software and hardware. The immediate question is how Muslims in each of these societies relate their attitudes toward democratic software and hardware to Islam. Direct questions were asked and the responses allowed for an aggregate and systematic classification of Muslims' schemas of thought.

Based upon the responses of Muslims to the MCB survey, four criteria were found to distinguish the respondents' attitudes toward democracy. These attitudes toward democracy are highly related to their reading of what Islam says about the legitimate form of government. These four criteria classified Muslims into four groups as stated in table 2. Question 2.8[51] in the survey is a very straightforward and reliable criterion to determine a respondent's position as a secularist or Islamist since it directly asks respondents to (strongly) agree or (strongly) disagree to the famous statement of Islamic groups that Islam is *deen wa dawla* (religion and state. Those who chose "Not sure" are excluded from the

TABLE 2. Classification of respondents' attitudes toward democracy.

	Islam as a source of political doctrine (Q. 2.8)	Are Islam and elected polity compatible? (Q. 2.7)	Associating democracy with negatives? (Q. 2.4)	Definition of democracy (open-ended) (Q. 2.28)
1. Traditionalist Islamists	(Strongly) Agree	(Strongly) Disagree	(Strongly) Agree	(Very) Negative
2. Autocratic Secularists	(Strongly) Disagree	Not Applicable	(Strongly) Agree	(Very) Negative
3. Modernist Islamists	(Strongly) Agree	(Strongly) Agree	(Strongly) Disagree	(Very) Positive
4. Liberal Secularists	(Strongly) Disagree	Not Applicable	(Strongly) Disagree	(Very) Positive

Source. Muslim Culture Barometer, 2002.

classification. However, since the attitude toward democracy specifically is much more delicate, the three other questions (2.4, 2.7, and 2.28) were used to differentiate between modernists (who argue for the compatibility of Islam and democracy) and traditionalists (who argue the opposite) among Islamists and between liberals (who advocate democracy) and autocrats (who advocate autocracy) among secularists.

The traditionalist Islamists have been identified in the survey as those who consistently refuse the values and institutions of democracy since they are believed to be un-Islamic. The best exemplification of this mentality is Ali Belhaj (a leader of Algeria's Islamic Salvation Front, which almost won the 1988 elections), who said: "[W]hen we are in power, there will be no more elections because God will be ruling." Hadi Hawang of Partai Islam Sel-Malaysia (PAS) echoed the same mentality, saying: "I am not interested in democracy. Islam is not democracy, Islam is Islam."[52]

Traditionalist Islamists have been identified by their opinions on:

(1)   Islam as state and religion;
(2)   their negative definition of democracy (an open-ended question); and
(3)   their belief that Islam and publicly elected and accountable government are incompatible.

Modernist Islamists, unlike traditionalists, have been identified as those who consistently accept both the values and institutions of democracy as being Islamic or Islamizable (condoned by Islam) in both their definition of democracy and their response to the same mentioned questions. In general, modernist Islamists argue that democracy is part of Islam since both are meant to fight dictatorship.[53] Modernists argue that, under the contemporary circumstances, democracy has a priority over *sharia*. This priority is not of supremacy, modernists argue, but priority of order. Analogously, the street is prior to the mosque since you need to pass by the street before you go to the mosque. Yet modernists argue that if the majority of Muslims do not want to apply *sharia*/Islamic legislation, then it cannot be applied by force. Both traditionalists and modernists are Islamists in the sense that they refuse the secularist reading that empties the state of its Islamic characteristics and its commitment to establish *sharia*.

Autocratic secularists are those who consistently (strongly) disagree with the political influence of Islam on the state apparatus and policies and also oppose democracy, claiming that is not suitable for, nor the top priority of, Muslim polities. Their main argument is that democracy is an evolving being, gets born and grows up. It is never created all at once. Whoever asks for something prematurely, one will be punished by not getting it. The baby that is born bigger than its natural size either will die; the mother will die; or both will die.[54]

According to autocratic secularists, Muslims are not ready for democracy: illiteracy, tribalism, apathy, emotionalism, and nostalgia are not conducive to democracy. They also argue that most of these problems are not necessarily the outcomes of wrong policies adopted by the autocratic rulers themselves.[55] They believe they were inherited from the distorting experience of colonialism that led to (1) urbanization without industrialization, (2) verbal education without productive training, (3) secularization without scientification (decline of religion without the rise of science), and (4) capitalist greed without capitalist discipline.[56] Autocrats' attitudes were captured in the responses to questions 2.4 and 2.28.

Liberal secularists are a subgroup of secularists who consistently accept democratic norms and institutions in their responses to these two questions (2.4 and 2.8). They argue that Islam, like all other religions, should be limited to the personal sphere. They believe that Islamists twist verses, sayings of the Prophet Mohamed, and interpretations of the Qur'an and Sunna to justify predetermined opinions.[57]

Eighty-six percent of the respondents could be classified into one of the four categories previously mentioned. The rest of the respondents could not be classified for various reasons.[58]

Based on tabulations of the 21,143 respondents who consistently fall into one of the four categories, the next step is to show the relative percentage of each one of these groups by country as demonstrated

TABLE 3. Percentages of the four categories in 33 Muslim societies.

	1 Trad.	2 Auto.	3 Mod.	4 Lib.	1+3 Islamists	3+4 Democrats	Democratizability
Turkey	1	5	31	63	32	94	Most
Senegal	9	0	68	23	77	91	Most
Morocco	9	0	72	19	80	91	Most
Albania	5	6	33	57	38	90	Most
Egypt	3	7	63	27	66	89	Most
Tunisia	6	8	37	50	42	87	Most
Iran	2	12	79	7	81	86	Most
USA	10	8	33	50	53	83	Most
Mali	2	15	50	33	43	83	Most
Gambia	3	15	54	29	56	82	Most
Turkmenistan	11	9	31	49	42	81	Most
Malaysia	14	6	62	18	76	80	Most
EU	15	5	47	33	62	80	Most
India	10	16	50	23	61	73	Possibly
Kuwait	17	11	41	32	58	73	Possibly
Bangladesh	20	8	48	24	68	72	Possibly
Jordan	20	9	48	23	68	71	Possibly
Qatar	23	8	45	24	68	69	Possibly
Bahrain	23	10	58	10	81	67	Possibly
Syria	26	7	40	27	66	67	Possibly
UAE	30	3	60	7	90	67	Possibly
Lebanon	20	14	31	35	51	67	Possibly
Algeria	25	10	33	33	58	66	Possibly
Indonesia	28	7	40	25	68	65	Possibly
Oman	31	5	46	18	77	64	Least
Libya	27	9	59	5	86	64	Least
Yemen	35	1	46	17	81	63	Least
Sudan	26	12	55	7	80	62	Least
Pakistan	24	15	42	19	66	61	Least
Nigeria	31	14	38	17	69	55	Least
Tajikistan	11	36	35	19	45	54	Least
Saudi Arab	46	2	48	4	95	52	Least
Average	18.34	8.41	47.69	25.72	65.13	73.38	Possibly

Source. Muslim Culture Barometer, 2002.

in table 3. This table is informative in a variety of ways. First, it suggests that educated Muslims are predominately Islamists (either traditionalists or modernists). This finding in itself confirms Islamists' argument that they control streets and mosques while secularists control palaces and armies in most Muslim countries. Only in Tajikistan (55 percent), Turkmenistan (58 percent), Mali (57 percent), Tunisia (58 percent), Albania (62 percent), and Turkey (68 percent) are secularists in the majority.

An Islamist modernist, commenting on the results of the 2003 elections in the Egyptian syndicate of journalism where the opposition (mainly pan-Arabists and Islamists) won two-third of the seats, said, "When true and genuine democracy prevails, it will definitely lead to the unequivocally opposite direction to the current trends in Arab politics."[59] Since the great majority of Muslim countries are not governed by liberal or modernist elites (according to the working definitions articulated in this article), this data, though not qualified to generalize about all Muslims, confirms that statement.

Second, the study finds there is a common factor that characterizes all the countries with a secularist majority: Muslims were forced through governmental policies to be secular (through secular systems of education, mass media, and governmental control over Islamic institutions) either by communist regimes (e.g., Albania, Tajikistan, and Turkmenistan) or Muslim rulers who decided to westernize their countries after independence (e.g., Turkey, Mali, and Tunisia). Unlike the elites, the majority of public attitudes in the five countries just mentioned (except Tajikistan) are more liberal than those of their predominantly autocratic rulers.

Third, since the modernist Islamists and the liberal secularists are the only two groups that accept political co-existence with each other—albeit with a very high level of self-restraint—they deserve more attention. It is almost impossible to imagine a scenario by which a peaceful alteration of power could ever happen in a country governed by traditionalists or autocrats. Yet one can imagine—assuming that each group of cultural entrepreneurs will act according to their declared discourses—that the only two groups that may accept, even if reluctantly, democracy to be the only game in town are the liberals and modernists. Added up together they have formed the seventh column in table 3 entitled 3 + 4. These two groups together form what can be called a "democracy-as-a-must" subculture, in contrast to the autocratic secularists and traditionalist Islamists who represent the apologetic "dictator, but..." subculture. In this subculture, individuals tend to justify their complacence and obedience to their autocrats by referring to their achievements in other areas such as fighting an outside enemy, achieving independence or social justice.

To avoid the arbitrary classification of societies, I have suggested a continuum where societies with the highest percentage of democrats (column 3 + 4) are the most democratizable and societies with the least percentage of democrats are the least democratizable. In this column, Muslims of Turkey, Senegal, Morocco, Albania, Egypt, Tunisia, Iran, USA, Mali, the Gambia, Turkmenistan, Malaysia, and the European Union countries are the most democratizable cultures. This list of countries (with the exception of Muslims of Turkmenistan and the EU) confirms the cultural map of democratic hardware and software as presented in figure 1. This confirmation is crucial since three of the four questions (2.8, 2.7, and 2.28) were not used in building the scales of democratic hardware and software as portrayed in figure 1. Thus, two different sets of questions lead to a similar result, which increases the relative reliability of the data and accuracy of the inferences. Additionally, table 3 suggests that while the average Muslim political culture may not be necessarily democratic, it is definitely democratizable. As shown, 73 percent of Muslims overall (irrespective of country) are either modernist Islamists or liberal secularists. The statistically significant correlations between the hardware (.762) and software (.784) scales and the percentages of modernist Islamists and liberal autocrats suggests that the ratio of people who adopt the subculture of " democracy-as-a-must" is a good predictor of the support of democratic hardware and software and vice-versa.

CONCLUSIONS

More public opinion and empirical political culture studies are necessary in order to arrive at a fuller understanding of how Muslims think about democracy.[60] This article is a step toward a series of articles that aim at encouraging students of the Middle East and Islam to use the same survey and come up with their own analysis. However, until we have panel data, we must ask: what does the first round of the MCB survey tell us about the cultures of Muslim societies? First and foremost, this survey provides some scientific basis for the claim that Muslims are attitudinally heterogeneous enough to defy easy generalizations, but that subtle and warranted categorization is a possibility. Second, some Muslim societies (e.g., Morocco, Tunisia, and Egypt) have enough democratic hardware and software at the mass level to become democracies, although in actuality they are not. For this reason, blaming the Muslim culture for dictatorship is not a fair assessment in these cases. Third, the mass cultures of some other Muslim countries are real obstacles toward democratization because they lack democratic software (Pakistan and Nigeria), hardware (the UAE, Oman, and Libya), or both (Saudi Arabia, Yemen, Sudan, and Tajikistan). Fourth, Muslims are divided not only between Islamists and secularists. Among Islamists there are both progressive modernists and traditionalists, and likewise, not all secularists are liberals. Some of them are autocrats. That is why assuming that all Islamists are by nature fundamentalists and inimical to democracy is as fallacious as assuming that a secular Muslim is necessarily democratic. Fifth, Muslim societies witness a struggle between the subculture of "democracy-as-a-must" versus the subculture of "dictator, but..." that justifies autocracy either in the name of Islam—as in the case of traditionalist Islamists—or on secular grounds. Tentatively and cautiously,[61] we find that societies that score high on democratic hardware and software are statistically correlated with high percentages of modernist Islamists and liberal secularists and low percentages of traditionalist Islamists and autocratic secularists. The evidence presently available from this article shows that Muslims' attitudes are obstacles toward democratization in certain countries, but not others.

The next step to reach a fuller understanding of how Islam influences the prospects for democratic transitions in the Muslim world is to conduct a micro-analysis of data at the individual level to discern what factors shape the individual Muslim's attitude toward democracy.

One last caveat should be taken into consideration: these results should not be seen as final answers but preliminary readings of a highly complicated and dynamic phenomenon that will require the efforts of many researchers over a long period of time.

Appendix A

This article uses survey data of literate Muslims from thirty-three countries via two tools: written surveys and Web-based surveys in five different languages—Arabic, English, French, Urdu, and Farsi. The survey was designed and tested by eleven Muslim area experts from Egypt, Iran, Pakistan, and Jordan, and tested fourteen times with literate Muslims of different countries and languages. The respondents to the written survey were drawn from a multistage cluster probabilistic sample of college and university students and graduates. After tossing away the ineligible respondents[62], around 6,699 responses from twenty-two societies were kept. These countries are listed in appendix D. The responses were collected during the period from March through August 2002. By examining the structure of bias in the written-survey data, one finds that there is an over-sampling of men versus women. However, this kind of over-sampling corresponds to the actual inequality of education in most Muslim countries.

Regarding the Web-based survey, a lengthy four-step process was undertaken to collect the e-mails of the potential respondents and to stratify them:

1. Collecting the convenience sample: The initial pool of e-mails was selected from over 200 public Web sites where people provided their e-mail addresses (e.g., chat rooms, petitioning sites, e-mail groups, comments on articles and news from various newspapers, etc.), in the same five languages. The initial process resulted in approximately 49,400 e-mails. The process of collecting these e-mails took about nine months (July 2001–March 2002).[63]

2. Expanding the frame of the network sample: These people were e-mailed in the first week of May 2002 and asked to anonymously participate in a worldwide survey of Muslims on political issues. Upon their agreement, they were asked to visit a Web page where they could provide anonymous preliminary information regarding demographics

(gender, age, income, and education), countries of origin, citizenship and residence (if different), and religious denomination (Sunni, Shiite, Ahmadi, or other) in Arabic, English, French, Farsi, or Urdu.

Additionally, they were asked to forward the inviting e-mail to other Muslims aged eighteen and above. By the end of May 2002, around 61,700 e-mails from sixty-four countries around the world were sent by Muslims who showed interest in participating in the survey. These 61,700 e-mails have become the network or snowball sampling frame. The main advantage of network sampling is to increase the diversity, but it may produce non-representative samples. That is why stratifying the e-mails according to known characteristics within each country was essential.

3. Stratification of the network sample: The 61,700 e-mails represented diverse individuals in diverse Muslim and non-Muslim societies, but nonetheless, their degree of representation technically remained unknown. To partially cope with this problem, I decided to subgroup the e-mails by country of citizenship or origin, if different. I eliminated the e-mails that belonged to a country with a total number of emails less than 480 as a convenient cut-off. The remaining list included thirty-nine countries where Muslims have a notable presence. Dealing with each country separately, I drew stratified proportionate random samples from the e-mails based upon the known national demographics of the population of each society. These national demographics were obtained from national censuses and the indexes of World Bank, IMF, and Human Development Reports.[64]

By stratifying the e-mails of each country according to their demographics and Islamic sect into homogenous discrete strata (with heterogeneity between subsets), the pooled respondents were found to represent educated Muslims of the middle and upper classes in only thirty-three countries. On the basis of the relative proportion of the population, I randomly selected the e-mails to represent literate Muslims between the ages of eighteen and fifty-five. The main advantage of this technique was to ensure the proper representation of the stratification variables, which, in turn, "enhances the representation of other variables related to them."[65]

4. Sending the final survey: About 55,100 e-mails were sent to representatives of the stratified samples from the thirty-three countries. About 24,681 people responded (a 45 percent response rate). The sample size of each society is provided in appendix D. Again, I eliminated the e-mails that belonged to a country with fewer than 480 respondents as a convenient cut-off. The respondents to the Web-based version had to respond to the same forty-eight questions of the written survey during the same period. Comparing the income gap between the average citizen (measured by GDP per capita) and the average income of the respondents to the survey implies that the respondents are relatively richer than the average citizen. I take this gap to imply that the respondents belong to the middle and upper classes. For instance, the Albanian respondents to the survey, as indicated in the last column of appendix D, are 21 percent richer than average Albanians. However the economic gap increases dramatically in the cases of the Gambia, Iraq, Mali, Nigeria, Senegal, Syria, Tajikistan, and Yemen. This large gap indicates that the pooled data can speak only for the upper class.

Though admittedly imperfect, combining the data from the Web-based survey and the written survey serves three desired purposes: (1) It provides a larger N with wider representation of a greater number of Muslim countries and thus more diversity in Muslim sects, ages, gender, and political ideologies. (2) It strikes a balance between the advantages of a written survey followed by deeper focus-group discussions and the Web-based survey where the researchers distanced themselves from any influence on the respondents.[66] (3) It controls for the effect of fear from responding to what can be seen as very politically sensitive questions given the fact that the Web-based survey does not meet the same level of censorship that written surveys may encounter. Additionally, other studies show that "[i]n the aggregate, Internet access appears to make little difference in the personal concerns of Arabs. Even where rankings and ratings do differ, the differences are slight."[67] Based on the current data, contrary to initial expectations, the one-way analysis of variance (ANOVA) and preliminary regressions suggest that there are no statistically significant differences between the two sets of respondents once we control for the effect of age in the Web-based sample. That is to say, we did not find statistically significant attitudinal differences between literate Muslims who have access to the Internet and literate Muslims who do not have access to the Internet. With all these measures to ensure the reliability and validity of data, one has to deal with this data and the results stemming from it as an attempt to explore an empirical puzzle that has been for so long tackled only from theological and historical perspectives.

A technical note should be made about the unknown representativeness of the Web-based survey. According to Smith, "Perhaps the most critical problem with Internet-based research is the practical impossibility of probability sampling, that one can only tentatively generalize to a very specific population, if at all."[68] After discussing different accounts of this problem, she concludes that "we do this all the time," whether we use Web-based, telephone-based, or paper-based surveys. None of them is completely random. The solution that Smith advances is to "learn more about [the respondents'] demographics," which will enable "generalizability to well-studied segments of the overall population." Others suggest that non-probabilistic samples are better at understanding relationships between variables than at making descriptive estimates about target populations.[69]

Two econometricians examined five decades of mathematical and theoretical sampling and suggested that the great majority of the sampling methods that social scientists use do not actually produce random samples unless we ignore the impracticality of most of the underlying assumptions.[70]

For the full survey, please visit the English version at http://www.chsbs.cmich.edu/fattah/islam/. And for the limitations of the survey, please read the appendix of my book, *Democratic Values in the Muslim World* (Fattah 2006).

Appendix B

The Factor Analysis

Q #	Democratic Hardware	Democratic Software
	(3 questions)	(4 questions)
2.6	Voting is some type of enjoining the good and forbidding the evil.	
2.7	Public elections of rulers will lead to taboos.	
2.10	Democratic institutions and procedures are against Sharia.	
	Alpha =.875	Alpha = .763
2.16	Attitude toward participation of Christian minorities in the political process.	
2.17	Attitude toward participation of Jewish minorities in the political process.	
2.18	Attitude toward participation of Muslim women in the political process.	
2.30	Attitude toward participation of Muslim minorities in the political process.	

Source. Muslim Culture Barometer, 2002.
Note. Principal component factor analysis was used with varimax rotation and Kaiser Normalization. The total model predicts 78.8% of cumulative variance. The support for democratic hardware scales were reversed so that a positive response expresses greater support for democratic hardware.
Cronbach's estimate of reliability and internal consistency is reported as Alpha.

Appendix C

The Wording of the Questions Used
Besides the questions shown in the factor analysis table (appendix B), the following five-point scale of agree/disagree questions were asked.

2.4. By allowing people to make their own laws, democracy replaces the will of Allah with the will of the people; that is why it is some type of disbelief (*kofr*).

2.8. One popular saying is that "Islam is both religion and state" (*deen wa dawla*). Do you agree?

2.28. In your opinion, what is democracy? (Open-Ended Question)

APPENDIX D

Respondents to the Survey

Country	Written Samp.	Web Samp.	Total N	College access (%)	Literacy rate (%)**	$GDP per capita (HDR)***	$GDP per capita (sample)	% GDP per capita gap
Albania		500	500	15	85	760	921	121
Algeria	198	570	768	15	60	5,900	7,050	119
Bahrain	102	530	632	21	86	15,100	16,300	108
Bangladesh	196	935	1131	7	39	1750	3,141	179
Egypt	1617	1346	2963	38	53	2900	4,139	143
EU	118	774	892	40	99	24000	25,149	105
Gambia		489	489	NA	33	1450	6,769	467
India		1497	1497	11	57	2500	3,690	148
Indonesia	154	1331	1485	15	85	3000	6,492	216
Iran	342	1138	1480	21	77	6000	8,399	140
Iraq		91	91	14	58	1600	6,921	433a
Jordan		687	687	31	88	3800	8,012	211
Kuwait	113	533	646	21	82	18,100	18,919	105
Lebanon		534	534	45	86	4400	5,505	125
Libya	266	597	863	58	80	6000	7,609	127
Mali		521	521	29	46	760	1,919	516a
Malaysia	683	1177	1860	28	88	8500	9,721	114
Morocco	125	627	752	10	50	3800	7,035	185
Nigeria	138	579	717	27	64	650	2,889	444a
Oman		494	494	11	72	13000	13,231	102
Pakistan	872	1685	2557	5	45	2000	3,398	170
Qatar		568	568	27	81	20000	20,441	102
S. Arabia	182	942	1124	22	73	11000	11,692	106
Senegal	187	569	756	4	39	1300	6,501	500a

(continued on next page)

Country	Written Samp.	Web Samp.	Total N	College access (%)	Literacy rate (%)**	$GDP per capita (HDR)***	$GDP per capita (sample)	% GDP per capita gap
Sudan	447	583	1030	7	53	1500	2,306	154
Syria		613	613	18	75	3000	3,991	323a
Tajikistan		497	497	15	99	1000	4,492	449
Turkmen		504	504	NA	98	5000	5,898	118
Tunisia	119	546	665	23	73	6300	7,489	119
Turkey	264	1058	1322	25	85	6500	7,749	119
UAE	185	595	780	12	76	21000	21,139	101
USA	223	1083	1306	71	97	37000	36,649	99
Yemen	168	488	656	11	50	850	3,271	385a
Total	6699	24681	31380					
Average				22.487	70.7	7285	8921	
Stand. Dev.				15	19	8415	7667	

UNESCO report on global education available at http://www.uis.unesco.org/TEMPLATE/html/Exceltables/education/enrol_tertiary.xls.

* World Bank, Human Development Report, 2002.

** This entry shows GDP on a purchasing power parity basis divided by population as of July 1 for the same year. World Bank, Human Development Report, 2002, and CIA World Factbook.

Endnotes

1. Lingemann, Hans Dieter. 1999. "Mapping Political Support in the 1990s: A Global Analysis," in *Critical Citizens: Global Support for Democratic Government*, ed. Pippa Norris, pp. xv. (Oxford; New York: Oxford University Press).
2. Inglehart, Ronald. 2000. "Political Culture and Democratic Institutions: Russia in Global Perspective," in *Annual Meeting of the American Political Science Association*.
3. Fish, M. Steven. 2002. "Islam and Authoritarianism," *World Politics* 55: 4–37.
4. Karatnycky, Adrian. 2002. "The 2001 Freedom House Survey: Muslim Countries and the Democracy Gap," *Journal of Democracy* 13: 99–112.
5. Gellner, Ernest. 1991. "Islam and Marxism," *International Affairs*. Huntington, Samuel. 1984. "Will More Countries Become Democratic?" *Political Science Quarterly* 99. Karatnycky, Adrian. 2002. "The 2001 Freedom House Survey: Muslim Countries and the Democracy Gap," *Journal of Democracy* 13: 99–112. Kedourie, Elie. 1992. *Democracy and Arab Political Culture* (Arlington: Washington Institute for Near East Policy). Lewis, Bernard. 1993a. *Islam and the West* (New York: Oxford University Press); 1997, "The West and the Middle East," *Foreign Affairs* 76; and 2002, *What Went Wrong: Western Impact and Middle Eastern Response*. (New York: Oxford University Press). Miller, Judith. 1997. *God Has Ninety-Nine Names: Reporting from a Militant Middle East* (New York: Simon & Schuster). Naipaul, V. S. 1981. *Among the Believers: An Islamic Journey* (New York: Knopf) and 1998, *Beyond Belief: Islamic Excursions Among the Converted Peoples* (New York: Random House). Pipes, Daniel. 1988. *Slaves, Soldiers, and Islam: The Genesis of a Military System* (New Haven, CT: Yale University Press).
6. G. W. Bush, November 6, 2003.
7. The actual survey is available at http://personal.cmich.edu/fatta1ma/islam/index.htm. Appendix A has a description of the data and how it was collected. A more detailed description of both the written and Web-based surveys is available by request from the author.
8. Brace, Paul, and Barbara Hinckley. 1992. *Follow the Leader: Opinion Polls and the Modern Presidents* (New York, NY: Basic Books). Harik, Iliya F. 1971. "Opinion Leaders and the Mass Media in Rural Egypt," *The American Political Science Review* 65 (September): 731–40. Heath, M. R., and

S. J. Bekker. 1986. *Identification of Opinion Leaders in Public Affairs, Educational Matters, and Family Planning in the Township of Atteridgeville* (Pretoria: Human Sciences Research Council). Kotzâe, H. J. 1992. *Transitional Politics in South Africa: Attitudes of Opinion-Leaders* (Stellenbosch: Centre for International and Comparative Politics, University of Stellenbosch).

9. In fairness to the research team, their effort to survey illiterate Muslims failed due to the sensitivity of the questions asked and their skepticism of strangers. In addition, the attitudes of the very few illiterates who responded to the interviewees reflected a very shallow and inconsistent understanding of politics in general. In other words, it was impossible to survey apolitical people about politics or to use surveys to discern the culture of people who do not have much familiarity with surveys.

10. John S. Mill noted that the thinking of the masses "is done for them by men much like themselves, addressing or speaking in their name, on the spur of the moment...." Weimann, Gabriel. 1991. "The Influentials: Back to the Concept of Opinion Leaders?" *The Public Opinion Quarterly* 55 (summer): 267–279.

11. Al-Mashat, Abdel Mon'em. 1983. "Egyptian Attitudes Toward the Peace Process: Views of an 'Alert Elite'," *The Middle East Journal* 37: 394–411. Harik, Iliya F. 1971. "Opinion Leaders and the Mass Media in Rural Egypt," *The American Political Science Review* 65 (September): 731–740. Suleiman, Michael W. 1973. "Attitudes of the Arab Elite Toward Palestine and Israel," *The American Political Science Review* 67 (June): 482–489.

12. Al-Mashat, Ibid. Hinnebusch, Raymond A. 1982. "Children of the Elite: Political Attitudes of the Westernized Bourgeoisie in Contemporary Egypt." *The Middle East Journal* 36 (4): 535–561. Tessler, Mark. 1987. *The Evaluation and Application of Survey Research in the Arab World*. Boulder, CO: Westview Press.

13. Krosnick, Jon, and Shibley Telhami. 1995. "Public Attitudes Toward Israel: A Study of the Attentive and Issue Publics," *International Studies Quarterly* 39: 535–554.

14. Discerning the factors that shape individual Muslims' attitudes toward democracy will be a topic for another article.

15. Inglehart, Ronald, and Pippa Norris. 2003. "The True Clash of Civilization," *Foreign Policy* (March/April): 63–70.

16. Pew Research Center. 2003a. *Views of a Changing World 2003* (Washington, DC: The Pew Research Center) and 2003b, *Religion and Politics: Contention and Consensus* (Washington, DC: The Pew Research Center).

17. Sartori, Giovanni. 1962. *Democratic Theory* (Detroit: Wayne State University Press).

18. Goodin, Robert E. 1996. "Institutions and Their Design," in *The Theory of Institutional Design*, ed. R. E. Goodin (Cambridge: Cambridge University Press).
19. Ronald Inglehart and Pippa Norris 2003. "The True Clash of Civilization," *Foreign Policy* March/April: 63–70.
20. Obeidi, Amal. 2001, *Political Culture in Libya* (Richmond, UK: Curzon).
21. Ibid.
22. Bianci, Steven. 2003. *Libya: Current Issues and Historical Background* (New York: Nova Science Publishers).
23. Beblawi, Hazem, and Giacomo Luciani. 1987. *The Rentier State* (London; New York: Croom Helm). Kechichian, Joseph A., and Gustave E. von Grunebaum. 2001. *Iran, Iraq, and the Arab Gulf States* (Houndmills, Basingstoke, Hampshire; New York: Palgrave).
24. Tahir, Umar, and Muammar Qaddafi. 1996. *Al-Qadhdhafi wa-al-Thawrah al-Faransiyah, 1789–1969* (Beirut: al-Multaq lil-Tibaah wa-al-Nashr). Zartman, I. William. 1982. *Political Elites in Arab North Africa: Morocco, Algeria, Tunisia, Libya, and Egypt* (New York: Longman).
25. Fandy, Mamoun. 1999. *Saudi Arabia and the Politics of Dissent* (New York: St. Martin's Press).
26. Al-'Alyan, Lubna Solayman. 2003. "Interview," *al-Sharq al-Awssat*, June 7, 2003.
27. Al-Fassi, Haton. 2003. "Saudi Woman: New Arguments and Reforming Visions," *al-Sharq al-Awssat*, June 14, 2003.
28. Al-Hamad, Turki. 2003. "Beyond Brain-Washing (Arabic)," *al-Sharq al-Awssat*, May 12, 2003.
29. Al-Hozzeffi, Abdulrahman. 1998. "Wipe out the Jews, Christians and Shiite from Arabia." Islamway.com Recordings available at: http://www.islamway.com/?iw_s=Scholar&iw_a=lessons&scholar_id=31.
30. Al-Iryani, Abd al-Karim. 1998. "The Role of the State in a Traditional Society," *Yemen Gateway*. Othman, Abdo Ali. 1998. "Tribe and Society in Yemen," *Yemeni Times* VIII.
31. http://www.aljazeera.net/news/arabic/2000/12/12-25-1.htm.
32. Chaudhri, Rashid Ahmad, Shamim Ahmad, and Ahmadiyya Muslim Association. 1989. *Persecution of Ahmadi Muslims and Their Response* (London: Press and Publication Desk, Ahmadiyya Muslim Association).
33. Suberu, Rotimi T. 1996. *Ethnic Minority Conflicts and Governance in Nigeria* (Ibadan, Nigeria: Spectrum: IFRA).
34. Aborisade, Oladimeji. 2002. *Politics in Nigeria* (New York: Longman).

35. Pew Research Center. 2003a. *Views of a Changing World 2003* (Washington, DC: The Pew Research Center).
36. Ibid.
37. Aborisade, Oladimeji. 2002. *Politics in Nigeria* (New York: Longman). Jafri, A. B. S. 2002. *The Political Parties of Pakistan* (Karachi: Royal Book Co). Jawed, Nasim. 1999. *Islam's Political Culture: Religion and Politics in Predivided Pakistan* (Austin: University of Texas). Ujo, A. A. 2000. *Understanding Political Parties in Nigeria* (Kaduna, Nigeria: Klamidas Books).
38. World Bank. 2001. *World Development Report* (Washington, DC: World Bank).
39. Al-Hayat, May 18, 2003.
40. Huntington, Samuel. 1996b. "Democracy for the Long Haul," *Journal of Democracy* 7: 3–13.
41. *Al-Sharq al-Awssat*, April 20, 2003.
42. Weaver, Mary Anne. 2000. "Democracy by Decree: Can One Man Propel a Country into the Future?" *The New Yorker* (November): 54–61.
43. *Al-Sharq al-Awssat*, June 8, 2003.
44. Hadenius, Axel. 2001. *Institutions and Democratic Citizenship* (Oxford; New York: Oxford University Press).
45. Al-Qashtini, Khaled. 2003. "Step by Step, Move by Move," *Al-Sharq al-Awssat* (June 22, 2003).
46. Gillespie, Richard, and Richard Youngs. 2002. *The European Union and Democracy Promotion: The Case of North Africa* (Portland, OR: Frank Cass Publishers).
47. Bourqia, R., and Susan Gilson Miller. 1999. *In the Shadow of the Sultan: Culture, Power, and Politics in Morocco* (Cambridge, MA: Distributed for the Center for Middle Eastern Studies of Harvard University by Harvard University Press). Layachi, Azzedine. 1998. *State, Society & Democracy in Morocco: The Limits of Associative Life* (Washington, DC: Center for Contemporary Arab Studies, Edmund A. Walsh School of Foreign Service, Georgetown University).
48. Saktanber, Ay'se. 2002. *Living Islam: Women, Religion and the Politicization of Culture in Turkey* (London: I.B. Tauris).
49. Ibrahim, Ferhad, and Gèulistan Gèurbey. 2000. *The Kurdish Conflict in Turkey: Obstacles and Chances for Peace and Democracy* (New York: St. Martin's Press).
50. Baghdadi, Ahmad. 1999. *Renovation of the Religious Thought* [in Arabic: *Tagdid Al-Fikr Al-Dini*] (Damascus: Al Mada Publishing Company).

51. The wording of the question is in appendix C.

52. Daniel Pipes, "There are no moderates: dealing with fundamentalist Iran.," in *National Interest* (22 September 1995).

53. Al-Ghannouchi, Rachid. 1993. *Public Freedoms in the Islamic State* [Arabic] (Beirut: The Center for Arab Unity Studies). Al-Qaradawi, Yusuf. 2001a. *On the Fiqh of the Islamic State* [Arabic: *Min Fiqh al-Dawla Fil-Islam*] (Cairo: Dar al-Shorouq) and 2001b, *Secularist Extremism vs. Islam: Turkey and Tunisia* (Cairo: Dar al-Shorouq). Tamimi, Azzam. 2001. *Rachid Ghannouchi: A Democrat within Islamism* (Oxford; New York: Oxford University Press).

54. Al-Rawabda is a former prime minister of Jordan. Al-Rawabda, Abdelraouf. 2001. "Forum on Democracy in the Arab World [Arabic: *al-Democrateya fi al-Watan al-Arabi*]," Jazeer.net.

55. Mahathir bin, Mohamad, and Makaruddin Hashim. 2000. *Politics, Democracy and the New Asia: Selected Speeches* (Subang Jaya, Selangor Darul Ehsan, Malaysia: Published by Pelanduk Publications for the Prime Minister's Office of Malaysia, Putrajaya, Malaysia).

56. Mazrui, Ali. 1990. *Cultural Forces in World Politics* (Portsmouth, NH; UK: Heinemann).

57. Al-Azmeh, Aziz. 1992. *Secularism from a Different Perspective* (Arabic: *Al-ilmaniyah min manzour mukhtalef*) (Beirut: Markaz Dirasat al-Wehda). Al-Arabiya, Baghdadi, Ahmad. 1999. *Renovation of the Religious Thought* (Arabic: *Tagdid Al-Fikr Al-Dini*) (Damascus: Al Mada Publishing Company). Surush, Abd al-Kar im, Mahmoud Sadri, and Ahmad Sadri. 2000. *Reason, Freedom, & Democracy in Islam: Essential Writings of Abdolkarim Soroush* (New York: Oxford University Press).

58. It is important to note that around 4.5 percent of the respondents did not respond to two or more of the questions mentioned in table 2. However, it is very difficult to assess why the remaining 9.5 percent of the respondents who actually responded to almost all the questions did not fall into any of the four categories. They may have misunderstood one or more questions, they may have simply been inconsistent, or they may have adopted an outlying position that could not be met by the suggested categorization.

59. Howaidi, Fahmi. 2003b. "The Message of the Elections of the Egyptian Syndicate of Journalism," *al-Sharq al-Awssat* (August 4).

60. Tessler, Mark. 2002. "Islam and Democracy in the Middle East: The Impact of Religious Orientations on Attitudes toward Democracy in Four Arab Countries," *Comparative Politics* 34: 337–354.

61. To avoid ecological and individualist fallacies, I do not suggest any micro-level causal relationships between one's ideological inclinations and the democratic hardware or software of societies since this is an issue to be discussed separately using the individual-level data. Scheuch, Erwin K. 1989. "Theoretical Implications of Comparative Survey Research: Why the Wheel of Cross-Cultural Methodology Keeps on Being Reinvented," *International Sociology* 4.

62. Ineligible respondents were either non-Muslims, under eighteen or above fifty-five years old, and/or refused to state their countries of origin.

63. I am indebted to Miss Ghada Sharaf of Egypt, Mr. Abdulhaq al-Jundi of Syria, Mohamed al-Ameen of Sengal, Mr. Hafez Noa'man of Pakistan, Hameed Siddiqi of Malaysia, and Mai Somani of Indonesia for their indispensable effort to collect these e-mails.

64. I am highly indebted to Dr. Susan Carlson (sociology department), Kevin Corder (political science), and Matthew Higgins (economics department) of Western Michigan University for their valuable advice and thorough guidance on the process of stratification.

65. Earl R. Babbie. 2004. *The Practice of Social Research* (Belmont, CA: Thomson/Wadsworth).

66. Christine B. Smith. 2002. "Casting the Net: Surveying an Internet Population." http://www.ascusc.org/jcmc/vol3/issue1/smith.html. D. J. Solomon. 2001. "Conducting Web-based Surveys," *Practical Assessment, Research & Evaluation* 7.

67. James J. Zogby, 2002. *What Arabs Think: Values, Beliefs and Concerns* (New York: Zogby International).

68. Christine B. Smith, 2002. "Casting the Net: Surveying an Internet Population." http://www.ascusc.org/jcmc/vol3/issue1/smith.html.

69. Jack Allen, 2002. *Randomness and Optimal Estimation in Data Sampling* (Rehoboth: American Research Press). Earl R. Babbie, 2004. *The Practice of Social Research* (Belmont, CA: Thomson/Wadsworth). Risto Lehtonen and Erkki Pahkinen. 2004. *Practical Methods for Design and Analysis of Complex Surveys* (Chichester, West Sussex, England; Hoboken, NJ: J. Wiley). S. Sampath, 2001. *Sampling Theory and Methods* (Boca Raton; New Delhi: CRC Press; Narosa Pub. House). Rebecca Wingard-Nelson. 2004. *Data, Graphing, and Statistics* (Berkeley Heights, NJ: Enslow Publishers).

70. Aman Ullah and Robert V. Breunig, "Introduction," in *Handbook of Applied Economic Statistics*, ed. Aman Ullah and David E. A. Giles (New York: Marcel Dekker, 1998), xi, 625 p.

CHAPTER 3

ISLAM AND DEMOCRACY IN ASIA

WHAT CAN WE LEARN FROM THE UNDERDOG STRATEGY?

Laure Paquette

INTRODUCTION

What, if anything, can the underdog strategy tell us about Islam and democracy in Asia? And if it does say something, is it worth using its framework to analyze the move toward liberal democracy of some Muslim countries? These are the broad questions this chapter will address. These questions are of interest to readers such as:

- policymakers whose countries have a Muslim minority and who want to promote either the development of democracy or the participation of this minority in democracy;

- policymakers whose countries have a Muslim majority and who also want to promote the development of democracy;
- governments that deal with the governments of weak or failed states with a Muslim majority; and
- scholars who study such governments or such minorities.

The framework of the underdog strategy specifically allows for the possibility of either Muslim minorities or majorities containing elements of extremism.

"Underdog strategy" can be characterized as the ancient "way of thinking of women and the vanquished," the form of strategy that Aristotle excluded from philosophical discourse,[1] but which did not disappear from practice. The word "strategy" has become something of a rubber band, stretched to fit whatever meaning is necessary. For the purposes of this chapter, however, "strategy" is defined as an idea that orchestrates actions to achieve a goal, as usually applied in business and military. The underdog strategy is a particular form of strategy, more flexible and more holistic than strong-side strategy. It can be employed outside the military or business world and applied to any interactions between individuals, groups, or governments. The underdog strategy answers the question, "What is the best thing you can do when the odds are against you?" Not all underdogs use strategy, but those who do are unusually successful in achieving their goals. The status of underdog, however, is meant to be defined by the actor in relation to other actors whom he considers important. It is also possible that an actor on the international stage who has long been at a disadvantage may retain the underdog mindset even after the conditions that led to it have ceased to exist.

The differences between the underdog strategy and the strong-side strategy are few in practice, but very significant. First, there is a difference in scope. For example, the former Soviet armed forces would apply strong-side strategy to the theatre of operations, but not to any smaller units. The underdog strategy, on the other hand, has a much smaller scope, down to an ambush over a few city blocks, for example. The strong-side strategy would call actions at that level tactical. Second, there is a difference in range of tactics. The U.S. armed forces, for example, would consider in an operation like that carried out in Afghanistan what their trained, specialized personnel and equipment could do. The underdog strategy uses a much broader range of political, economic, and social means to achieve its end. It is almost certainly not going to be confined to using military means. Finally, there is a difference in what is acceptable. The U.S. armed forces, for example, behave in a way that reflects their chain of command, discipline, laws, treaties, and national policies. Underdog strategists will also have rules of behavior, but they are fewer and much less rigid. These few differences taken together account for the differences in characteristics between the strong-side and the underdog strategy, as well as the mistakes underdogs often make.

The underdog strategy as an idea has given rise to a framework made up of four components: (1) the description of the main characteristics of the underdog strategy; (2) a list of the mistakes actors using this approach most commonly make; (3) a distinct general theory of strategy; and (4) an analytical method that can analyze and predict what underdogs using strategy will do. Trying to analyze Islam and democracy in Asia through the lens of the underdog strategy may be new, but the approach itself is not new to the study of relations between states, of domestic politics and policy, or of Asian politics.[2] The methodological development of the framework and its wider range of applications have also been published elsewhere.

Investigating Muslim democracies in Asia using the underdog strategy in enough detail to analyze and predict developments requires a considerable investment of time and energy. It makes sense, then, to ask whether it is worth making such an investment at all. To make that determination, this chapter will ask the following questions:

- Is there evidence that any Muslim governments, groups, or individuals in Asian democracies are underdogs?
- If so, are they using the underdog strategy, or are they behaving in some other way?

These two specific questions can be explored by studying Afghanistan—a southwestern Asian nation with both a Muslim majority and a violent extremist Islamic minority—which has tried to democratize since 2001. There are several reasons to choose Afghanistan. First and foremost, Afghanistan's war with the Soviets in the 1980s and its present situation have contributed to the revival of Islam in Asia.[3] Second, Afghanistan's Shiites make up a significant portion of the population, and Shiites are of considerable interest for the development of democracy in other Muslim Asian countries. The same can be said of Al Qaeda, which maintains a presence in Afghanistan.[4] Third, Afghanistan is clearly struggling toward liberal democracy at a time when there are few liberal democratic countries with an Islamic majority.[5] Fourth, the status and outcome of democratization in Afghanistan is a prominent concern in international affairs at the time of this writing, so there is information widely available. Finally, Afghanistan is afflicted with an extremist minority dedicated to the destruction of the nascent democratic institutions: the Taliban. With the study of a single country, we can examine two types of situations: a government with a Muslim majority that is an underdog in the international system, and a government afflicted with a violent extremist Muslim movement, who are in turn underdogs within their own country.

In the next section of this chapter, we will consider *prima facie* evidence regarding a government or group being in a disadvantaged or underdog situation, and determine whether this justifies assigning them underdog status. We will then examine whether there is evidence that some governments or groups are using the underdog strategy. We will make that determination by looking at whether they show some characteristics of the underdog strategy and/or commit some of its mistakes. But before our investigation begins, a comment about Islam is in order. This chapter will only be considering political Islam; a discussion of the faith by which 1.2 billion Muslims live is outside our scope.[6] Nor do we intend to discuss Muslim governments in terms of their Islamic character, since "[m]ost governments in Islamic countries today are, in fact, secular in operation and practice, as has been most governance in Islamdom historically."[7]

PRIMA FACIE EVIDENCE OF UNDERDOG STATUS

The Afghanistan Government

The case that Afghanistan is an underdog in the international system rests on evidence of its political instability and inability to implement social and political reforms as compared to other nations. Once the government takes on the characteristics of an underdog, however, those characteristics will show up in both domestic and international actions. Unfortunately, Afghanistan has suffered from such chronic instability and conflict during so much of its modern history that its economy and infrastructure are in ruins, and many of its people are refugees.

Afghanistan state institutions have been weak for decades, giving rise to instability and unsuccessful attempts to modernize the society. These efforts go back to 1926 and the defeat of King Amanullah's social reforms by conservative forces. In 1953 Prime Minister (and General) Mohammed Daud introduced social reforms again, including the abolition of the seclusion of women. After he left power, the introduction of a constitutional monarchy led to political polarization and power struggles. But in 1973, Daud seized power again. In playing the USSR against Western powers, he alienated left-wing factions, which overthrew and killed him in 1978. The victors, the People's Democratic Party, were made up of Khalq and Parcham factions. The Khalq faction eventually purged and exiled most Parcham leaders, as conservative Islamic and ethnic leaders in the country revolted against social changes. In 1979 the Soviets backed the Parcham faction leader, Babrak Karmal, who was duly installed, while the United States, Pakistan, China, Iran, and Saudi Arabia supplied money and arms to anti-Soviet mujahedeen groups. Civil war raged from 1988 to 1993 as rival militias vied for influence after the Soviets withdrew. These militias eventually agreed to form a government with Burhanuddin Rabbani, an ethnic Tajik, as president, though factional contests continued. In 1995 the Pashtun-dominated Taliban emerged, and they seized control of Kabul the following year. By 1997, they and their extremist version of Islam controlled about two-thirds of country.

There matters rested until terrorists attacked the United States on September 11, 2001. In October, the United States invaded Afghanistan after the Taliban government refused to hand over Osama bin Laden, the architect of those attacks. Once the U.S. had defeated the Taliban government, meetings of various Afghan leaders, sponsored by the United Nations, produced an interim government and an agreement to allow a peacekeeping force to enter Afghanistan. Hamid Karzai, who headed the provisional administration, won a five-year term in Afghanistan's first direct presidential elections in October 2004, with 55.4 percent of the vote. Karzai, a Pashtun, was an effective player on the world stage who also enjoyed strong American backing, persuading international donors to pledge $US 4 billion in 2002.

Given this history, it is no wonder that in November 2006 the UN Security Council found Afghanistan at risk of becoming a failed democracy because of its fragile state institutions, the increase in Taliban violence, and the growing illegal drug production. In addition to these reasons, the Karzai government has yet to achieve national unity. National unity has been elusive both because the nation is diverse and because it has a poor history of human rights. In the 1980s, the Soviet invasion brought mass killings, torture, and a landscape littered with land mines. The subsequent civil war brought extensive abuses by the armed factions vying for power. When the Taliban were in power, they were particularly notorious for their human rights abuses against women. Without a tradition of shared respect and participation by various groups, it is not possible to hope for a strong central government being established other than by force.

If the government of Afghanistan can be considered an underdog because of political reasons, the Taliban after 2001 can be considered underdogs for military ones. The case here rests on the military defeat of the Taliban government by the United States in late 2001 having an impact on future governments.

The Taliban Insurgents
Once the Taliban were summarily defeated by the U.S.-led coalition in 2001, they were reduced to the status of an insurgent group with no place

in the political system. At the time of the U.S. invasion, the Taliban controlled perhaps 90 percent of the territory and was opposed only by an alliance of minority factions in the north. Although the Taliban's version of Islam had attracted widespread criticism, the United States invaded only after the Taliban's refusal to hand over Osama bin Laden. The invasion proved decisive in very short order, and showed the degree to which the Taliban were outmatched militarily.

The air war against the Taliban began in October 2001. The U.S. enjoyed immediate air supremacy. They lost no aircraft to enemy fire because the Taliban relied mostly on leftover arms and weapons from the Soviet invasion, and they operated almost without opposition throughout the country. Cruise missile strikes initially focused in and around the cities of Kabul, Jalalabad, and Kandahar. Within a few days, most al-Qaeda training sites had been severely damaged, so the campaign then focused on command, control, and communications. Thousands of Pashtun militia from Pakistan poured into the country, reinforcing the Taliban, but to no avail. The Taliban support structure began to erode under the pressure of the air-strikes.

The ground war began with Special Forces launching a raid deep into Kandahar, even striking one of the Taliban leaders' compounds, that of Mullah Omar's. Poor Taliban tactics magnified the effects of U.S. attacks, as when Taliban fighters made easy targets by standing on top of bare ridgelines. By November 2, Taliban forces were so weak that foreign fighters from al-Qaeda took over security in the Afghan cities. On November 9, the U.S. bombed Mazar-i-Sharif, allowing the Northern Alliance forces to seize the city's military base and airport, and triggering a complete collapse of Taliban positions. On November 12, Taliban forces fled Kabul, and within twenty-four hours all of the Afghan provinces along the Iranian border had fallen. The last Taliban stronghold, Kandahar, fell by the end of November, and the Taliban regrouped in the wilds of Tora Bora, on the Pakistan border. There was only a week-long revolt by Taliban prisoners to mark the end of combat. The calm was not destined to last, however: within a year, the Islamic radicals had shifted to a new mode of operation. The rapid and devastating defeat by an invader-turned-occupier is certainly enough to make the Taliban feel they are underdogs.

As we have seen, there is ample *prima facie* evidence for both the Afghanistan government and the Taliban to be underdogs. We can now turn to the question of whether either shows the characteristics of using the underdog strategy.

CHARACTERISTICS OF THE UNDERDOG STRATEGY

For the most part, governments, groups, and individuals using the underdog strategy share many of the same characteristics. These characteristics are meant to be relative: all countries, for example, can expect to be aware of what greater powers around them are doing, but underdogs devote more energy and time to such a consideration. The identification of the characteristics was made through direct observation of individuals and groups. (The analytical framework, on the other hand, was primarily developed for and applied to states and governments.) We can now review what evidence exists for both the Karzai government and the Taliban insurgents.

1. Underdog strategists are more aware of what the stronger groups or governments may do. During the election campaign of 2004, for example, the smaller political parties watched Hamid Karzai's party to take advantage of any misstep. For its part, the Taliban were clearly observing what the Afghan and foreign police were doing—in the spring of 2005, they moved some of the Helmand opium trade to Nimroz when they realized that province was more weakly policed.[8]

2. Underdog strategists are always adapting. The Taliban changed its methods repeatedly after the initial U.S.-led invasion, then after its defeat, and finally after the arrival of the NATO troops. These methods included assassinations, kidnappings, insurgency tactics, suicide bombings, and improvised explosive devices.[9] Among the examples of each are:

- Assassinations: the death of Vice President Haji Abdul Qadir in July 2002 and attempts on President Hamid Karzai in September

2002, on a vice-presidential candidate in 2004, and on the former governor of Badakhshan in October 2007

- Kidnappings of groups of foreigners in both July 2007 and October 2007
- Insurgency tactics including recruitment and training on the Pakistan border and the repeated ambush of soldiers
- Sixty-four suicide bombings between January 2005 and August 2006
- Improvised explosive devices used against U.S. and NATO troops and against Afghan military and civilian vehicles, with the number steadily increasing.[10]

The Taliban also quickly developed a symbiotic relationship with the opium traders in order to finance these and other operations.[11]

3. Underdog strategists are much more likely to play a waiting game. Groups, governments, and individuals who practise the underdog strategy do not have circumstances in their favor, so they have no choice but to wait. After its defeat by the United States in 2001, for example, the Taliban took a few months to regroup and start recruiting. The violence fell to nothing during that period, before increasing again later. The Karzai government has had a gradual and slow approach to the development of several democratic institutions, most significantly the rule of law.[12] The 2006 Afghanistan Compact followed up on the Bonn initiative by providing rather modest benchmarks for reconstruction.[13]

4. Underdogs are more creative because their means are so limited. The Taliban imported the use of improvised explosive devices from the Iraq insurgency. It showed creativity in the adoption of the opium trade to finance itself.[14] The Taliban-based opium trade also showed creativity in effectively exploiting Afghanistan's harsh terrain, the easy corruption of some of its officials, and the insecurity of the population.[15]

5. Underdog strategists are more holistic. Because they live and act in hostile and unpredictable environments, they need to see beyond their immediate circumstances just to survive. It is clear, for example, that the Taliban are no longer seeking a military victory over NATO or the

U.S.-led forces. Instead, they are targeting the unwillingness of NATO's domestic populations to take casualties. The Taliban are also exploiting certain tactics to which the U.S. or NATO troops cannot respond in kind, for legal or ethical reasons. Those tactics include NATO troops threatening relatives of dangerous Taliban, blackmailing the civilian population into providing information, and exploiting the widespread poverty. Taking advantage of such opportunities would be impossible without a holistic perspective. The willingness of the Karzai government to work with governments of other countries on development and reconstruction also reflects a holistic perspective. It has also repeatedly shown its awareness of the link between economic development and the growth of liberal democratic institutions.

6. Underdog strategists spend more time scanning the environment for possible threats and opportunities. The Taliban are quick to spot their opportunities, something that is made more obvious by their ruthlessness. For example, they quickly identified the poverty of farmers as a possible way to exert power over them by offering them money, by extortion, or by promoting the opium trade. Since farm prices for poppy have declined as production has increased, many farmers are falling into debt, making them vulnerable to Taliban blackmail.[16] Poverty also makes exploitation easy: the Taliban have recruited for as little as US$20 a day.[17] Unemployed civilian men may be inferior to NATO troops, but they can easily be used to conduct reconnaissance on NATO or Coalition forces, arrange roadside bombs, or harvest opium.[18]

7. Underdogs are more likely to design each action specifically to suit their strategy. This is because their difficulties train them to think globally and act locally. The Karzai government is clearly conscious of the necessity for development and economic progress to support their efforts at democracy.

8. Underdogs are much more likely to forecast for even the unlikeliest tactic and scenario. Some of the Karzai government's best decisions were made possible by this characteristic. Before the U.S. invasion, there were fears of widespread starvation and large refugee populations. In fact, the worst was avoided, despite the fact that the United Nations

World Food Programme suspended activities when the U.S. invaded. The World Food Programme actually resumed its activities quickly after the fall of the Taliban. Focus Humanitarian Assistance (FOCUS) also continued its rehabilitation and relief activities despite border closures. With respect to the Taliban, however, there is no evidence from open sources about any forecasting capability.

9. Underdog strategists usually assume they will lose any direct confrontation. The Taliban as a government may have been attacked directly by the United States, but once defeated and reduced to the status of an insurgent political group with no place in the political system, it avoided any direct military or political confrontation. The Taliban did not participate in the Afghanistan elections. For its part, the Karzai government has repeatedly, if indirectly, acknowledged its own poverty and the weakness of its institutions by accepting both foreign aid to alleviate poverty and foreign troops to maintain security; it has done so even when the foreign troops were unpopular.

10. If the situation gets bad enough, underdog strategists are much more likely to break their own rules of behavior. While the Taliban were in power, as late as 2000, they banned opium production. As insurgents, however, they have quickly come to rely on the opium trade in order to finance their operations.[19] Similarly, Afghanistan warlords operate outside the law, maintaining private armies and jails and threatening people who speak out against them in the Loya Jirga.[20] Despite the Karzai government's efforts to introduce the rule of law and encourage freedom of speech, it has been forced to bargain with warlords, even going so far as including some former warlords in government.

11. Underdog strategists are usually much more (even passionately) committed. Despite long-standing adverse circumstances, Taliban supporters are willing to fight on, even though they face a much more powerful military enemy. Similarly, Karzai government ministers continue to accept high office and exercise their functions in government, despite the repeated and obvious dangers of assassination.

Overall, there is a good level of evidence that the Taliban and the Karzai government both use the underdog strategy. Table 4, Evidence of

TABLE 4. Evidence of characteristics of the underdog strategy.

Characteristic	Karzai government	Taliban insurgents
They are always thinking about what the strong are about to do	Smaller political parties watched Hamid Karzai's party to take advantage of any misstep	Opium traders moved to Nimroz from Helmand because it was more weakly policed
They are always adapting	N/A	Changed from regular warfare to assassinations and kidnappings, insurgency, suicide bombings and improvised explosive devices, financing by opium trade
They play a waiting game	Slow, gradual development of legal system, modest Afghanistan Compact benchmarks on development	Took time to regroup after losing control of country
They are creative	N/A	Adopted the method of roadside bombs, imported from the Iraq insurgency; opium traders exploit harsh terrain, easy corruption of officials, poverty of the population
They are holistic	Willingness to work with governments of other countries on development and reconstruction	Abandoned goal of military victory over ISAF; now targeting unwillingness of domestic NATO populations, using unanswerable methods
They are always scanning their environment	Starvation, refugee problems failed to materialize	Quickly identified the poverty of farmers as a possible way to exert power over them

(continued on next page)

TABLE 4. *(continued)*

Characteristic	Karzai government	Taliban insurgents
They specifically design each action to suit their strategy	Clearly conscious of the necessity for development and economic progress to support their efforts at democracy	N/A
They are always forecasting for all events	Decision-making processes slow and ineffectual	N/A
They are convinced they will lose a direct confrontation	Accepts foreign troops, even when unpopular	Gave up regular warfare; did not compete in elections
They will break their own rules	Bargains with warlords who operate outside the law, maintaining private armies and jails and threatening people who speak out against them in the Loya Jirga	Banned opium when in power, rely on opium trade as insurgents
Their commitment is complete	Ministers continue to hold office despite the dangers of assassination	Willing to fight on despite facing a much more powerful enemy

Characteristics of the Underdog Strategy, summarizes the findings for the Karzai government and the Taliban insurgents. The next section examines the evidence that the Karzai government and the Taliban insurgents are making some of the mistakes underdog strategists have in common.

MISTAKES UNDERDOGS MAKE

1. Underdog strategists may not keep things simple and straightforward. For example, an underdog government may get bogged down in details, or be easily derailed from its intended agenda. This mistake is one possible explanation for the Karzai government's slow progress in reconstruction, economic development, and democracy.

2. Underdog strategists may not exploit momentum as they should. During the U.S. invasion in 2001, the Taliban had massed nearly 10,000 fighters in its last stronghold in northern Afghanistan. There, it was besieged and defeated by the Northern Alliance with the support of American Special Forces and air support. They had massed these fighters even though their own defeat must have been obvious. Since 2001, however, the Taliban insurgents only made this mistake once: they massed their fighters at Dai Chopan in August 2003, and the outcome was punishing: a quarter of them were killed outright.[21]

3. Underdog strategists may rush into action. Difficult circumstances may drive underdog strategists to act prematurely. There is no evidence of this in open sources for either the Karzai government or the Taliban insurgents.

4. Underdog strategists may ignore unintended consequences. There is no evidence in open sources of either the Karzai government or the Taliban insurgents ignoring unintended consequences. There is one example of this sort of mistake, however, when the Taliban regime was in its last months. In February 2001, the regime had announced its decision to destroy two giant Buddha statues that had been designated a World Heritage Site by the United Nations Educational, Scientific and Cultural Organization (UNESCO). The Metropolitan Museum of New York had offered money to move these statues to their own, more secular environment, in an effort to preserve them. Some Afghan clerics were enraged when money was offered for the statues, but not for starving Afghan children.[22] When the Taliban inquired whether the money offered could be accepted for the children, the museum refused. Incensed, the Taliban regime destroyed the two priceless Buddhas. In this instance, it was the Metropolitan Museum that failed to take into account the unintended consequences of their offer.

5. Underdog strategists might work on the wrong problem. The U.S. invading force certainly conquered the country, but it did not definitively destroy the Taliban. After the Taliban reorganized, they adopted insurgency tactics that NATO troops who succeeded the U.S. were not well prepared to combat. In insurgencies, the regular armed forces often become the underdog. In this situation, the forces failed to recognize the Taliban's potential, and failed to address that potential definitively.

6. Underdog strategists may not specify their objectives enough. The Karzai government could have clarified the constitutional arrangements of Afghanistan much earlier. As late as 2007, few ministries and provincial offices had clear terms of reference, rules, or procedures. Similarly, the central institutions had few checks and balances to prevent patronage, the misuse of public funds, the abuse of public land management, or corruption in the privatization of state-owned enterprises.[23] When it came to democratic processes, government policies sidelined increasing popular dissatisfaction. The same policies favored marginalization and intolerance of political opposition and stunted the development of a pluralistic system in the 2007 parliamentary elections.[24] With an absolute divide between the executive and legislative branches, only the Office of Administrative Affairs could link the two, and its role was still unclear. Finally, the elected provincial councils' specific mandates also remained undefined.[25]

7. Underdog strategists might not develop enough alternatives for their tactics. This mistake is one possible explanation for two notable failures of the Karzai government. First, the Karzai government has not been able to control the opium problem. Second, the Karzai government has failed to eliminate or decisively defeat the Taliban, with the result being increased human rights violations against women, the killing of teachers, the abduction of aid workers, and the burning of school buildings in areas outside of central government control.

8. Underdog strategists may not give adequate thought to tradeoffs. To achieve their goal, underdogs may have to set aside other desirable outcomes or actions. These costs need to be weighed carefully. Before 2001, when the Taliban was still in power, it refused to hand over Osama bin Laden after the terrorist attacks on September 11, 2001. Provoked, the United States invaded shortly thereafter and the regime was overthrown. There have been occasions when the Karzai government did not consider tradeoffs, as well. Inadequate vetting of Afghan police and army candidates, for example, has resulted in political organizers and journalists often being threatened and harassed.

9. Underdog strategists may disregard uncertainty. There is no evidence available in open sources for either the Karzai government or the Taliban insurgents.

10. Underdog strategists may fail to account for the limited tolerance of their people. A politician like Karzai has to consider what his ministers and party members will accept, especially given that political alliances might be fragile because they are new or unusual. This is one explanation for the problem of corruption in the government. When a political situation is fragile, it can change very quickly, and politicians uncertain of their future may be more vulnerable to corruption. Also, Afghanistan has a poor history of national unity, whether between ethnicities, languages, or tribes, making it particularly easy for one group to ignore the situation of the others.[26] Finally, violence and tribal and ethnic conflicts have frequently resulted in the domination of the country's politics by one group to the exclusion of the others. Such a government would not take into account the tolerance and sensibilities of excluded groups in their decision making.[27]

11. Underdog strategists may fail to plan ahead when decisions are linked over time. This happened to the Karzai government early on when it did not address the opium problem immediately. The trade then developed to the point where it became a competing power structure. And Afghanistan, the world's newest democracy, also became its largest producer of heroin.[28]

In summary, there is little evidence available in open sources that the Taliban makes these kinds of mistakes, with one exception. The evidence is not quite as limited for the Karzai government, but only when their processes are more transparent.

Table 5, Evidence of Strategic Mistakes, summarizes the findings to date.

TABLE 5. Evidence of strategic mistakes.

Type of Mistake	Karzai Government	Taliban Insurgents
Not keeping things simple and honest	N/A	N/A
Going against, instead of with, the flow of events	N/A	Taliban insurgents committed this mistake in massing their fighters at Dai Chopan, and had a quarter of them killed outright
Ignoring the need to wait, rushing headlong into action	N/A	N/A
Ignoring the unintended consequences of actions	N/A	N/A
Working on the Wrong Problem	Foreign forces conquer the country, but not well suited to counterinsurgency	N/A
Not Specifying Objectives Enough	Unclear terms of reference and procedures for ministries, provincial offices, liaison between legislative and executive; too little accountability to prevent patronage, misuse of public funds, abuse of public land management, and corruption in the privatization of state-owned enterprises; policies sidelined increasing popular dissatisfaction and favored marginalization and intolerance of political opposition	N/A
Not Developing Enough Alternatives	N/A	N/A
Giving Inadequate Thought To Tradeoffs	Inadequate vetting of army/police candidates led to harassment and threats to political organizers and journalists	N/A

(continued on next page)

TABLE 5. (continued)

Type of Mistake	Karzai Government	Taliban Insurgents
Disregarding Uncertainty	Corruption of government officials	N/A
Failing To Account For Risk Tolerance	History of ethnic and tribal lack of unity; domination of one ethnic group to the exclusion of others	N/A
Failing to Plan Ahead When Decisions Are Linked Over Time	Allowing the opium trade to develop to the point of being a parallel power structure	N/A

CONCLUSION

There is ample *prima facie* evidence that both the Afghanistan govern-ment, as part of the international community of states, and the Taliban, as a minority within Afghanistan, show evidence of being underdogs. When it comes to the use of the underdog strategy, the Karzai government shows evidence of the most characteristics of underdog strategists, with some evi-dence showing it makes typical underdog strategic mistakes. Meanwhile, the Taliban insurgents present open source evidence for all of the underdog strategy characteristics, but only one of the typical mistakes. This suggests that the problem is information, that is, that open sources are not sufficient for a thorough study of them. It stands to reason that there is not enough open information about the inner workings of the Taliban at this point to make a determination regarding their underdog strategy mistakes.

Readers knowledgeable about the situation in Afghanistan may object that they are aware of alternative explanations for some of the evidence cited. Indeed, it is maybe even possible to find alternative explanations for all of the evidence presented earlier. The argument being made here, however, is about the pattern of characteristics and/or mistakes. Alter-native explanations for those are much fewer than for any individual occurrence.

This assessment using characteristics and mistakes of the underdog strategy leads to some interesting hypotheses. For example, if the Taliban behaves like an underdog, then it will target the smaller countries contributing soldiers to the international force. If the insurgents are truly targeting the domestic willingness to take casualties, a small number of casualties would have a greater effect on a smaller national population.

Of more interest to readers of this chapter are the numerous interesting hypotheses regarding the promotion of democracy. If the Taliban insurgents again use violence to disrupt future elections, then their behavior is more predictable. That means it will be easier for police or the military to protect the population from violence. The Karzai government could be assisted in the setting of its priorities by this understanding; for one, it would have probably screened police candidates better and prevented the intimidation of politicians and reporters. Similarly, if governments understood that the Karzai government is an underdog, then governments wanting to develop policy to assist it in its democratic development would behave differently than they do currently. Given the circumstances of the central institutions, foreign governments might more easily identify the clarification of the terms of reference of provincial councils, for example, as a significant contribution to the government of Afghanistan. It would be even more obvious to those donor governments that development aid is linked to democratic advances for the Afghan people, as would also be true of the fight against the opium trade.

Anr avenue that was not explored in this chapter is how the understanding of the underdog strategy could lead to the recruitment of former warlords, militia members, or political extremists into the political sphere, where they would of their own volition abandon violence and criminality in order to participate in the political life of the country.

It is also clear that there is enough evidence to support a much more detailed investigation of democracy in Muslim nations with extremist factions in order to provide insight and policy advice. Given its record in studying domestic and foreign policy, the framework of the underdog strategy could be applied in several contexts. It has the potential to help manage and promote how a fledgling democracy can encourage political participation from radical Islamic groups. It could also be used to predict the behavior of a Muslim minority in a period of democratization, either to improve that minority's political effectiveness, or to help the government predict and manage that minority. It can also help guide the strengthening of a Muslim weak or failed state.

Future research could focus on other cases not assessed in this article, for example, how states deal with Muslim extremist states, how states deal with Muslim weak or failed states, how states deal with struggling liberal democracies with Muslim minorities (especially in south, southeast, and northeast Asia). It would also be of interest to select case studies that are more historical. While they may be of less interest for policymakers, they could still provide some answers about the applicability of the framework.

ENDNOTES

1. Marcel Détienne, *Les Ruses de l'intelligence* (Paris: Grasset, 1956).
2. Laure Paquette, *Security in the Pacific Century* (New York: Nova, 2002), *Strategy and Ethnic Conflict* (New York: Praeger, 2002), *Building and Analyzing National Policy* (Lanham, MD: Lexington, 2002).
3. C. Mark, "Islam: A Primer," *Congressional Research Service (CRS) Report* RS 21432 and F. Armanios, "Islam: Sunnis and Shiites," *CRS Report* RS 21745.
4. Bruce Vaugh, "Islam in South and Southeast Asia," *CRS Report*, February 8, 2005, 2 and A. Kronstadt and B. Vaugh, "Terrorism in South Asia," *CRS Report* RL32259.
5. Although there is no consensus on the definition, we define democracy here as a government having competitive elections, freedom of speech, freedom of the press, the rule of law, civilian control of the military, and popular sovereignty. See Takashi Inoguchi, Edward Newman, and John Keane, *The Changing Nature of Democracy* (New York: United Nations University Press, 1998), 255. See also Rein Taagepera, "Prospects for Democracy in Islamic Countries," in *Democratic Development and Political Terrorism/ The Global Perspective*, ed. William Crotty (Boston: Northeastern University Press, 2005), 93–101, *See esp.* p. 93.
6. Bruce Vaugh, "Islam in South and Southeast Asia," *CRS Report*, February 8, 2005, 1.
7. Donna J. Stewart, "The Greater Middle East and Reform in the Bush Administration's Ideological Imagination," *Geographical Review* 95:3 (July 2005), 400–425. James W. Robert, "Political Violence and Terrorism in Islamdom," in *Democratic Development and Political Terrorism/The Global Perspective*, ed. William Crotty (Boston: Northeastern University Press, 2005), 101–20, 103.
8. Andrew North, "Losing the War on Afghan Drugs," *BBC News*, April 12, 2005.
9. Scott Baldauf and Faye Bowers, "Afghan Riddled with Drug Ties," *Christian Science Monitor*, May 13, 2005.
10. "IED, A Weapon's Profile," *Defense Update/An International Online Defense Magazine* (2004), 3, updated August 23, 2006.
11. Hayder Mili and Jacob Townsend, "Afghanistan's Drug Trade and How It Funds Taliban Operations," *Terrorism Monitor* 5:9 (May 10, 2007).

12. Laura Barnett, "Afghanistan: The Rule of Law," Parliamentary Information and Research Service, PRB 07-17E (Library of Parliament of Canada), 2007.

13. Ali Wardak, Daud Saba, and Halima Kazem, *Afghanistan Human Development Report 2007, Centre for Policy and Human Development (CPHD)* (Army Press: Islamabad, 2007).

14. Anthony Cordesman, "Testimony to the U.S. House Armed Services Committee," January 2007.

15. Hayder Mili and Jacob Townsend, "Afghanistan's Drug Trade and How It Funds Taliban Operations," *Terrorism Monitor* 5:9 (May 10, 2007).

16. Gregg Zoroya and Donna Leinwand, "Rise of Drug Trade Threat to Afghanistan's Security," *USA Today*, May 13, 2005.

17. Senlis Group, Afghanistan, *Countering the Insurgency in Afghanistan: Losing Friends and Making Enemies* (London: MF Publishing, 2007).

18. Hayder Mili and Jacob Townsend, "Afghanistan's Drug Trade and How It Funds Taliban Operations," *Terrorism Monitor* 5:9 (May 10, 2007).

19. Unofficial comments by international staff working in the region, April 2007, cited in Hayder Mili and Jacob Townsend, "Afghanistan's Drug Trade and How It Funds Taliban Operations," *Terrorism Monitor* 5:9 (May 10, 2007).

20. Kenneth Katzman, "Afghanistan: Government Formation and Performance," *CRS Report for Congress*, June 2007, 3.

21. *Voice of America*, "Unstable Afghanistan," August 5, 2003, from American Forces Information Service on Globalsecurity.org.

22. Sahar Kassaimah, "Afghani Ambassador Speaks at USC," *IslamOnline*, March 12, 2001, retrieved February 19, 2008.

23. Seema Patel and Steven Ross, *Breaking Point: Measuring Progress in Afghanistan*, Center for Strategic and International Studies (CSIS), February 2007; report of the UN Secretary General, *The Situation in Afghanistan and its Implications for International Peace and Security*, A/62/345, September 21, 2007.

24. "Political Parties in Afghanistan," *Asia Briefing* 39 (June 2, 2005).

25. Ali Wardak, Daud Saba, and Halima Kazem, *Afghanistan Human Development Report 2007*, Centre for Policy and Human Development (CPHD) (Army Press: Islamabad, 2007).

26. *CIA World Factbook* (Washington, DC: Central Intelligence Agency, 2007).

27. Hafizullah Emadi, "Ethnic Groups and National Unity in Afghanistan," *Contemporary Review* (January 1, 2002).

28. Gregg Zoroya and Donna Leinwand, "Rise of Drug Trade Threat to Afghanistan's Security," *USA Today*, May 13, 2005.

PART II

SOUTH ASIA

CHAPTER 4

ISLAM AND PAKISTAN

Touqir Hussain

Islam is not new to Pakistan, nor is political Islam. In fact, political Islam is not new to Islam, either—it is as old as Islam itself. The Islamic world may have become weaker over the course of history, but the unity that the faith provided has transcended political decline and fragmentation and remains strong even up to today, at least at the emotional level. This has helped political Islam to survive as a transnational force, getting entangled with many regional and global issues. And in countries like Pakistan that have had varying degree of problems in nation building, political Islam has merged with societal tensions and served as a substitute national purpose. This has given space to political Islam, of which a portion has become extremist in recent decades.

Much of this chapter focuses on a historical analysis of the rise of religious extremism in Pakistan and how it has come to pose an existential threat to Pakistan's state and society. It also focuses on where we go from here. Democracy could be a way to defeat extremism but faces defeat from extremism itself. Democracy may bring stability to Pakistan, but can it survive instability? The chapter concludes with a section on democracy and the Islamists specially the challenges Pakistan's democratization faces from the extremists.

Religious extremism is variously referred to in the West as extremist or fundamentalist Islam, or radical or militant Islam. This chapter avoids such nomenclature. These descriptions suggest that Islam is prone to extremism, is intrinsically radical, or that there exists a radical version of Islam, a view vehemently disputed by Muslims, even more so in the context of current tensions between the Islamic world and the West. In defense, they go on to insist that Islam is in fact a moderate and tolerant religion, something that is also open to question by some in the West. These two views polarize the debate, making it unproductive.

This contentious debate and the unresolved tensions between Islam and the West end up harming Islamic societies as much as they do the West. They make it difficult for Muslims to challenge the radicals and extremists, who do not consider themselves as such, anyway, and feel they are practicing a "true" and "authentic" version of the religion. This view subverts the more moderate and mainstream Muslims' understanding of the religion, particularly as they have been seduced by the radicals' claims that they are the defenders of a faith under siege from the West, and have become vulnerable to their propaganda. This complicates the debate, not only with the West but among Muslims themselves.

THE PICTURE OF ISLAM IN PAKISTAN

Islam in Pakistan has several dimensions. One is Islam as a religion that is followed by the vast majority of population who are essentially traditionalists. About 12 to 13 percent of the population are Shias, but the Shia and Sunni Muslims have historically coexisted peacefully—that is, until the Iranian revolution in 1979 and the beginning of the process of the Islamization of Pakistan at about the same time by Zia ul Haq. This changed not only sectarian Islam but also Islam itself, which has not been the same since.

The picture of Islam in Pakistan becomes clearer in the historical context. Islam is embedded in Pakistan's historical roots, as the country was created as a homeland for Muslims of British India. But while it was easy to understand the demand for Pakistan by defining what it was not—it was different though not distinct from India—it was neither possible nor was it politically desirable for the Pakistan movement to fully articulate what Pakistan was. And the challenge continues today, made more difficult by the independent Pakistan's failure as an idea, a theme well explored by Stephen Cohen.

Pakistan's identity crisis and its security problems have arguably been at the heart of this failure. In Pakistan's formative years, when it had a weak national identity, Pakistanis looked for a surrogate identity. They defined it in opposition to India but paid a price by creating an administrative military state. Then they asserted Islamic identity and ended up boosting the Islamists. And now the Islamists have become a dominant stakeholder in the struggle for the soul of Pakistan, which they want to turn from a homeland for Muslims to a homeland for Islam.

By the term *Islamists* this chapter refers only to the pacifist elements seeking an electoral route to power, that is, the established Islamic political parties and a range of religious scholars and political activists inclined to inject religious laws or values into governance. But the problem is the boundaries of Islamists have been touching the extremist organizations like Jihadi outfits, sectarian organizations, and Al Qaeda and the Taliban. And since 9/11 and the war on terrorism, the line dividing the Islamists and the extremists—who are related yet independent—is getting so blurred that we now end up using these terms interchangeably. This whole complex is often referred to as political Islam, yet it might be useful to keep the distinction between the Islamists and the extremists in mind.

The fact is the Islamic parties that form the mainstay of political Islam had initially opposed the creation of Pakistan but saw a good prospect for prospering in the post-independence Pakistan that was struggling to find a national identity, survive economically, and maintain its security and territorial integrity. Indeed, the viability of the state was at stake. The Islamists in a way came to Pakistan's rescue by keeping the focus on religion among the ordinary population and thus sanctioning a religious foundation to Pakistan's national identity. As a payoff they grabbed a stake in the political life of the country by insisting on being a party to the process of constitution making. The passage of the Objectives Resolution as a prelude to the constitution making, which took nine years after the independence in 1947, was a major victory for them.

In this period the largely feudal politicians, who derived their political support not from public acclaim but from their social position and economic status and influence, dominated the balance of power and wanted no change in the regressive social structure. They found good allies among the Islamists, as religion ensured unity, stability, and status quo, as well as some national purpose. They let the Islamists interlope into the political process, as their demands for Islamization helped delay the creation of a constitution, postponing the electoral process and the commencement of democratic experience.

The civil military bureaucracy who watched this drama from the sidelines found in this democracy vacuum a potential recipe for the failure of politicians, giving them an excuse to appropriate political power. The Islamists, who saw no realistic chance of coming to power, became a pressure group, placing their facility for agitation and arousing public emotions at the service of politicians and meddlesome and ambitious civil military bureaucracy. Their concern was limited to a few narrow conservative social values such as sexuality, the subordination of women, and opposition to Western culture. But more importantly, they were acceptable to the West for their anti communism stance and benefited from this liaison. So in time they came to acquire both internal and external benefactors.

The Islamists had no broader social and political agenda that could appeal to people. They were basically playing the role of spoilers trying to get their foot in the political space, and they managed to achieve that. Pakistani politics had no lasting place for them yet, and until that happened it suited them to keep the politics unstable and on the boil.

Their chance was not to come until the break up of Pakistan in 1971, when a number of factors brought Islam into the center of the national agenda. First was the trauma of the separation of East Pakistan and Zulfiqar Ali Bhutto's slogan about Islam, democracy, and socialism, which invested Islam with a new populism. Second was the prospect of exporting manpower to and economic aid from newly rich oil-producing Arab countries. A weakened and fallen country was desperately looking for a tighter embrace with a new external benefactor after the United States was seen as once again having let down Pakistan in 1971, just as it was believed to have done in 1965. Pakistan began ingratiating itself with the oil-rich Arabs by promoting the study of Arabic and popular Islamic culture.

This was the Islamists' second chance to advance their presence on the political scene. They managed to get more Islamic clauses inserted in the 1973 Constitution than in any previous constitution. They lost in the 1970 election yet became emboldened and started demanding the enforcement of sharia laws.

SECTARIANISM AND ISLAMIZATION

The first stirrings of "Islamization" happened during Zulfiqar Ali Bhutto's time. Bhutto "seized upon the idea of an Islamic Pakistan" and went with the growing Islamist movement[1, 2]. Islam became another dimension to his populism as it became more than just a slogan—democracy is our politics, socialism is our economy and Islam is our religion,"[3] as well as the slogan of *"Roti, Kapra, aur Makan"* ("Bread, Clothing, and Shelter"), which appealed directly to the aspirations of ordinary citizens.[4] In 1974 he supported a move to declare the Ahmadiyya sect "non-Muslim." It was a popular move. Islam also began encroaching on culture and entertainment. In early 1977, when he was under siege from the Islamist forces acting as the army's cat's paw, he banned alcohol and declared Friday as a weekly holiday in a desperate move to save his rule.

But it was the action against the Ahmadiyya community that had far-reaching repercussions. It emboldened the Islamist forces and incited sectarianism, thus adding another stimulus for conflict in society that went on to wreak havoc, especially during the time of Zia Ul Haq, the military dictator who ruled Pakistan from 1977 to 1988. Segments of the population began viewing the other religious sects or groups and secularists as the "enemy." They were not seen as committed to the idea of an Islamic Pakistan.[5]

Under Zia the domestic and international contexts soon converged to launch the Islamists as an autonomous force. This was the third wave of the Islamization of Pakistan, and it affected more than the politics of the country. Religious consciousness started becoming more pervasive in all segments of society. It showed particularly in the rise of conservative attitudes as everywhere, the second generation of Pakistanis whose major formative influences were indigenous, and not British, began anchoring their identity in their local cultural values, to which religion, of course, remained central. Nowhere was the religious surge more visible than in the army, where it got mixed with culture, ideology, and opportunism.

Zia increased the role of Islam exponentially as it came to penetrate several societal institutions. He initiated what came to be known as the process of the "Islamization of Pakistan,"[6] with several laws aimed at creating a "true" Islamic state. It was a personal, political, and ideological project built on opportunism and ostensible conviction to strengthen Pakistan and Islam; he ended up doing neither. Instead, we saw the birth of extremism, the consequences of which have been horrendous for Pakistan and indeed for the world. But he was not the sole architect of this adventure. Many players and strategic purposes contributed to this witches' brew. What follows is some background.

HISTORICAL FOUNDATIONS OF RELIGIOUS EXTREMISM IN PAKISTAN

The Pakistan of today has become both a tributary and a confluence of religious extremism that has been responding to local, regional, and global stimuli whose distant origins are buried in the colonial and imperialist past of the Western world. The wider Islamic world and its relations with the West have been the main historical levers of this phenomenon.

Much of the Islamic world is resource rich and has been under Western domination for most of its modern history. Part of this world rests on artificial borders sundering ethnic, linguistic, or sectarian communities, and in a few cases leaving dissatisfied and restless minorities. Some of it is host to regressive social influences—feudalism, tribalism, or oligarchic monarchism claiming religious lineage or superiority to seek obedience. There are also class and cultural wars between the elite—who have inherited Western liberal traditions but practice illiberal values—and the masses, practitioners of conservative and religious values who are crying out for a just social order and political empowerment.

The West had made a common cause with the ruling elite of the Islamic world, thus helping to reinforce the status quo and block social change. Modernization of these societies was sacrificed to the strategic and economic interests of the West.

Taking into account these factors, it is no wonder the Islamic world has been struggling to come to terms with the challenges of social change, political reform, and modernization. And religion has gotten entangled with this struggle that is taking place simultaneously on two fronts, at home and abroad. Nowhere is this conflict more evident than in Pakistan, which has given an enormous boost to the extremists, especially as the history of Islam in Pakistan in the last three decades has gotten entwined with the forces of religious radicalism that arose from the Middle East.

The oil and the new economic power in the Middle East in the 1970s gave a sudden sense of pride to Muslims all over the world and became an important factor in the search for and reassertion of Islamic identity globally. Muslims now thought they had something to be proud of. A revival of the Islamic glory of the past began stirring in many Muslims' dreams. As a result, beginning in the late seventies and early eighties, money and patronage started flowing into Pakistan from all directions, including private sources, in support of religious or pseudo-religious causes. The private money came from the Gulf, where much of the expatriate Pakistani community came from the conservative areas of the North West Frontier Province (NWFP). Many of them had become even more conservative while living in the fundamentalist system of Saudi Arabia.

The Iranian revolution of February 1979 provided a political framework for an Islamic system. At the same time, the incipient Afghan jihad was beginning to train political Islam in militancy, largely spearheaded by "Afghan Arabs"—the Arab dissidents who began looking for a religious paradigm on which to organize their resistance to the unpopular regimes back home. Afghanistan became their training ground and Pakistan the logistics base. But they were not the only ones to exploit Pakistani soil, particularly in the tribal areas, which were becoming more radical than ever before.

With the 1979 Iranian revolution and ensuing Saudi-Iranian rivalry that flowed from the internal dynamics of Saudi Arabia and the regional rivalries and tensions, along with the U.S.-led jihad against the Soviets, Pakistan's domestic order became susceptible to the foreign policy goals of the external patrons on whom Pakistan was becoming dependent because of its poor governance. And if it was a military government it would also be desperate for international support to overcome the problem of legitimacy. The United States and Saudi Arabia fulfilled this need for financial, diplomatic, and political support, and in return used Pakistan to advance their own strategic purposes.

Other Muslim countries, especially Iran and Iraq, also exploited Pakistan's religious infrastructure to further their own political and strategic agendas. The Saudi-Iranian rivalry triggered and continues to fuel sectarian tensions in Pakistan. Along with this rivalry has come a lot of money. Madrassa education mushroomed in Pakistan thanks to Saudi money. The madrassas[7] became the most potent vehicle of dissemination of Wahabi Islam and were expected to serve as a counterweight to the Shia Islam propagated by Iran. This strengthened Islamists of all manner.

All this fitted in well with the Pakistan army's own strategic ambitions. The army, helped by the Islamic parties, continued to fuel the Islamic fervor in the country. Islam came to underpin a security-denominated nationalism, and in a larger context, religion, politics, social order, national security, and foreign policy became rolled into one in Pakistan.

Zia began giving new meanings to the concepts of war, conflict, and jihad. Jihad was no longer defensive but became instead an offensive war—a concept that has been refined by today's radicals in order to find rationale for suicide bombings. Thus was born during Zia's time a Pakistani-style jihadist Islam that spawned a whole generation of militants, with the army becoming its big stakeholder. Many personal ambitions also came to find focus on this militancy. Understandable security concerns became inflated by the army's political ambitions and institutional pride, making rivalry and competition with India an end in itself. This powerful army began feeding on a weak and insecure state, and, of course, on the U.S. aid.

The Pakistan army began making pretensions of being an army of Islam, bringing under its banner a new breed of military adventurers and Islamic revolutionaries, such as some of the heads of Pakistan's intelligence agency, the ISI (Inter Service Intelligence Directorate). First Afghanistan and then Pakistan became the home of this radicalism that soon began searching for new targets in the region and beyond.

Pakistan became "the base for Islamic extremists from all parts of the Islamic world, setting up seminaries under the auspices of religious parties, allowing free movement of five million Afghan refugees in Pakistan, winking at the induction of Afghan destined weapons into Pakistan, conniving at the forced 'Islamisation' of Pakistan's polity. These policies ensured that while the United States emerged from this decade-long effort as an unrivalled hyperpower, Pakistan emerged as the detritus—striven by internal religious and political strife, saddled with a huge refugee population, confronted with a deteriorating law and order situation, and habituated to profligate spending by the dollops of external assistance both overt and covert.

Importantly and tragically, Pakistanis were also left harboring unrealistic ambitions about the further utility of jihad. It achieved nothing in Afghanistan or elsewhere, but strengthened the extremists in Pakistan's body politic."[8]

The traditional Islamic parties saw benefit in cohabitation with the radicals beginning with the Afghan jihad, as there was money and political capital to be made by providing leadership to such Islamic causes as Kashmir, which thanks to the army's patronage had become the leading national priority. In the process, they came to strengthen their traditional bonds with the army. The army and the Islamists collaborated to instigate positive public opinion and support for these causes, and then went on to claim that by fighting for them they were only responding to popular impulses and serving the national interest.

RELIGIOUS EXTREMISM AND PAKISTAN'S TROUBLED DEMOCRACY

It was not only the boundaries of the traditional Islamic parties that started overlapping with the jihadists; when democracy was revived in the 1990s the agenda of the so-called secular liberal parties also started lapping at the Islamists. The army in the middle, on who both had depended, not only blessed but also overtly and covertly encouraged this liaison.

By colliding with Pakistan's internal dynamics, especially its flawed politics and ambitious army with its strategic overextension in the region, along with global Islamic revivalism, the problems of Muslim diasporas, and the war on terrorism, religious extremism has been on the rise in Pakistan. One stimulus has been the gradual growth of an extremist mindset in the Pakistan state and society.

Extremism essentially reflects Pakistan's long but unsuccessful struggle to find a national purpose and identity and an open and stable political process that promotes tolerance and liberal habits of the mind and supports justice for all, not only for the citizenry but also for the minorities and smaller provinces. Pakistan's existential struggle with issues of security, national identity, and state power has historically led to national priorities that fed on emotions, a perfect environment to host an extremist mindset.

Years of authoritarian rule, degraded rule of law, deformed democracy, and weak institutional architecture have intersected with Pakistan's societal tensions, especially crosscurrents of sectarian, ethno-linguistic, and civil-military differences, encouraging a public tendency over time to resort to extremist solutions. Such institutions as existed to mediate the differences either lacked integrity or autonomy, being subservient to the centers of power. No wonder there has been an inclination to resort to militancy and extremism as instruments of redressing the imbalances and wrongs. Once force becomes an acceptable way of settling differences it turns on itself and breeds its own imbalances and injustices. Thus, extremism thrives.

Obviously this kind of politics, especially as it was laced with bad governance, brought Pakistan to grief. Over the years, beginning with 1971 and then with Zulfiqar Bhutto's time, Pakistan has been losing control of itself. Even in the 1990s during the so-called decade of democracy neither Benazir Bhutto nor Nawaz Sharif attempted to moderate the extremist tendencies, which they could have done by reversing Zia's legacy of "Islamization."[9] But they did not. Benazir continued the religious populism of her father. Like him, she was secular but did not shy away from using "Islamic causes for short-term political gain."[10] It was during her time that the Taliban was created and its godfather was the same man who was advising her father. General Nasiurllah Babar was close to her father and authored his Afghanistan policy, later joining his PPP party, and as Benazir's interior minister he continued the same Afghan policies.

Both Nawaz and Benazir started raising the ante to serve Islam. During his second term, Nawaz set up a system of Khidmat Committees, a kind of grassroots system of sharia. Before he fell, he was about to institute the sharia system of government, with himself as Amir.

The politicians paid lip service to Islam in order to acquire public support without having to provide good governance, which they could not, given the rapacity of politicians and unethical politics. They also supported the radicals in a Faustian bargain with the army, which wanted to use the jihadists in Kashmir. By 2000, at least eighteen militant groups preaching jihad in Kashmir were operating out of Pakistan.[11]

Because they ended up serving some national purpose, such as fighting for Kashmir and serving Islam, the militants began acquiring legitimacy and public support. This hollow national purpose was achieved at the expense of national stability, good governance, a working rule of law, and effective law and order. Meanwhile, Pakistan's problems—social and demographic changes, a dysfunctional public school education system, and slowing economic growth[12]—had been mounting. These conditions benefited the Islamists, especially the extremists.

People facing socioeconomic pressures or in search of work had been moving to urban areas from rural ones in the 1980s and all through the early 1990s. The poverty migrated with them, however. Now these people were not only economically deprived, but emotionally deprived, as well, since their rural support systems were gone. The government was unresponsive to their problems. This void was filled by Islamists, particularly the extremists, who became the mediators to this large population looking for hope and solace. As more and more people migrated from rural to urban areas, Pakistan's government ignored the fact that these same people would remain poor (only this time, they inhabited a different location) and susceptible to the views and objectives of the religious extremist groups, who in turn claimed to have all the answers.[13]

No wonder there developed a reciprocal linkage between rise of socioeconomic discontent, growth of religious extremism, poor governance, and political instability. In this weakened state it was not only the minority provinces that began asserting their latent nationalist tendencies, but the substate or nonstate actors became powerful, as well. This further weakened the state capacity to confront these Islamic extremists. The growing influence of militants also meant greater sectarianism and divisions within society, not to mention the fact that it fostered intolerant social attitudes—especially toward minorities. This was hardly an ideal mindset for democracy.

Once Musharraf came to power, Islamic extremism got a further shot in the arm. He came in the name of "enlightened moderation," but this turned out to be no more than a ruse to get Washington's support and that of the liberal segments of society. He liberalized the media, essentially to use it as an ally—the liberation was merely cultural while his politics remained anything but liberal. He made bedfellows with the jihadists by supporting the MMA (Muthida Majlis e Amal—the coalition of Islamic parties). MMA, which during much of Musharraf's rule governed the province of NWFP and was a partner in the government of Baluchistan, gave a free hand to the Taliban and by extension their Al Qaeda backers. The militant groups became even stronger and better organized despite the fact that they were no longer dependent on state patronage. They had a place under the sun in Pakistan society.

In January 2002, Musharraf gave a landmark speech aimed at burying the Islamization agenda of Zia. He announced that that the "day of reckoning" had come.[14] He claimed to support a more "moderate," a more "progressive" Islam within Pakistan.[15] But even though he banned some of the major extremist outfits, some of them resurfaced shortly thereafter under different names.[16] It was clear that the time to effectively deal with these groups just by proscribing them had gone. And as it turned out, even his ban was just a window dressing.

Some 2,000 extremists were put in jail but released soon after. The government dragnet acted too late, however, and most escaped. Their bank accounts were closed, but only after most of the money had already been moved. It was becoming apparent that there were sympathies for the militants in many quarters both official and unofficial. By now too many individuals and institutional players had come to have vested interests in these organizations and their causes.

The Impact of the War on Terrorism

The war on terrorism has incited anti-Americanism in Pakistan and raised the stock of Islamists and extremists in more ways than one. First, the campaign against terrorism was launched in conjunction with a dangerous war hysteria in the West that led to the profiling of Islam as a universal creed of terrorism. Everything wrong with Muslim societies was equated with religion, making the war on terrorism look like a war on Islam, and the distinction between the terrorists and their societies was blurred.

The West then claimed it was a war of ideas, provoking Muslims to uphold and defend their value system. Elements on both sides began seeing their basic values and self-image as being under siege and exaggerated their mutual fears, defaming and demonizing each other. Moral issues were undifferentiated or confused, or sacrificed to self-righteousness. As the war on terrorism began looking like a war on Islam—especially as it led to U.S. occupation of two Muslim countries—many felt that Islam was under siege and the only way for Muslims to break free would be to wage jihad.

Muslims felt they had to defend their religion and what it stands for. Extremists took up this cause and were tolerated, even applauded for doing so. The Islamists and extremists alike began "winning" this war of ideas. The extremists in particular were able to present Muslims as victims and the West as oppressor. Specifically with respect to Pakistan, religious extremism thus came to find wider sponsorship and popular support.

All of this made the war on terrorism very unpopular and intensified anti-Western and especially anti-American sentiments. The feelings of identity, honor, and dignity that the war on terrorism ignited have asserted themselves through nationalism.

A majority of Muslims are convinced that the United States was using the tensions between Islam and the West and the opportunity provided by the 9/11 tragedy to pursue an aggressive foreign policy agenda whose prime example has been the Iraq war. In Pakistan, the Afghanistan war came to be seen by people in the same light as the Iraq war, fueling an insurgency in the tribal areas.

THE INSURGENCY IN THE TRIBAL AREAS AND ITS IMPACT ON PAKISTAN

It will be pertinent to explain here what is going on in the tribal areas (FATA[17]) of Pakistan and how it is affecting Islam and the rest of the country. A core tribal value on both sides of the border is resistance against control, by the foreigner or the state. Whenever such a conflict has happened in the past, particularly when the invader was also an "infidel" like the British or the Soviets, the resistance has been provided leadership by the mullah. The mullah has then employed the Islam that first got mixed with Arab culture centuries ago, but is now entangled with a social order that rests on strong tribal and clan dynamics in the tribal areas on either side of the Pakistan-Afghanistan border.

The U.S.-led war on terrorism in which the Pakistan army has been a partner has re-ignited a similar resistance now. The war on terrorism is regarded by much of the Pashtun-dominated tribal territory straddling the Pakistan-Afghanistan border as an assault on its religious and ethnic identities. This is happening in a society where the weight of the past oppresses the present, and continuity and change are locked in a bitter contest. This struggle typifies the internal contradictions in the Islamic world, touching on deep-rooted socioeconomic structures and traditions. Exposure to the West has externalized this reality, affecting as well as reflecting inner tensions.

As Akbar S. Ahmed tells us in his book, *Resistance and Control in Pakistan*, jihad has come to voice material and spiritual needs and has become an instrument of many intangibles, such as ambition for power and control, which are burnt into the human psyche. It therefore transcends a purely religious significance. Ahmed writes, "It tells us more about the Muslim society in which jihad is articulated than Islamic theology or law" (p. 138) and that "[u]nderstanding of religion is not the issue here, the affective and connotative power of its symbols in society is" (p. 139).

This is what the current struggle in Pakistan's tribal areas—in which local, regional, and global agendas have gotten entangled—is all about. The population on either side of the border considers the cause of its kinsmen on the other side as its own. Support for the Taliban by Pakistan's tribal areas is thus becoming a surrogate for their own nationalist aspirations. No wonder the Taliban of Afghanistan have inspired the rise of a Pakistani Taliban,[18] led by Baitullah Mehsud, trying to replicate the same movement in Pakistan.

Pakistan thus has two insurgencies on its hands, one whose origins lie in Afghanistan and the other of Pakistani extraction. The militancy radiating from the tribal areas is now spreading throughout Pakistan, threatening its future. The siege of Red Mosque[19], its aftermath, and the wave of suicide bombings are only part of this story.

The fact is that post-9/11 events, especially U.S. foreign policy, have added a whole new dimension to the religious radicalism in Pakistan that is seriously threatening the country's stability and territorial integrity, and indeed its future.

COMPETING VISIONS OF ISLAM

The events in Pakistan since 9/11 and the war on terrorism cannot be understood without understanding what is going on in the broader Islamic world.

Much of the Islamic world is struggling to come to terms with the continuing perceived Western domination and the related challenges of social change and political reform.

Unfortunately, against the background of a lack or weakness of institutions of social and democratic change and the absence of a just international order, for the majority of Muslim societies this struggle has been very troubling. Over the years, the general populace has been kept on the periphery and prevented from being a part of true nation-building; the socially dominant groups have managed to marginalize the proletariat and have kept it from having an active say in democratic rule.[20] Such democracy as has existed in a few places—without social restructuring—empowers not the people but the elite, which goes on to strengthen its class and institutional interests.

This has caused a high level of discontent that is seeking avenues for self-expression. This quest has coincided with a religious revival that had previously been independent of the stream of discontent, but has now merged indistinguishably with it, releasing uncontrollable forces that threaten to aggravate the very failure of nation and state that caused the social turmoil in Muslim societies in the first place.

But that is not all. There is also a resurgence of Islam as a moral and spiritual force hovering between personal and political Islam. There are some Islamic thinkers engaged in an intellectual effort to bring Islamic values to the center of the debate in the Islamic world as a means of renewing their societies that are under siege from Western cultural and political assault. Many Islamic scholars, for instance, are working on the institution of Islamic banking with some success. And then there are others among the educated and the moderate who yearn for a soft Islamic revolution.

Many young minds are also opening up to religion. For some, religion has become a medium of idealism while others are prone to extremist thoughts, especially those getting their first dose of religion administered not by scholars but by those who have mixed their social or political agenda with the message of Islam. This enhances the appeal of their message even though it distorts the religion, and an activist media in Pakistan is helping them. Through this kind of religion, the young are seeking expression of their anger, fear, and hopes, spurred by social discontent, economic dissatisfaction, political frustration, and personal unhappiness.

Islam is thus becoming a mix of idealism, ideology, religiosity, populism and moral and political activism, social discontent, economic dissatisfaction, political frustration, and personal unhappiness. The debate has drifted into religious channels because of multiple factors. There is the political and economic failure of leadership in Islamic societies that has ceded ground to the better organized and motivated Islamists, who have become the only mediators with the common man. They fill the critical vacuum both in the political landscape and civil society. Equally important is the rise to dominance of moral and cultural issues that have been triggered by modernization. These cut across classes and are related to the resurgence of honor, ideology, and nostalgia for the past that is typical of societies experiencing a nagging sense of failure, or at least a lack of self-fulfillment, and a collapse of traditional values with no substitute sense of national purpose.

Ideology serves a reassuring purpose in these troubling and capricious times. According to Khalid Abou el Fadl,[21] professor of law at the UCLA Law School, as quoted by Pakistani academic Suroosh Irfani in his article, "After the Flogging," in a Pakistani newspaper,[22] the "puritanical orientation" of Pakistan is a supremacist ideology "that compensates for feelings of defeatism, disempowerment and alienation with a sense of self-righteous arrogance vis-à-vis the 'other'—whether that other is the West, nonbelievers in general, Muslims, or even women."

At the same time, Puritanism is alienated not only from modernity, "but also from Islamic heritage and tradition, literature, aesthetics, music, mysticism, intellectual and cultural history." Religious texts are used "like a shield to avoid criticism or escape challenges that mandate the use of reason and rationality." Indeed, for puritans, "religious texts [are] whips" wielded to further the aims of regressive forces in society.

Puritans "are ignorant of jurisprudential theory and methodology, and therefore treat law in whimsical and opportunistic fashion. They search through thousands of statements and sayings attributed to the Prophet Mohammad (Peace be upon him) in order to find anything that they could use to support their already preconceived positions." They end up projecting "their social and political frustrations and insecurities upon the text." Consequently, "if a puritan is angry at the West, he will read the religious text in such a way as to validate this hostility. And if he needs to compensate for feelings of powerlessness by dominating women, he'll read the text to validate the subjugation and disempowerment of women."

In fact, "in every situation we find that the proverbial arm of the text is being twisted to validate whatever the puritan orientation wishes to do. All along the puritan claims to be entirely literal and objective and faithfully implement what the text demands without personal interference."

Fadl further notes that given the intellectual vacuum in the Muslim world, "virtually every Muslim with a modest knowledge of the Quran and the tradition of the Prophet considers [himself] qualified to speak for Islamic tradition and sharia law."

Small wonder then that the leaders of Wahhabi-Salafi movements such as Al Qaeda, LeT and Jama'at-ud Dawa are not trained jurists but "engineers or medical doctors." "Such self-proclaimed jurists have reduced Islam to a combustible mix of intolerance, hatred and isolationist arrogance, exploding across the world, but most notably among Muslims themselves" (chapter 3, "The rise of the early puritans," and chapter 4, "The story of contemporary puritans").

CHALLENGES IN FIGHTING EXTREMISM

The rise and sustainability of religious extremism within Pakistan owes itself to many factors and players. There are internal and external stimuli, direct and indirect. Since no single phenomenon helped create this specter, no single force can dismantle it.

In the past three decades, the external support for extremism has come from Saudi Arabia and Iran, partly because of geopolitical rivalry and partly because of Saudi fear of the export of revolution by Iran, not to mention ideological and sectarian objectives.[23] The United States has made its own contribution to extremism.

The most significant role, however, has been that of Pakistan itself. It supported the Taliban in Afghanistan, and earlier, the Pakistani government nourished and used this Islamic extremism to support insurgency in Kashmir during the 1990s.[24] There are suspicions that there are still extremist-group sympathizers within the ISI.[25] Even if Pakistan (especially after 9/11) may have dropped its active support of these groups, its lack of forceful action against them, for whatever reasons, had the effect of sustaining them.

But more than the government, the ISI, the politicians, or the Islamic parties the ownership of extremism has now passed on to the general public. The Afghan war of the 1980s had left in its trail much stronger forces of militancy. Among other things, it bred a whole crop of adventurers, political opportunists, and religious fanatics—including former ISI operatives who were trying to harness these forces of extremism in pursuit of their ambitions for power in the name of Islam.

As Pakistan's religious extremism is no longer dependent on state patronage for survival, state power, therefore, will not be sufficient to fight it. But the problem is that Pakistanis not only lack national consensus on the issue, they are confused and disoriented. In some cases they even lack moral clarity. Public sympathy has become a big factor in the support of extremism, as it has made it politically difficult for the government to take action against extremist elements.

People are generally afraid of speaking against extremism for fear it might be misconstrued as speaking against religion—at least, this is what is happening in Pakistan.

Let us look us at the reaction to the Red Mosque episode in 2007, when government troops stormed the mosque in Islamabad that had been taken over by radicals sympathetic to the Taliban and Al Qaeda. It is true the government botched the operation, resulting in the deaths of many innocent people. But in an atmosphere of charged emotions against the army and the United States and their cooperation in the war on terrorism the debate on the issue took on the wrong color. Pakistanis ended up lionizing the fanatics for their resistance. In addition, many thought an attack on them would be tantamount to an attack on religion. This is an instance where a clear moral stand that both sides were wrong would have been critical. But it did not happen.

According to noted Pakistani analyst Hassan Askari Rizvi,[26] Pakistanis condemn terrorism and suicide attacks in principle but advance odd reasons to rationalize their behavior in not taking action against it. Suicide bombings and other terrorist attacks are typically described as nothing more than reactions to American military presence in Afghanistan or revenge for American drone attacks in the tribal areas. This mindset conceives of terrorist attacks as a U.S., Indian, and Israeli conspiracy to destabilize Pakistan. In their thinking, the United States wants to destabilize Pakistan in order to justify taking over Pakistan's nuclear weapons and making it subservient to India.

Whether it is caused by lack of political will, loss of capacity, or denial (or perhaps all three), in addition to a loss of hope and sense of failure, a paranoia and fear of state collapse are inducing people to clutch at false icons of national honor and dignity.

And collective paranoia is particularly dangerous, as we saw in Germany. Pakistan is not there yet, but could get there if things continue to go like this. The task of fighting extremism and terrorism—perceptions of which have been submerged in the wave of nationalism, anti-establishment sentiments, anti-Americanism, anti-India sentiments, the religious surge, and tensions between Islam and the West—thus remains daunting.

The central dilemma for many in Pakistan is whether by opposing the Taliban (which is now a generic name for the extremists) they are opposing Islam and supporting the U.S. policies. On the flip side, the other question is whether by opposing the United States and its policies toward the Islamic world they are supporting the Taliban. It is a tough choice. What follows is a look at how different strands of society are addressing this dilemma.

The masses, which generally are more traditional and conservative, tend to view the Taliban favorably and consider them good Muslims, except in areas such as FATA that have suffered the brutal effects of insurgency and counter-insurgency. Yet even there the local people's hostility to the government and the United States and the killing of innocent civilians by both exceeds their hostility to the militants. If the Taliban kill ten civilians in their insurgency it arouses less angry response than that provoked by the killing of just two by the drones or by the actions of the Pakistan army.

As for the intelligentsia, it may hate the Taliban for its attack on liberal values and human freedoms, but acquiesces to, if not admires, their resistance to the United States. And the religiously inclined among the intelligentsia have their own hang ups—they are afraid of criticizing the Taliban's sharia for fear that they may end up criticizing Islam. In their convoluted view, bad Islam is perhaps still better than no Islam.

ISLAM, ISLAMISTS, AND DEMOCRACY

Whether personal or political, moderate or extremist, this emphasis on Islam has boosted not only the prospects of extremists—whatever their agenda may be—but also the hopes of the Islamists such as traditional Islamic parties like Jamaat Islami in Pakistan, which is dallying with modern political ideas and offering an amalgam of traditional values and modern institutions to broaden their political appeal.

All manner of Islamists have become mediators with the wider population, offering "solutions" to their problems, which is something that the so-called democratic political leadership has failed to do. This leadership felt confident of its electability because of its wealth and social influence and because of the vulnerability of the poor and the uneducated, who could be swayed by populist slogans. The same vulnerability to populism is being tested now by the Islamists, who are inciting religious sentiments with greater facility, especially as they have been able to create the false impression that Western democracy has failed and is not the answer to Pakistan's problems, while Islam is.

Interestingly, while Islam is rising in Pakistan, so is the surge for democracy, as witnessed in the unprecedented activism of the civil society in the agitation against Musharraf in 2008. A public opinion poll released in January 2008 by the U.S. Institute of Peace found that the majority of Pakistanis want their country to be an Islamic democracy.

There is something in the Islamists' agenda or rhetoric that touches a sympathetic chord in the hearts of a wide range of people. Their nationalism is appealing to some, and to some their moral conservatism, while others respond to rhetoric about the honor and glory of Islam, and by extension its ideals of social justice and egalitarianism. The Islamists compete with the Western liberal elite, who are themselves divided between pseudo-liberals in league with the ruling elite who run authoritarian and unrepresentative systems and practice half democracies, and disempowered intelligentsia with aspirations for liberal democracy. The intelligentsia thus ends up fighting on two fronts—with the Islamists on the one hand and with the ruling elite on the other.

The fact is that the propagation of ideas is no longer monopolized by the state or the intelligentsia. They are now available at the grassroots level, making this truly an era of mass politics and activism. As a consequence, the political thinking in Muslim societies has come to reflect predominantly the values and assumptions of the masses—who are more traditional and religious than the elite—and of the disaffected youth whose anger finds an easier outlet in an ideology and politics of protest and rejection than in the nonexistent institutions of democratic change.

The masses especially felt betrayed by the Western-oriented elite and the failure of the pseudo-liberal institutions to provide them with economic and physical security. Whatever little modernization their societies accomplished brought hardly any material difference to their lives, but plenty of corrosive potential for their traditional values.

This pressure-vacuum for change in the Islamic world, especially in some Arab countries that have lacked a modicum of open and credible political process, is coming from Islamists. After all, Islam holds the promise of social justice and an egalitarian system. It does seem to be an answer to the moral dilemmas detonated by rapid modernization and is beginning to attract conservatives and liberals alike to its alternative model of society. While in the past it was possible to synthesize religious tradition and elements of modernization, it is now becoming increasingly difficult to bridge the widening gap between the two as modernization, at least in terms of cultural values, is moving too fast. More and more people are therefore falling back on traditional values for stability.

This has been exploited by the Islamists, who have also preyed on the anti-West feelings, undercurrents of class and cultural wars, and above all the presumed failure of the so-called Western liberal democracy, which has made no material difference to the daily life of the vast majority of the population.

The fact is, it is not the idea of democracy that has failed but its practice; however, the majority of people do not realize that. Islam may be incompatible with a Western liberal democracy that rests on individualism and secularism, but it is not incompatible with democratic ideals such as basic human rights, respect for human dignity, and social justice. Right now, the democratic and the religious waves are not reconciling, but this is not to say that they are irreconcilable.

Yet the question is being raised, both in the West and in the Islamic world, of whether liberal democracy, much less Western liberal democracy, can be promoted in Muslim societies at all. In these essentially traditional societies would the concepts of man, freedom, social order, and world view be the same? Or would we be looking at an alternative societal model?

To answer that, some definitions will be helpful. Is the presence of an electoral democracy enough for a society to be defined as democratic or are we talking here of other qualifications, particularly the quality of governance, as well? The term *governance* is equally confusing. Its definition ranges from a narrow and restricted view of it as merely an administrative phenomenon to an all-encompassing system of stable social order, efficient economic management, and maintenance of law and order. This means that governance is merely an administrative bureaucratic concept that can extend to authoritarian or semi-authoritarian rulers who may or may not have come to power through elections that may or may not have been very credible. An example was Musharraf's performance-based authoritarianism. Or the governance could be a system of liberal constitutionalism allowing civil liberties, rule of law, an independent judiciary, and a moderately free press like in Singapore, but lacking a free or credible political process, representative institutions, or participatory democracy.

But does not true democracy go well beyond the half democracy of Singapore and half governance of Musharraf? Does it not also include a different value system? The issue here is whether these values can be represented only by the Western liberal models, or whether they can be associated with other value systems, such as those of Islam.

Where do Muslim countries stand in regard to the Western democratic model? As Mr. Sharfuddin has observed in an article in the *Dawn*, the leading English-language newspaper of Pakistan, while Muslim countries are largely authoritarianism, Western democratic countries are in the advanced stages of liberal democracy, where the focus is entirely on individualism. This democracy is also secular, "where the emphasis is on the separation of state from religion in all aspects of social and political issues, such as the constitution, administration, legislation, policy-making and culture."[27]

Such a secular democracy raises questions in the minds of many Muslims as to its implications for their religious and family values. Malaysia, for instance, has been arguing in favor of a compromise between illiberal democracies or authoritarian regimes and secular or liberal democracies with "decent democracies," where human rights, democratic and institutional reforms, and constitutions "correspond to the core values of the local population and sit well with the social makeup of their respective communities."[28]

This middle model might resolve the never-ending debate as to whether Islam is compatible with democracy or democracy is compatible with Islam. Decent democracy lays emphasis on those positive aspects where there is no difference of opinion between the West and Islam, Sharfuddin concludes.

The Islamic world began with a great humanitarian and ethical revolution, but its outstanding civilization declined with the rise of the West and has been struggling since to come to terms with the modern age. Leaving aside the tiny minority of radical fundamentalists, the fact is the mainstream Islamic world has no serious issues with the modern humanistic values that have been universalized—basic human rights, respect for human dignity and security, equality of people in the eyes of law, gender equality, social justice, and so on.

There is a broad unanimity over the inviolability of these values. The question lies in how these values are enshrined in the social charter—within what institutions and political structure—as well as how to reconcile them with personal and family laws and with religious traditions and values. There is also the question of how the Muslim diasporas can live in a Western society that overemphasizes individual freedom. These are the challenges for the Islamic world. To this end, there are competing visions of society. It is very hard to build a consensus as to what really constitutes an Islamic way of life and governance in this age and day. The dilemma is how to be a good Muslim in this so-called modern age.

Unfortunately, this quest is not only affecting the current tensions between Islam and the West but also the search for democracy in the Islamic world, since democracy is associated with Western values, some of which violate the Muslim sense of propriety and ethics. And the extremists who have mixed political agenda with their opposition to the West have also joined the debate by demonizing democracy as a Western concept and thus something to be rejected.

The unrepresentative regimes in some of the Arab countries have joined the extremists in subverting public perceptions of democracy by inciting a debate as to whether Islam is a better system. While this debate rages, authoritarian rule, underpinned in some places by nominated consultative institutions called Shura that are presumed to represent the will of the people and claim to reflect the traditional Islamic way of participatory democracy, continues to thrive. This is certainly no democracy, Islamic or otherwise.

As this debate is not going to be resolved any time soon—in fact in many Islamic countries it has not even begun—the Islamists will remain relevant to Pakistan's future regardless of the unimpressive record of their past electoral success, particularly as the U.S. policies in the region will continue to provoke anti-Americanism, which the Islamists are likely to exploit. While in the past the struggle against an unpopular regime has been generally led by secular parties, there is a good chance that such struggle in future will be led by Islamists, who can package a moral and social agenda and anti-Americanism to a telling effect. U.S. policies in the region in years to come will provide the Islamists with exploitable causes that will appeal to popular emotions.

CONCLUSION

It is well and good to sit here in the West, talking of democracy as a natural human condition and wondering why the Islamic societies are defying this logic. Muslims do aspire for democracy, especially if it means empowerment of people and social justice, and they know that democracy is indeed the answer to their problems; however, it is their failure to democratize that has caused them to start looking at religion to provide the basis of an alternative model of society. But here again, paradoxically, the main impulse to turn to religion may have come from democratic ideals that have focused on the search for a just society.

The fact is that religion has not caused this frenzy; it is only giving expression to it. This is happening mostly in societies that were already troubled or stagnant, where social change and political process had been blocked and economic progress remained stillborn. The common man cries out for justice and he does not care if it is dispensed through secular or religious channels, though he would remain privately religious either way.

It is true that there has been a religious revival in countries that have not failed, such as Turkey and Malaysia, but there revivalism takes on a different character. It is more in the nature of finding the soul within modernizing societies. The West has its own creeds, such as freedom, equality, and individual self-fulfillment, which claim their origins, at least in the United States, from Protestant ethics and values. So it is not surprising that Muslims should be looking to their religious roots to impart moral content to their national purpose and strengthen their sense of identity. The West has found its answer only after centuries of struggle.

But the problem is this search has gotten entangled with the difficulties of nation- and state-building in many countries, aggravated by unjust social and international orders. As a consequence, competing and compelling visions of Islam have emerged in the Islamic world that are inducing Muslims to revolt against their modern history. While their religion does offer a vision based on its humanitarian and ethical values, it is very hard to build a consensus as to what really constitutes an Islamic way of life and governance in this age and day. The moderates and extremists differ vehemently on this question, further complicating the search for democracy in the Islamic world.

Yet, in my view the appeal of Islam to an average Muslim remains more moral, cultural, and emotional than political. There may be incompatibility between Islam and Western democracy, but not between Islam and liberal democratic values—once the Islamic world has resolved its internal conflict over competing visions of religion. Liberal democracy can indeed flourish in traditional societies.

But this will not happen if there is no enlightened and scholarly debate in the Islamic world as to where it stands in relation to the modern world. Whatever passes for a debate is actually a confused and confusing political discourse mixed with a half-baked view of religion dominated by the extremists. The onus is on Islamic scholars and the traditional Islamic parties to rescue the debate from the clutches of the extremists, otherwise the Islamic world is headed for a great historical failure. One cannot ignore Islam, but one must reject extremists. Let the Islamists stand up and be counted, and become and be allowed to become part of a democratic process.

Political Islam, in my view, is essentially a resistance movement. In the ultimate analysis, the Islamists will fall and stand on whether they can respond to people's aspirations for a better quality of life and not so much on appealing to their religious instincts. The leadership will be judged not by its religious content but by the quality of its governance. Islamists have to change or they will become extinct, having outlived their utility as a cutting-edge for social and political change.

Eventually, after religion has served its main purpose of giving leadership to political change, it may struggle to survive as a political force, especially if external stimuli like tensions between Islam and the West have moderated. Islam's moral, cultural, and emotional appeal may, however, live on.

Meanwhile, democracy cannot be transplanted and be up and running overnight. It is a graded experience that nations acquire by hard work in schooling themselves in literacy and appropriate habits of thought, accommodation, and tolerance, and by modernizing social structures with openness to such concepts as rights of man, the people's sovereignty, and humanistic values. It also involves harmonizing the tribal, ethnic, regional, religious, and sectarian divisions, if any, and restructuring the economic system.

In the ultimate analysis, democracy is hardly distinguishable from nation building, and historically the United States has complicated this struggle by becoming a party to the internal conflicts on behalf of the ruling elite that protected its economic and strategic interests.

ENDNOTES

1. Cohen, Stephen Philip. *The Idea of Pakistan* (Washington, DC: Brookings Institution Press, 2004.
2. Ibid., 169.
3. From the manifesto his Pakistan People's Party.
4. Traub, James. "Can Pakistan be Governed?" *The New York Times*, March 31, 2009.
5. Haqqani, Husain. Pakistan: Between Mosque and Military (Washington, DC: Carnegie Endowment for International Peace, 2005), 318.
6. Ibid., 193.
7. There are several good reports on Pakistani madrassas, including the World Bank/Harvard Study (2004), International Crisis Group Report (2005), and a study by Christine Fair for the USIP (2006).
8. Najmuddin Shaikh Dawn.com Feb 18, 2007 Flash Forward: America, Part of the problem or solution
9. Jones, 282.
10. Cohen, 174.
11. Ibid., 301.
12. Cohen, 259.
13. Barsalou, Judy. "Islamic Extremists: How Do They Mobilize Support?" *United States Institute of Peace: Special Report 89* (July 2002): 8. Online at http://www.usip.org/pubs/specialreports/sr89.pdf (accessed April 12, 2008).
14. Ibid, 282.
15. Ibid.
16. Haqqani, 305.
17. Federally Administrated Tribal Areas.
18. The organization known as Tehrik Taliban Pakistan (TTP).
19. Red Mosque is a mosque in Islamabad, Pakistan, where in 2007 government troops attacked suspected radicals and madrassa students who had initiated a campaign to harass music and video shops in the city and act as a vice squad.
20. Hippler, Jochen. "Nation-Building in Pakistan." http://www.jochen-hippler.de/Aufsatze/Nation-Building_in_Pakistan/nation-building_in_pakistan.html.
21. *The Great Theft: Wrestling Islam from the Extremists* (New York: Harper One, 2005).

22. *Daily Times*, April 16 2009.
23. Cohen, 306.
24. Ibid.
25. Ibid., 5.
26. "Can Pakistan Cope with Terrorism?" *Daily Times*, April 12, 2009.
27. Dawn, "Muslim States and Democracy," by Syed Sharfuddin May 25, 2007.
28. Ibid.

CHAPTER 5

BANGLADESH

THE NEW FRONT-LINE STATE IN THE STRUGGLE BETWEEN ASPIRING PLURALIST DEMOCRACY AND EXPANDING POLITICAL ISLAM

Tariq Karim

The past is never dead. It is not even past.

—William Faulkner

Those who ignore history are doomed to repeat it.

—George Santayana

INTRODUCTION

Marginalized and pushed to the periphery as the smaller nations of South Asia are by the all-consuming, seemingly epic struggle between India and Pakistan, people might well ask: does Bangladesh matter at all? And why?

Bangladesh, with its over 147 million people who are hostage to widespread poverty, presents itself as a most interesting case study of a third-world nation struggling to establish, preserve, and consolidate democracy against the grain of a legacy of deep-rooted political schizo-phrenia that is apparently imbedded in its identity and history. Its bloody birth itself was indelibly framed within the larger contestation that then defined the Cold War paradigm. At its independence in 1971 it emerged as a uniquely homogenous nation in South Asia, with its population comprised 98 percent of ethnic Bengalis. Despite 88 percent of its peo-ple being Sunni Muslims, Bangladesh had rejected political Islam as the defining logic for state-foundation and consolidation, and proclaimed secularism along with democracy, nationalism, and social justice as the core pillars of the state.

Bangladesh was considered until recently as a possible role model for developing Muslim nations because of its inherited secular tradition, its democratic aspirations, and its inclusive world vision. With a long his-tory of struggle against authoritarianism for democratic rights, a very large number of the Bangladeshi population believes strongly that their country is a democracy in which voting gives each individual a say in electing leaders of their choice and in governance issues.[1] However, the progressive abdication of the pluralist vision of democracy and good governance by successive political parties elected to government, whose indulgence of a zero-sum politics relentlessly undermined and corrupted the core institutions on which any democratic nation must rely, has been concomitant with creeping inroads made by Islamist extremism. Thirty-seven years after its independence, the nation's political fabric a little over a year ago revealed a deeply divided people, pitting Benga-lis against Bengalis, and described by some hyperbolically as pushing the nation to the perilous edge of civil war. Only the intervention by the army and the installment of an army-backed government in January 2007, marking a disturbing return of the military to the political arena after a hiatus of fifteen years, prevented that scenario from becoming reality, but the divisions remain, waiting to burst out and whether they will be resolved peacefully or not, as well as which direction the country will take remain to be seen.

The present contestations wracking the country may be viewed as struggles for the heart and soul of Bangladesh, and are being played out on at least two levels: at one level is the struggle between defining oneself as Bengali (culturally) or Muslim (by religious denomination); at a second level is the contestation between its many centuries' legacy of Sufi Islamic tradition being challenged by the widespread and deep inroads that have been made by Wahabi-Salafi-Deobandi doctrinaire interpretation of Islam during the last few decades, which peaked in 2005 with brazen displays of the capacity and organizing powers of militant Islamist groups. These contestations have had a profound impact on the fledgling democracy that was Bangladesh at its emergence as an independent nation.

These conflicts have in effect transformed Bangladesh into a front-line state, fighting simultaneously on several fronts: against a return to despotic authoritarianism; to reestablish democracy, rule of law, and good governance; and against militant Islam to wrest back their traditional Sufi-inspired moderation and tolerant world vision. While these battles are waged, the fight against poverty to win economic emancipation that has been waged from Bangladesh's inception continues unabated, with some remarkable successes but vast areas yet uncovered, with over 50 percent of the populace barely surviving below the poverty line. The outcome of the fighting in each sector will influence its efforts in the others, since they all simultaneously cut across the entire fabric of today's Bangladeshi society. That outcome will also have profound implications for the stability of the region and for larger world security.

Today, much hinges on whether the army-backed interim civilian government is successful in restoring the integrity and viability of the core institutions of the state, and whether it will fulfill its pledge to hold fresh elections by December 2008. On the success or failure of these efforts will rest the ultimate direction that Bangladesh will take—a moderately oriented, largely Muslim nation returning to pluralist and secular-oriented democracy, or a cloning of the Pakistan model from which the Bengalis of then—East Pakistan province deliberately tore themselves free in 1971. Fortunately for Bangladesh, in the general elections held on December 29, 2008 an overwhelmingly large turnout of elected voters, defying conventional wisdom, voted in the Awami League-led grand alliance, awarding it almost three-fourths of the seats in the Parliament and thus giving it a huge mandate for return to secular, pluralist democracy.

This chapter will attempt to explain the historical factors that led Bangladesh to this impasse. Woven into this historical fabric of a part of what was known as the Indian sub-Continent are the tales of the content and advances in each battle front that Bangladeshis wage today, in the hope that a better understanding of that history and the processes that worked through it in shaping the battle lines will help the country, the region, and the world keep a potential powder keg from exploding.

THE PARTITION OF BRITISH INDIA AND INDEPENDENCE AS PART OF PAKISTAN (1940–1947)

What is Bangladesh today was a part of undivided British India until August 1947, when the latter was partitioned at independence and reconfigured into the two separately independent states of India and Pakistan. Modern Bangladesh at that point in time emerged as East Pakistan, one of the five provinces of independent and supposedly federal Pakistan. The creation of Pakistan was the result of the dynamics of the "two-nation" rubric that dominated Muslim politics in the final phase of the Indian independence movement that ended British colonial rule over India. Bengali Muslims lent critical mass to the Pakistan movement, and the creation of Pakistan perhaps would not have been possible without their support.[2]

However, what is important to note here is that while the Muslim leadership of Bengal voted for the All-India Muslim League's resolution in 1940 at Lahore for a separate homeland, there already existed among them and their leadership the latent seeds of division in how they envisioned their future free from the British yoke. Two great political leaders from Bengal presented different visions of national configuration at that fateful conference of the All-India Muslim League at Lahore, which on March 23 resolved as follows:

> ...that it is the considered view of this session of the All-India Muslim League that no constitutional plan would be workable in this country or acceptable to Muslims unless it is designed on the following basic principles, viz. that geographically continuous units are demarcated into regions which should be so constituted, with such territorial adjustments as may be necessary, that the areas in which the Muslims are numerically in a majority as in the north-western and eastern zones of India should be grouped to constitute Independent *States* [italicized here to draw attention of readers], in which the constituent units shall be autonomous and sovereign....Adequate, effective and mandatory safeguards should be specifically provided in the Constitution for minorities...for the protection of their religious, cultural, economic, political, administrative and other rights.[3]

While A. K. Fazlul Huque, who was a member of the officially invited Muslim League delegation from Bengal and who tabled the final draft resolution for approval by the conference went along with the concept of a separate homeland, for many Bengalis the concept of such a homeland differed fundamentally from their northern compatriots' vision, since they were driven by differing concerns. For the Muslims of Northern India,

> the demand for Pakistan was the culmination of the Muslim renaissance movement initiated by Sir Syed Ahmed Khan in the latter half of the nineteenth century...to safeguard the religious, cultural, and political rights of the Muslims of the entire subcontinent. They assumed a linguistic and cultural unity of Muslims which was not there.[4]

The Muslims of Bengal wanted primarily an assurance of insulation from the economic domination of the Hindus, since linguistically and culturally they had no problems with the latter. At the same time, "caste prejudices of the neighboring Hindu community and, particularly, the anti-Muslim, exclusive and communal attitude of the upper and middle class Hindu *bhadralok*,[5] also generated anti-Hindu feelings among the

Muslims."[6] It is noteworthy here that Huseyn Shaheed Suhrawardy,[7] also representing Bengal at the Lahore Conference, had argued that "each of the provinces in the Muslim majority areas should be accepted as a sovereign state and each province should be given the right to choose its own constitution or enter into a commonwealth with the neighboring province or provinces."[8]

Suhrawardy was to later found the Awami Muslim League party in June 1949 as a party that presented an alternative vision for the country's future that was in opposition to the Muslim League's. Significantly, it was renamed as the Awami League in 1955, dropping the word "Muslim," after the routing of the Muslim League in East Pakistan in the general elections of 1954—symbolizing the rejection of the non-secular and monolithic unitary state in favor of a secular, pluralist (and federalist) orientation for the state.[9] Subsequently, it was the Awami League under Sheikh Mujibur Rahman's leadership that led the country to independence from Pakistan in 1971. The historical continuity of events and their linkages through over half a century is palpably clear here.

One could perhaps assert here with hindsight that the differing perceptions of their end-goals at the Lahore Conference were never really reconciled into an overarching consensus that could have firmly bonded together and united the disparate parties within the Indian Muslim community. Instead, the final document of that fateful conference, the Lahore Resolution that drove the demand for the creation of a separate Pakistan, fudged magnificently on the fundamental issue of defining the national configuration envisaged, leaving the hubris of violent dissent firmly imbedded within the nascent polity of the new nation-to-be. It is not at all surprising, therefore, that it took Pakistani leaders nine long years of bitter wrangling before they were able to finally cobble together a constitution, which was doomed to a singularly short life span before it was jettisoned two and a half years later by the country's first military coup d'état.

Given this complex history, East Pakistan/Bangladesh was bound to develop a somewhat schizophrenic political psyche, the yin and yang of its *politiae* pitting its very distinctive Bengali (cultural) identity against its Muslim (religious) identity—the former rooted deeply and indigenously in centuries, even millennia-old historical traditions, the latter a more recent acquisition through a process of active conversion to a new faith brought in by Muslim invaders/conquerors and Sufi proselytizers following in their wake. Most Muslim Bengalis had adapted to disciplining these two aspects of their identity to coexist peacefully within them. However, the clash between these two inner personalities was stirred up, and then progressively inflamed by the policies of the Pakistani (predominantly West Pakistani) establishment—policies that were meant to suppress the "Bengaliness" and accentuate the "Muslimness" in the identity of the average East Pakistani.

AFTER THE PARTITION OF INDIA: THE STRUGGLE FOR DEMOCRATIC RIGHTS AND LIBERTY (1947–1970)

In his first speech as Governor General to the Constituent Assembly of Pakistan on August 11, 1947, Jinnah had declared:

> Now, if we want to make this great State of Pakistan happy and prosperous we should wholly and solely concentrate on the well-being of the people, and specially of the masses and the poor. If you will work in cooperation, forgetting the past, burying the hatchet, you are bound to succeed...
>
> I cannot overemphasize it too much. We shall begin to work in that spirit and in course of time all these angularities of the majority and minority communities, the Hindu community and Muslim community...will vanish...You are free, you are free to go to your temples. You are free to go to your mosques or to any other places of worship in this State of Pakistan. You may belong to any religion or caste or creed; that has nothing to do with the business of the State....
>
> ...you will find that in course of time Hindus will cease to be Hindus and Muslims would cease to be Muslims, not in the religious sense, because that is the personal faith of each individual, but in the political sense as citizens of the State.[10]

Drawing inspiration from this speech, the Bengalis of East Pakistan at Partition after independence, separated as they were geographically from the rest of Pakistan by over a thousand miles of Indian territory and also providing a homeland to a sizeable Hindu minority, no doubt aspired to autonomous self-fulfillment within a federal and indeed secular Pakistan. However, post-1947, the Punjabis and Urdu-speaking immigrants from Uttar Pradesh and Bihar in India dominated the new Pakistani ruling establishment, virtually trashed the federal principles on which the state was founded, and embarked upon what most Bengalis perceived as a systematic exploitation of the resources of East Pakistan largely for the benefit of West Pakistan. Effectively, and increasingly, East Pakistan was perceived by the rulers ensconced at Karachi as a colony of West Pakistan, even though the majority of the population of post-1947 Pakistan comprised Bengalis who resided in East Pakistan. The efforts to foist Urdu upon them as the sole state language of Pakistan (announced by Jinnah himself in Dhaka in 1948) was an affront to the cultural sensitivities of the Bengalis, who were proud of their language and rich cultural heritage. Continuing economic discrimination and oppressive political disenfranchisement sparked the beginnings of their consciousness of a distinctly separate and secular national identity. The Awami League under Sheikh Mujibur Rahman became the logical platform for espousing the national aspirations of the Bengalis of East Pakistan. Its unwavering and undeterred movement (despite numerous crackdowns by the full force of the state) progressed through its six-point program of 1966,[11] burst out into the mass democratic uprising in 1969, and translated through the general elections of 1970[12] into Mujib's emerging as the undisputed national leader of "federal" Pakistan. The denial of this democratic outcome by the military dictatorship of General Yahya Khan, aided and abetted by a cabal of West Pakistani politicians, inevitably led to the separation of East Pakistan from Pakistan and its emergence as independent Bangladesh in December 1971.[13]

INDEPENDENT BANGLADESH: THE COLD WAR PARADIGM PLAYS MID-WIFE AND NURSE (1971–1975)

In separating from Pakistan, Bengali nationalism had finally triumphed over systematic institutional attempts to de-signify the Bengali culture.

It was a bitter body-blow to the "two-nation" theory on which Pakistan had been created in the first place, resoundingly reasserting the ethnic Bengali aspect of the people's identity, while unequivocally rejecting political Islam and religion as the constituent bases of nationhood. The constitution that free Bangladesh adopted in 1973 defined nationalism, democracy, secularism, and socialism[14] as constituting the four pillars of the new state. However, the new state's birth pangs and early years were very much hostage to the dynamics of the Cold War paradigm that dominated global politics in that era, with India-USSR facing off against Pakistan-USA in a complex and tangled skein. Bangladesh's emergence was opposed by the U.S. administration of those days, which had a decidedly pro-Pakistan tilt, and China and most Arab and many Muslim countries initially denied recognition to Bangladesh and held up its admission into the United Nations. The Cold War fault lines were also reflected within the Bangladesh liberation movement and subsequently its domestic politics as well. One of the biggest prices that Bangladesh had to pay was that it was not permitted by regional and global politics to try the perpetrators of the crimes against humanity that were committed against the Bengalis during 1971. This denial of justice may be viewed, with hindsight, as the original sin that would come back to haunt the Bangladeshis in the course of time.[15]

After liberation/independence, Bangladesh embarked upon the painful path of reconstruction. Sheikh Mujibur Rahman, who had been incarcerated in prison in Pakistan during the entire nine-month period of war, on his triumphant return to his homeland began the process of nation-building, largely bringing to bear upon this process his personal charisma that dwarfed all others. The real initial challenges came "from the vast number of youth who were radicalized by the liberation movement without any precise ideological commitment"—and whose alienation could spell disaster for the Awami League.[16] While initially continuing to ride on the crest of its undisputed leadership of the struggle against West Pakistani domination and liberation of the country from Pakistan, a notable feature of the new political polarization taking place domestically was also nested in the dominating Cold War paradigm of that era.

While the Awami League (AL) tended to brand its opponents, ironically and oxymoronically, as agents of "U.S.-Chinese imperialists" (by implication Pakistan was also associated with this lumping),[17] the main parties in opposition to the AL[18] accused it and its allies of being pliant tools of "Soviet-Indian imperialism."[19] The first national elections in independent Bangladesh, held in 1973, although serving to consolidate the AL's grip on power through popular mandate, also served to crystallize the polarization of the opposition.

The post-1973 period was also marked by the growing threat to the AL establishment of militantly inclined, underground Marxist-Leninist Communist parties and factions, much as the Naxal movement had done to the Congress government in the adjoining Indian state of West Bengal around the same time. The compulsions of containing this burgeoning threat to the new state inevitably led to a flexing of state muscles and the resorting to draconian measures that served to consolidate state power and muzzle any dissent, slowly transforming what had ambitiously begun as parliamentary democracy into a one-party authoritarian state. Debate within the AL party—between those who advocated change of the constitution to strengthen state powers and those who opposed such change and wanted the evolutionary process of democracy to continue its course—was stifled as well.

The Cold War paradigm had another significant fallout for Bangladesh in its fledgling years. War-ravaged Bangladesh was heavily dependent on external food aid to sustain its vast population, and it received much of this food aid under the US PL-480 program. In 1974 the mysterious "diversion" of vitally needed food-grain shipments and the late arrival of food aid resulted in famine and numerous deaths in Bangladesh, pushing the government into crisis.[20] That same year, with Bangladesh's admission into the United Nations after three years of hard diplomatic struggle to win international recognition, Sheikh Mujibur Rahman traveled to New York to address the United Nations General Assembly. On the sidelines, his efforts to establish any meaningful contact with the U.S. administration, which were motivated by his own personal desire and inclination to establish close relations with the United States and the West, were rudely rebuffed. The dynamic that was generated by this rejection largely shaped the events that followed after his return from New York, having strengthened the hands of the hardliners within his party.

In January 1975, Sheikh Mujib lent his indomitable charisma and weight to the side of authoritarianism by having Parliament amend the constitution and initiating the so-called "second revolution." Under this amendment, the parliamentary form of government was replaced by the presidential form, a one-party system was instituted, and the administrative structure was to be reorganized with politically appointed district governors. Compulsory, multipurpose village cooperatives were also to be established. All this entailed a massive curtailment of civil liberties. This so-called "second revolution" not only alienated large sections of society (notably the nationalist bourgeoisie and many middle class and urban elites), but also the large numbers of surplus farmers adversely affected by the compulsory cooperatives scheme, the media (with its history of freedom), traditionally non-partisan but professional civil servants, and many elements within the armed forces (Jahan). In short, the move was arguably a direct *casus belli* for Mujib's overthrow. The majors who planned and executed the coup d'état (and brutally murdered Mujib and most members of his family[21]) had calculated to cash in on this alienation.

MILITARY RULE AND PROGRESSIVE REGRESSION TO THE RIGHT (1975–1990)

Following the assassination of Sheikh Mujibur Rahman, a right-wing, pro-U.S. faction within the AL was pushed forward by the young officers to form the new government. It was during this period that several of Mujib's most senior ministers were shot in cold blood while incarcerated in prison. The AL was thus effectively decapitated and rendered incapable of mounting any serious challenge to this insurgent act. After a period of grave uncertainty and coups and counter-coup attempts within the armed forces, General Ziaur Rahman, who had taken over as Chief of Army Staff following the coup in August 1975, was able to finally consolidate personal power in November 1975, ironically with the help of the radical left forces within the army. However, after having consolidated his power, he had no qualms about eliminating this leftist faction that had played so critical a role in thrusting him into power. In the process, he won the support of the bulk of the large middle class in Bangladesh, who were essentially centrists and fearful of the extreme ideologue slogans of the radical left. At the same time, he cultivated and won the support of the anti-Soviet/anti-India/anti-AL groups. Political parties were initially banned along with all political activities, but in July 1976, twenty-three parties were given permits to function again with the requirement that they confine their activities indoors. In order to break the backbone of the Awami League, factions were encouraged or induced to split away to form their own new parties or join Zia's new party.

General Ziaur Rahman "civilianized" himself on assuming the presidency and established his own political party, the Bangladesh Nationalist Party (BNP). Questions of identity that most people thought had been settled in 1971 were reopened—"Are Bengali-Muslims Bengalis first and Muslims second, or Muslims first and Bengalis second?" "Should Bangladesh have a parliamentary democracy or a presidential system of government?"[22] Zia made fundamental changes to the constitution, dropping one of its main pillars (secularism), redefining a second pillar (socialism), and adding an Islamic preamble that acknowledged the primacy of Islam and the Muslims of the country—thus emphasizing the Muslim identity of the country over its cultural identity. He also declared that the citizens of the new nation would be identified as "Bangladeshi" rather than as "Bangalees" (the term favored by the Awami League) so as not to be confused with the (Hindu) Bengalis of West Bengal. Notably, he promoted the rise of right-wing parties and permitted the return of the Jamaat-i-Islami (JI) leaders (notably its Amir, Moulana Gholam Azam, accused by the AL of war crimes), who had fled Bangladesh or had gone underground for fear of reprisals, as well as allowing them to reactivate their political functioning as Jamaate Islami Bangladesh (JIB). Sheltered thus under the wings of the BNP, the JIB and other smaller

Islamic parties gradually grew in size and extended their political activities. These parties, working in tandem with the BNP while initially not directly coalescing with the latter, served the purpose of projecting pluralism while also acting as a powerful firewall against the AL, rendered headless and in disarray with its leadership dispersed or muzzled.

With hindsight, all these acts may be seen as having served to set the new nation on its path to regression. The BNP projected itself as a centrist party, leaning to right-of-center to distinguish itself from the AL, which was viewed largely as a left-of-center party. The gradual process of Islamization may, therefore, be said to have commenced during Ziaur Rahman's watch. Ironically, despite having fought against Pakistan for Bangladesh's independence, he chose to replicate the style of Pakistan's first Martial Law under Ayub Khan and Khan's subsequent format of a civil-military bureaucracy taking control of the affairs of the nation and then gradually "civilianizing" and "democratizing" the junta. The zero-sum culture in politics was also triggered during this period, whether wittingly or otherwise. To this day, the AL has never quite shaken off its conviction that Ziaur Rahman's rise and his subsequent efforts to de-signify Mujib link him, even if indirectly, with the events that resulted in the tragic and cold-blooded murders of Mujib and almost his entire family.

General Ziaur Rahman was himself assassinated in May 1981 by an army aide. Once again, there was a period of chaos marked by attempted coups and counter-coups, and the civilian "elected" BNP government of Zia was rendered ineffective. To "save the country" from plunging into chaos, Lt. Gen. Hussain Mohammed Ershad, then Chief of Army Staff, assumed power through a military coup on March 24, 1982. He dissolved Parliament but co-opted the same elites who had helped Zia rule. He basically followed the same path that Zia had embarked upon, wooing the same constituency but going much farther than his military predecessor by seeking to institutionalize permanently the role of the army in the political governance of the country (taking inspiration from the system then prevailing under Suharto in Indonesia). He also donned civilian "mufti" and then created his own political party, the Jatiya (National) Party (JP) in 1986 as the springboard and base for consolidating power, drawing his political foot soldiers from break-away factions of the late Zia's sinking ship as well as willing defectors from other parties seeking a share of the spoils.

Ershad declared Islam as the state religion of Bangladesh, effectively driving in the last nail on the coffin of secularism. He drew considerable inspiration from General-turned-President Ziaul Huq of Pakistan in "Islamizing" Bangladesh, promoting the influence of the mosques within the army cantonments as well as in the urban areas and rural countryside. Just as the BNP had shifted ideologically to right-of-center to distinguish itself from the AL, Ershad found it necessary to shift more conspicuously to the right to distinguish his own new party from the BNP. A consummate political manipulator, he also realized the necessity of establishing for himself a pluralist image, so he "permitted" the return of the AL leadership to participate in the political process once again (which would also serve as a check upon the BNP). At the same time, to dilute the power and ability of the JIB (who owed a debt of gratitude to the BNP for its resurrection and with whom they were allied), Ershad promoted the formation and growth of splinter Islamist parties as foils, which actively promoted the agenda of adopting sharia law in Bangladesh. Under pressure from his Islamist "alliance partners," Ershad declared Bangladesh an Islamic state in 1988 through a constitutional amendment.

However, all these civilian-political activities were carried out while he maintained an iron grip on the army itself, his mainstay and actual source of power (as it was for General Ziaul Huq of Pakistan). Ershad did hold "general elections" (under strictly controlled conditions) in Bangladesh in 1986 and 1988, with multiparty participation, but these elections, like the earlier one in 1979 under General Ziaur Rahman, lacked credibility and legitimacy, having been held under quasi-military rule that controlled the mechanics and dynamics of the electoral process to advance its own agenda. However, allowing the political parties to function in such a process, even under such muzzled conditions, was sufficient space for these parties to slowly pry apart increasingly more ground for pluralistic politics to play more meaningfully. Ershad was able to play them off against each other in the earlier elections, but the parties increasingly started viewing Ershad as their common enemy. They eventually forged a broad coalition that included all parties from right to left (even including some breakaway factions of the JP), and was able to galvanize civil society across the nation into a mass social movement for the restoration of democracy. This movement wrested back democracy, forcing President Ershad to step down and the army to return to their barracks. But what sort of democracy did the Bangladeshi people get?

ZERO-SUM BATTLES FOR BANGLADESHI HEARTS— AND THE BETRAYAL OF DEMOCRACY (1991–2006)

The mass mobilization of civil society in 1990 that led to the downfall of the last military regime and forced the military back to the barracks in November of that year, was a defining moment in Bangladesh's political history—a defining moment in wresting democracy from the clutches of the military and embarking on its post-independence democratic transition. It was heady moment for Bangladesh civil society at large and marked by a process of consensus-building on some basic parameters regarding the mode of holding the next elections and the transition to democracy. This consensus resulted in the formation by civil society of an interim, Non-party Caretaker Government (NCG), headed by the Chief Justice, which was mandated to hold fresh and free elections within ninety days. The head of the Caretaker Government was assisted by a council of advisers, again drawn by consensus from civil society.

The first free and fair elections in over twenty years were held in February 1991, in which the BNP managed to secure 140 seats (having sucked away the constituency of the JP, which secured only thirty-five seats) and the Awami League, in second place, secured eighty-eight seats, despite having secured 41 percent of the votes—a vote bank that has remained stable and constant to date. The Jamaate Islami (JI) secured eighteen seats, and independents/other parties won nineteen seats. The JIB allied itself in Parliament with the BNP (but remained outside the government), enabling the BNP to form the government. There were calls at this stage by some sections of civil society for the parties to form a government of national unity, but this was ignored by the BNP/Jamaat. That was a golden opportunity lost for consensus-building on a number of issues that would continue to plague the second transition. With hindsight it appears that the JIB was playing its cards to be able to wedge itself further into the national political process, riding on the bandwagon (or back) of the BNP.

The euphoria of consensus forged during the anti-Ershad movement was quite short-lived. During the period of 1991–1994, relations between the two main parties deteriorated sharply, with the BNP succumbing to the temptation of taking advantage of the state power under its control to sway the results of several by-elections to the Parliament in its favor. In the process, it also managed to alienate its ally, the JI. A new broad coalition of the opposition parties (ironically including both the JIB and the JP) launched another civil mobilization movement, this time against the ruling BNP, demanding that the constitution should be amended to provide for having at least three more general elections under the Non-party Caretaker Government system. The BNP adamantly refused to concede this, and held elections in February 1996 under its stewardship, which were not participated in by any other party. Voter turnout was only in the mid-20-percent range, despite the fact that the BNP controlled all the levers of power. However, this time, even large segments of the bureaucracy joined the movement, rendering the government virtually ineffective and unable to organize the rigging of votes, and it was abundantly clear that the party in power was out of synch with civil society and the mood of the times. With the results announced, the parties in opposition launched a mass mobilization movement that paralyzed the government (very reminiscent of the situation after the 1970 elections in Pakistan) and the BNP realized it had to bow to the pressure from the entire civil society as well as reverberating international condemnation. It convened Parliament once and adopted an amendment to the constitution that institutionalized permanently the concept of a neutral Non-party Caretaker Government for holding all future elections. The Parliament and government resigned thereafter and ceded power to a NCG headed by the just-retired chief justice. Fresh elections were held in June 1996.

Once again, under this unique system the elections were deemed by domestic and international observers to be largely free and fair. This time the BNP lost to the AL 146:116. JP managed to retain thirty-two seats, but parties from the right and left were routed, with only three seats on each side. The people had clearly opted against extremism of any kind, and overwhelmingly voted in favor of the centrist parties that occupied the middle ground. The JIB's routing in this election indicated two things—that its earlier association with the BNP had worked against it, and that given the nation's existing inclination, it could not aspire to win seats on its own.

The NCG institution was born out of the prevailing widespread lack of mutual trust and confidence by the various political actors in each other, reinforced over time by their propensity to succumb easily to the temptation of abusing state power when in government to skew the system in its favor in any electoral process. It is a unique system, and apparently as with any new model, unless used, faults are not immediately visible. It would appear that the system needs to be amended suitably to ensure transparent neutrality and more completely exclude personal partisan biases from affecting the outcome of the elections. Essentially, it can work best if there is complete trust among all parties involved, as well as a considerable degree of good faith and self-disciplined abjuring of partisan bias by whoever is called upon to head the NCG.

Although Bangladesh did manage to conduct three largely free and fair elections under the Caretaker Government system in 1991, 1996, and 2001, and these elections were followed by relatively smooth transfers of power to the elected governments, the lesson of the last sixteen years is predominantly that elections alone and the resultant smooth transfer of power by themselves are insufficient and do not guarantee an efficiently functioning democracy, good governance, and stability unless there is a commitment by all parties to play by the rules of the game, and also to uphold the integrity and independent neutrality of the core state institutions—particularly the judiciary, the Election Commission, the bureaucracy, the Anti-Corruption Commission, the Public Service Commission, and the University Grants Commission. However, none of the political parties who came to power played by the rules of the game. On the contrary, they lost no opportunity in subverting these core institutions and undermining their authority and independence by stacking the decks so as to favor the party in power. Between 1991 and 2001, the two major parties had succeeded each other in turns;[23] regrettably, however, each viewed its term in power not as an opportunity to develop the state and the economy with a far-sighted vision for the people's greater benefit, but instead with a short-sighted view of furthering their narrower party and personal interests at the cost of the greater national good—a perspective that induced each party to look on its tenure in power as a short-lived period of opportunity to be exploited to the maximum for personal and party aggrandizement only.[24]

The Consequences For the Fight against Poverty and the Improvement of People's Lives

These zero-sum contestations not only militated against the people's welfare, but against the consolidation of democracy itself, imperiling it gravely. They also opened up increasing political space for the Islamic fundamentalism creeping in, at the same time rejecting a pluralism tolerant of other faiths. These policies made for poor governance, endemic and rampant corruption on an unimaginable scale (as unraveled only recently after the military-led government took over in January 2007), and widening disparities in income. The Asian Development Bank, in its Quarterly Economic Update of September 2002, had observed that Bangladesh's main challenge ahead was unemployment, and unless the country could increase its growth rate from between four and five percent to around seven to eight percent, it would not be able to create the 25–30 million new jobs it needed by the year 2015.[25] However, Bangladesh was creating only 0.7 million jobs annually for the 2.7 million new job-seekers entering the market every year, increasing the unemployment gap by 2 million people per year, thus creating a time bomb for society.[26]

It is moot to remember here that Islam was, and is, the faith of the majority of the Bengalis in Bangladesh, and that most Bengalis tend to be observant Muslims, flocking to the mosques in large numbers on Fridays and during the religiously important periods in the Islamic calendar. Historically, this had in no way mitigated against their secular, moderate, and accommodating world view of other faiths and cultures. However, when you have the phenomenon of a rapidly growing population within very limited geographical space, relatively few resources of which no significant amount trickles down to the vast majority of the people, who continue to remain poor, and when successive governments and indeed leadership across the political divide abdicate from governance, being preoccupied with narrower agendas of self or party consolidation at the expense of national consolidation, the mosque (or church) tends to become the refuge of last resort. When people have nowhere else to turn, they tend to turn in droves to divine dispensation for solace and comfort—and that is where, at their most vulnerable, they can easily become prey to agents with an extremist or malevolent agenda. This would appear to be entirely in keeping with trends that have been observed in other Muslim societies where authoritarian regimes muzzled political voice and repressed pluralist participation.

While the secular NGOs in Bangladesh were running remarkably successful programs to reduce poverty, subsequent governments during this period appear to have entirely abdicated their role and responsibilities for good governance. As a result of these failures in good governance, overall budgetary allocations for education were either insufficient or reduced. Against UNICEF's recommended spending target of at least 6percent of the GDP in 2003, Bangladesh's spending stood at only 2 percent of its GDP.[27] The secular NGOs, who through their microcredit financing programs were proactively engaged in poverty alleviation, and through their combined primary education programs actually exceeded the government's primary education activities, started facing increasing threats from thugs and Islamist groups as part of pressure tactics on their activities, forcing them to request increased police protection to be able to continue with their programs and activities safely.[28] At the same time, the reach of the *madrasas*[29] increased significantly, with all the Islamic parties working to extend their footprint over Bangladesh. There are no accurate figures for *madrasa*s in Bangladesh, but they are said to range from around 40,000 to close to 100,000.[30]

As is clear from this narrative, the separation of East Pakistan had hit hard against the very heart of the "two nation" theory that had prioritized the logic of political Islam in the formation of the state of Pakistan. The transformation of that province into the new nation-state of Bangladesh was as much a rejection of political Islam as it was an assertion of its secularly oriented Bengali identity, in which the Bengali-Muslim majority would coexist peacefully alongside the Bengali-Hindu minority as the basis for the underpinning of the new state. Tragically, after 1971, the operation of party politics with the goal of winning the hearts of the people turned increasingly into a zero-sum contestation that militated against democracy while using the vehicle of democracy. After the military-led coup of 1975, ironically, each subsequent phase of militarization marked a progressive return of political Islam in domestic politics and a dilution of the secular agenda. It also complicated the domestic political scenario further by allowing the intrusion of yet another level of contestation over the kind of Islam to be embraced: the heterodoxical Sufi tradition that was tolerant of other faiths and visions of Islam versus the more orthodox Wahabi/Salafi and Deobandi versions of Islam that brooked no dissent or deviation from the path as revealed and enjoined by the Prophet of Islam. A number of developments augured this change.

REDEFINING ISLAM: THE STRUGGLE FOR THE SOUL OF THE BENGALI MUSLIM

The vast majority of the Muslims of Bangladesh were converted to Islam and greatly influenced by Sufi teachers.[31] The Sufi tradition, embracing as it did the local cultural traditions that it found on first arrival and then giving them a new dimension or interpretation, was conducive to heterodoxy and tolerance for other faiths and beliefs. It was during the military era that the influence of the less tolerant versions of Islam started making steady inroads into Bangladesh, notably Wahabism and Salafism from

Saudi Arabia and its neighboring region and Deobandism in its more strictly defined version from Pakistan. Saudi and Gulf money poured into mosques, charities, social organizations, and madrassas, which promoted Gulf-backed orthodox versions of Islam.[32] The expansion of the Gulf-backed Islamist agenda was increasingly permitted by both the post-AL era mainstream parties and their respective leadership, who must be deemed responsible for this development to various degrees. In their bid to counter the secular AL as well as each other, both the party founded by General Ziaur Rahman and that subsequently founded by General Husain Mohammed Ershad courted the rightist Islamist parties in defining themselves, not taking into account the long-term consequences of their narrower agenda. As well as providing an increasingly open door for the surreptitious ingress by stealth of militant Islam, this process was concurrently accompanied by an increasing marginalization of the minority and a steady decline in their population caused by migration from Bangladesh on account of their increased sense of insecurity. Over the last few years, a large number of minority civil servants, police personnel, and armed forces recruits were deliberately and systematically superseded for career advancement and marginalized through being relegated to unimportant postings, tantamount to faith-based discrimination and cleansing of these services. This was perhaps the logical trajectory of the return of political Islam to Bangladeshi politics over the last three decades.

The Islamist elements thrived most when an authoritarian oligarchy was in power in Bangladesh. Having gained that invaluable space, they continued to expand and extend their turf through a process that can best be described as creeping annexation. Within the legitimate political process provided by the process of parliamentary democracy, the Jamaate Islami Bangladesh (and other smaller Islamic parties) wedged themselves ever deeper into vacated or laxly guarded political space, eventually occupying a critical "king-maker" role that even the historically secular Awami League had to take into consideration and accommodate in its electoral strategy.[33] One of the tools used by the Islamic right was to launch the anti-Ahmadiya movement. The Ahmadiyas, also known as Qadianis, are followers of Mirza Ghulam Ahmed, who was born in the village of Qadian in Amritsar, in East Punjab. He founded his sect in 1889, when he proclaimed that he had had "a divine revelation authorizing him to receive the allegiance of the faithful [Muslims]"[34] and that he was also the Mahdi[35] and the Messiah,[36] who would ultimately return to this world to rid it of all evil. Bangladesh has some Ahmadiyas, but they comprise a very small fraction of the total Muslim population. Pakistan had, under pressure from the Jamaat-i-Islami Pakistan and Saudi authorities, declared the Ahmadiyas as non-Muslims in the early seventies, even though most of the beliefs and practices of the Ahmadiyas conform to the tenets of orthodox Sunni Islam. The anti-Ahmadiya movement was used by Maulana Maududi, founder of the Jamaat-i-Islami (essentially followers of the Deobandi school), as a political platform to demonstrate street power and pressure the new state of Pakistan to conform to sharia law and practices. Some of the more radicalized Islamic parties in Bangladesh, led by a group called Hifazate Khatme Nabuwat Andolon (HKNA—Movement for Protection/Preservation of the Last Prophet), launched a similar aggressive street movement in 2003, attacking the places of worship and gathering of Ahmadiyas in Bangladesh in order to pressure the government to shift farther to the right. Most observers viewed this as essentially an effort to strengthen the hard-line faction within the BNP and the Jamaate Islami Bangladesh as coalition partners of the BNP-led government (2001–2006), not dissimilar to the tactics used by General Ershad before he amended the constitution to declare Bangladesh an Islamic Republic.

On another significant doctrinaire front, the Ahle-Hadith[37] movement of Bangladesh also sought to further dilute, weaken, and ultimately reject the traditional Hanafi practice of Islam, enjoining strict and uncompromising adherence to ritualistic observance, which in the ultimate analysis are tools for the expansion and exercising of the disciplinarian power of the clergy over the followers. The Ahle-Hadith's leader, Maulana Asadollah Ghalib, was arrested in cases linked to the terrorist activities of some other Islamist groups acting outside the state's legitimate parameters. This movement received generous financial assistance through covert channels from a senior but shadowy Salafi leader operating from adjoining West Bengal in India.

Outside the legitimate parameters of the state, militant Islamist groups like the Harkat-ul Jihade Islami (HUJI),[38] Jamaatul Mujahideen Bangladesh (JMB), Jagrata Janata Muslim Bangladesh (JMJB—Awaken! Muslim people of Bangladesh),[39] among others—many of whose members had at one time or another in their early formative years been members of the Jamaate Islami—asserted their presence and militant Islamic agenda on the political landscape and appeared to enjoy immunity from police or judicial action. These forces, it became progressively and abundantly clear, had wrested for themselves sufficient space to consolidate their organizational structure and their planning and execution capacities for the furtherance of their agenda. Despite numerous reports in the media about the growing strength of the militant Islamist groups by investigative journalists (who deserve kudos for their brave reporting), the BNP-Jamaate Islami coalition government entrenched themselves in a cocoon of denial. The extremely well-coordinated 400 bomb blasts that shook the entire nation on August 17, 2005, were designed so as to intimidate civil society and force it indoors, as well as to send a loaded message to the establishment—particularly the judiciary—and the secular media who had been reporting on the Islamists' activities, rather than cause actual damage. In recent years, some of the NGOs, notably Grameen Bank and BRAC,[40] were also targeted, no doubt because they catered to women's empowerment programs, and their activities were primarily geared to broad strengthening of civil society. Cinema halls, village fairs that commemorated local minority cultural/religious events, and even Sufi shrines (which have always been part of the Muslim culture of Bangladesh) were methodically targeted and bombed, principally to warn people away from them. All of these actions fall within the rubric of the Wahabi-Salafi-Deobandi nexus that accompanies what we now associate with Talibanization. It was also a demonstration of their capability and capacity to the establishment and the media, since targets chosen were government offices, lower courts (controlled by the executive branch), and media offices.

The fact that it was almost eight months before the government started rounding up suspects—and then only after very serious and severe arm-twisting by foreign donors (primarily the United States)—has most disturbing implications. It is a serious indicator that either (a) the government was not in control of the situation at all or (b) that a network within the government (which after all is drawn from society at large) was acting independently, thwarting measures at bringing these people to book—again reflecting the schizophrenic persona of the polity.

The increasing link between the Jamaate Islami party and the various militant groups was exposed during the second term of the BNP-Jamaate Islami alliance government, after the arrest of several militants in conjunction with the August 17 serial bombings.[41] At the very least, these Islamist groups enjoyed administrative support and protection from sections of the government, if not the entire government machinery itself.

Another disturbing, and related phenomenon, was the startling discovery of clandestine arms shipments and the discovery of arms caches across the country. The largest-ever arms and ammunitions seizure was made in the port city of Chittagong in April 2004, when security forces apprehended ten truckloads that included various types of submachine guns and AK-47 assault rifles; in all, 10,000 arms, 2,000 grenades, and 300,000 bullets.[42] Recently, there have been reports that the JMB was regrouping in some areas of Bangladesh and on a recruiting drive for their organization.[43] At the same time, it was reported that the Bangladeshi security forces, on the basis of intelligence that they had obtained, had unearthed several caches of grenades and assorted firearms from numerous places.[44]

Standing at the Crossroads:
Averting Disaster and Initiating Damage Control (2006–2007)
The term of the last elected parliament ended on October 26, 2006, and as per the constitution, the BNP-Jamaate Islami coalition government handed over power to a caretaker government. But the machinations of the preceding government had succeeded in subverting even this institution to the extent that the mainstream opposition parties did not trust it or the bureaucratic and law enforcement machinery, which had clearly been

politicized and stacked heavily to favor the BNP-Jamaat. The opposition poured out on the streets and resulted in serious clashes between the two sides. The neutrality of the caretaker government was called openly into question even by the international community, with civil strife continuing and spreading and becoming uncontrollable, finally prompting the army to move in—obliquely. On January 11, with the overt backing of the armed forces, the Fourth Caretaker Government was forced to resign and was replaced by another interim government that promised to act neutrally. The President, a BNP party person who had been elected to the post in 2001 on a clearly partisan basis and had openly abandoned neutrality to play a partisan role during the brief tenure of the Fourth NCG (October 26, 2006–January 10, 2007), was forced by the new situation to now play a neutral and nonpartisan role for the remaining period of his tenure (until the next parliament is elected).

The new dispensation in Bangladesh suspended the constitution and proclaimed a state of emergency. It also announced its commitment to holding the delayed parliamentary elections before the end of 2008. In the meantime, it set about in earnest to clean up the administration and restore the core institutions of the state. It has, in the last twelve months in office, succeeded in separating the judiciary from the executive and making it truly independent, as it was envisaged to be (something that all previous governments had repeatedly promised but held back from actually doing, because they all wanted to use, or rather, abuse the institution to consolidate their own political positions at the expense of the "other"—or the opposition of the day). The Election Commission, the Public Service Commission, the Bureau of Anti-Corruption, and the University Grants Commission were totally revamped. The Election Commission embarked on its first job of drawing up a completely fresh and credible voters list, and at last reports, had completed more than half their job already. The independent judiciary is showing signs of cleaning itself up institutionally, removing politically appointed judges of dubious credentials and instituting measures for the recruitment of capable persons at the level of the higher courts. The bureaucracy and the police have been purged of appointees whose sole criterion for getting jobs was loyalty to the political party in power. The Anti-Corruption Commission has cast its net far and wide to snare corrupt politicians, former members of government, bureaucrats, and businesspeople. The two former lady Prime Ministers, and a number of their former senior advisers and cabinet ministers, were arrested and imprisoned and are facing various charges of corruption, extortion, and abuse of power. Some of those arrested (some along with members of their immediate family) have been speedily tried and convicted by special courts under the Emergency Powers Act. Not a few, notably the incarceration of the two former lady Prime Ministers, were ill-advised and clearly intended to intimidate them into leaving the political scene. However, a number of these cases have been challenged in the High Court on procedural and legal grounds. As of now, the appeals processes on numerous cases are pending final hearings and disposal. Many of these cases may not stand the test of constitutionality and may well be ultimately thrown out.

Most people of Bangladesh appeared to welcome the present military-backed government when it took over on January 11, 2007. However, the government has also had to face more mundane issues of governance, like tackling the after-effects of natural calamities such as cyclones and floods that destroyed two crops, acute power shortages, shortages of fertilizer and essential consumer items, the rising cost of gasoline and the shortage of gas for domestic use, and the rising inflation, which is a globally viral phenomenon that is hitting poorer nations harder. Running any government with such problems as Bangladesh faces is by no means an easy task. With a truncated cabinet of only ten ministers—the constitution limits the size of a caretaker government—that job is made so much more difficult, with each minister in charge of multiple ministries/departments. Questions have been raised about whether this government can legally and constitutionally call itself a Neutral Caretaker Government, and that may at some point in time be challenged in the courts, since much of what it is doing is by dint of its emergency powers. One must ask the question: how can one preserve the constitution by suspending it? And how does one restore law and order and respect for the institutions and processes of justice by flouting them? The longer a government of this nature stays in power, the more tenuous may its actions become, regardless of the good intentions behind them. The road to perdition is often paved with the best of intentions. The sooner a credibly and fairly elected parliament and government take office, the better for the nation.

Some observers, including myself, feel that this interim government should have remained focused on a narrow agenda—of putting the core institutions of the state back on their feet and ensuring that they are insulated from future political tampering and subversion by whoever comes into power, and then holding free, fair, and credible elections as quickly as feasible. Statements made by some members of the present establishment that they intended to go after all crooks everywhere in the nation and erase all corruption from the face of Bangladesh could well turn into a self-perpetuating agenda. The indiscriminate drive to round up suspects from almost all walks of life has had the effect of stopping business-people from investing further in the country, or simply going slow, while the bureaucracy has cocooned itself in inertia. While most of the people incarcerated and either convicted or awaiting trial are widely perceived to deserve what they have received, many also feel that in bringing them to justice the due process of law must be scrupulously observed and meticulously followed; otherwise, the cases could later be thrown out on legal grounds, resulting in their emerging free and donning the halo of injured innocence. That could well result in an unraveling of all the excellent, critically essential, and long overdue reforms that have already been carried out and achieved. Should that happen, these immediate gains could well mutate into long-term damage. Bangladesh cannot afford that.

Democracy and Islam in the Bangladeshi Context
So in the end, we come back to the question: Are democracy and Islam compatible in a society like Bangladesh's? Bangladesh's saga as narrated earlier reveals the following:

- The overwhelming majority of the Bengalis were Muslims, and without their critical mass perhaps the birth of Pakistan would not have made much sense.

- Bangladesh's birth in 1971 was the culmination of the prolonged struggle of the East Pakistanis for democracy and their rightful voice and place within a supposedly federal democratic structure, on the basis of which Pakistan was originally configured when carved out of India in 1947. Throughout their history as part of Pakistan, the people of Bangladesh fought relentlessly against military dictatorship and quasi-military authoritarianism for the restoration of their democratic rights and liberty. Their split from Pakistan was triggered by the Pakistani-dominated military and a cabal of West Pakistani politicians who were unwilling to share power with their compatriots from East Pakistan, even when the latter had clearly demonstrated their electoral power by winning the majority of the seats in the national Parliament in the general elections of 1970.
- Even during the fifteen years of military or quasi-military inter-regnum in independent Bangladesh, when the voice of the people was forcibly subdued, it remained irrepressible. The demand for democracy was and remains high, even when disillusionment with their political leaders was equally high. Conversely, even if they have welcomed the role of the army from time to time to straighten wayward leaders and set things right, Bangladeshis have shown a consistent pattern of resenting any prolonged stretch of military rule. The military are an instrument of the state, but they cannot become the state.
- The Islamic parties on their own have never been able to win power through elections. In fact, in one of the elections they were almost completely wiped from the political scene. It was only during military rule that they were able to occupy political space in any meaningful measure, and even then they had to share power with a larger right-of-center party.
- When the Islamists tried to use tactics of intimidation, there were more voices of outrage than fear among most Bangladeshis, while members of the media (largely secular in orientation) risked their lives in persevering fearlessly with investigative journalism to

expose the nexus between the Islamists and members/sections of the ruling coalition government.

- In 2007, during the interregnum, some members of the Jamaate Islami party sought to change the parameters and context of national discourse by publicly asserting that:
  - ° The war of 1971 was not a war of liberation but a civil war. This implied that the outcome of that war had not yet been definitively established, and therefore the trajectory of 1971 could possibly be reversed—ergo, the reestablishment of the two-nation theory in the subcontinent and the reassertion of political Islam as the logic for state foundation and consolidation.
  - ° It has not been established that any war crimes were committed at all, and therefore no war criminals exist.
- These statements provoked widespread backlash across a broad spectrum of civil society, Muslim and non-Muslim.
- This reaction and anger has now fueled a growing demand across Bangladeshi civil society for bringing to justice war criminals that collaborated with the Pakistani occupation regime in 1970–1971, and are accused of having perpetrated crimes against humanity during that period. The vast majority of those voicing these demands are Muslim, although members of the minority communities have also joined their voices with their fellow Muslim-Bangladeshis. Even some of the less fundamentally oriented, but smaller, Islamic parties have joined in this demand (although perhaps that is as much for tactical reasons as strategic ones).

All these factors, to my mind, clearly demonstrate that the greater majority of the Bengali-Muslims of Bangladesh, while retaining their Muslim identity, demand democratic practice and governance. That is all the more reason that the present government should usher in an elected government earlier rather than later. The temptation to fix everything to a state of near perfection is perhaps strong, but that is neither within the realm of the feasible nor desirable. Consolidation of democracy can only be achieved by a democratic process, not by authoritarian fiats; reassertion

of constitutionalism cannot be achieved by suspension of the constitution and resorting to the indefinite use of emergency laws, and restoration
of the rule of law cannot be done by bending or subverting the rule of
law. These are all inherently self-contradictory. The longer an unelected,
military-backed regime stays on to "clean up the landscape," the stronger will be the urge to stretch out that period to the limits of elasticity
or beyond. While the present military-backed regime may have initially
appeared on a beleaguered Bangladesh's horizon as the fabled knight in
shining armor on a magnificent white charger come to the rescue of a
people sorely fed up with the shenanigans of unscrupulous politicians
and a corrupt bureaucracy, with the passage of time the savior-knight is
increasingly likely to mutate in people's perceptions into the image of
a tyrant riding a tiger that he is unable to dismount. The rumblings of
discontent among the people are already beginning to surface. A look at
the analogous situation and events in Pakistan during the last eight years
should serve as an eye-opener for those still unwilling to face reality or
prone to using the wrong lens to correct their vision of the landscape.
A permanent military-backed regime would have grave implications for
the future of a pluralist, tolerant, and democratic Bangladesh, and indeed
for the greater South Asian region, and even beyond.

THE LARGER IMPLICATIONS FOR STABILITY AND SECURITY

This much is undeniable—the continuing and festering state of internal instability in any country does not remain internalized for too long,
not in a globalized world where borders are increasingly permeable and
porous. Instability in the smaller entities in South Asia will spill over, in
some form or other, to their adjacent larger neighbors. When enemies
melt into local populations, they are usually very difficult to find. The
forces of unleashed globalization ease their rites of passage to distant
shores, cobbling together a network of "distant proximities" (to borrow
a term used by James Rosenau), which may not all be benevolent in
nature.

An even more important factor is simply this—Bangladesh is home to the fourth-largest concentration of Muslims in any single place in the world (after Indonesia, India, and Pakistan). If the world was concerned about the Talibanization of Afghanistan that allowed Al-Qaida to use the Afghan state as a base and launching pad for its agenda, Pakistan potentially posed (and perhaps continues to pose even now despite the routing of pro-Taliban parties in the elections just held [February 2008]) an even more serious cause for concern.[45] If Bangladesh were to tip in this balance toward Islamization, let no one doubt that the Muslims in India will not escape being affected or influenced by this spreading pincer-like process (India's secular democracy notwithstanding). In fact, because Bangladesh has long been under the radar of scrutiny, the spill-out from the crackdown on the Taliban and its accompanying allies in Afghanistan perhaps served to scatter not a few of them to seek less conspicuous bases not too far away. Certainly whatever has been gleaned from the interrogation of those apprehended so far tends to substantiate this.

The importance of helping Bangladesh regain its original moorings cannot be overemphasized. Its original revolution for a pluralist, secular democracy needs to be assisted toward successful closure and consolidation, but not by taking a one-dimensional approach to conducting the war on terrorism, as has so long been the case in Pakistan and elsewhere[46]. Otherwise, the world should be prepared to witness there a different revolution replacing it—a revolution of the far right.

On the other hand, should Bangladeshis win the multi-pronged battles described earlier, they could well present a shining beacon for other similarly struggling Muslim nations to follow and emulate. Bangladeshis, perennially struggling against natural and man-made disasters as they do, have so far demonstrated a virtually bottomless capacity to survive. As survivors, they possess innate entrepreneurial skills and capabilities that enable them to innovate against the most daunting of odds. The cynic in me is fearful for its future, but the optimist in me continues to hope that this time, too, the ordinary people of Bangladesh shall once again innovate, and overcome—provided its leaders assimilate and take to heart the lessons of history.

ENDNOTES

1. Thomas Carson, *Issues and Priorities for Bangladesh: The 2000 IFES National Survey*, IFES (November 2001), 9. (IFES is a Washington, DC–based non-profit election-assistance organization, formerly known as the International Foundation for Election Systems.)
2. A. F. Salahuddin Ahmed, "Bangladesh: History and Culture—An Overview," in *Bangladesh—National Culture and Heritage*, eds. A. F. Salahuddin Ahmed and Bazlul Mobin Chowdhury (Dhaka: Independent University, 2004), 4.
3. http://www.worldsindhi.org/publishedreports/5July05.html, from the "The Lahore Resolution, March 23, 1940." This document is also often referred to as the "Pakistan Resolution."
4. Hasan Zaheer, *The Separation of East Pakistan* (Karachi: Oxford University Press, 1994), 6.
5. Literally translated, the word means "gentleman," but also refers to the landed gentry.
6. A. F. Salahuddin Ahmed, "Bangladesh: History and Culture—An Overview," in *Bangladesh—National Culture and Heritage*, eds. A. F. Salahuddin Ahmed and Bazlul Mobin Chowdhury (Dhaka: Independent University, 2004), 4.
7. Chief Minister of undivided Bengal from 1944–1947.
8. Zaheer, 6.
9. The British plan for India's independence presented a loosely federal state configured more as a confederation, with all powers except defense, foreign affairs, and communication being vested in the provinces.
10. Government of Pakistan, Ministry of Information & Broadcasting, Directorate of Films & Publications, Islamabad, "Presidential Address to the Constituent Assembly of Pakistan at Karachi, August 11, 1947," in *Quaid-i-Azam Mohammad Ali Jinnah, Speeches and Statements as Governor General of Pakistan 1947–48* (1989).
11. The six-point formula for regional autonomy, ironically, was a reinstated demand for reversion to the "confederal" structure for India, as had been originally envisaged under the British colonial government's formula for India's independence.
12. The elections of 1970 have been very recently described by Stephen Cohen (a leading scholar and expert on South Asia at the Brookings Institution), in response to a question in a BBC interview, as perhaps the only free and fair elections that Pakistan has ever had in its history (until February 2008).

13. It was Zulfiqar Ali Bhutto (who had emerged with the largest majority within West Pakistan) who actually first voiced the demand for Pakistan to have two Prime Ministers, one for each wing—a fact that has tended to be glossed over by many in recent times.

14. It should be understood here that in the context of the times, socialism symbolized more the idea of social justice than doctrinaire socialism per se, and was entirely in consonance with the anti-colonial wave that defined the mood of most post-colonial states.

15. Most of these people escaped to Pakistan or went underground, but many were rehabilitated after General Ziaur Rahman assumed power, sowing the seeds of rekindled divisions within the polity.

16. Rounaq Jahan, *Bangladesh Politics* (Dhaka: University Press Limited, 2005), 114.

17. A charge that was also echoed by one faction of the leftist National Awami Party of Bangladesh, NAP (Muzaffar), and the Communist Party of Bangladesh (CPB), which tended to ally with the AL.

18. The leftist National Awami Party-Bhasani group (NAP-B) and the Jatiya Samajtantric Dal (JSD).

19. Jahan, 129. This also reflected the ideological schism then existing within the Communist world.

20. A combination of factors, most importantly inappropriate domestic policies and a corrupt distribution system, the use of food aid as a foreign policy political tool used extensively by Henry Kissinger, who had a "pro-Pakistan tilt," and a slowdown of shipments triggered a famine situation. For further details on some of these aspects, see Donald McHenry and Kai Bird, "Food Bungle in Bangladesh," in *Foreign Policy* 72 (summer 1977): 77–88.

21. Mujib's wife, three sons, and two daughters-in-law were all shot in cold blood. Only his two daughters, who were abroad in Europe at the time, escaped the massacre. The elder daughter, Sheikh Hasina Wazed, was later to head the party her father had led and eventually become Prime Minister in 1996.

22. Jahan, 228.

23. BNP (with JIB support in Parliament) in 1991; AL in 1996; BNP-JIB coalition in 2001.

24. As well as recover, with as much profit as possible, the huge "investments" in capital spent on electioneering.

25. *Daily Star*, Dhaka, October 16, 2002.

26. *Daily Star*, Dhaka, June 16, 2003.

27. *Daily Star*, Dhaka, June 6, 2003.

28. *Daily Star*, Dhaka, June 3, 2003.
29. Islamic religious institution of learning.
30. EuropeAid Studies of Asia—Analysis of Madrasas in Bangladesh and Pakistan.
31. Salahuddin Ahmed, 5, op cit Muhammad Enamul Huq's *A History of Sufism in Bengal* (Dhaka: Asiatic Society, 1975).
32. To this must also be added the fact that very large numbers of Bangladeshi workers are employed in Saudi Arabia and the Gulf region for long periods of time, and apart from their very valuable (and considerable) remittances to their homeland, they also serve as an agent of osmosis for the eastward flow of ideas and ideology.
33. While preparing for the 2006 elections, in a desperate act to get on the right side of electoral arithmetic, the Awami League announced an electoral alliance with an Islamic party that it had hitherto always denigrated and shunned.
34. Banglapedia.
35. The tenth Imam who mysteriously disappeared. Muslims believe that he will return to this world to fight the anti-Christ.
36. Jesus Christ. Muslims also believe that Christ will reappear on the earth on doomsday to save the world and its people. Ahmadiyas, unlike Christians and other Muslims, do not believe that Christ died on the cross, but that he was taken down and subsequently traveled to India to propagate his faith, where he died of old age.
37. Literally, followers of the Hadith, with commitment to the doctrine of Unity of God, complete obedience to the ways and practices of the Prophet Muhammad, enthusiasm of jihad, and complete submission to Allah. The roots of the movement go back to around 1919 in British India. In doctrinaire matters, it is close to Wahabism. In Bangladesh, the movement was established in 1830 by Haji Shariatullah in Faridpur, who propagated a softer and indeed enlightened approach that fought against popular superstitions, but who at the same time remained faithful to the Hanafi school of Islamic jurisprudence, thus displaying and advocating an inclusive pluralism. The less tolerant, or radical practice of this creed was followed by Titu Mir, the revolutionary freedom fighter of Bengal in the earlier part of the nineteenth century, who fought the British relentlessly and died in 1831. The Jamiyat-e-Ahle Hadith of East Pakistan, while keeping aloof from the liberation war of Bangladesh, did not act against it, unlike the Jamaate Islami, which actively colluded with the Pakistani authorities and are accused of war crimes.

38. Reportedly having links with banned Islamic militant groups in Pakistan, such as Jaish-e-Mohammed and Lashkar-e-Toiba, and in the Middle East. See Bertil Lindner's "Bangladesh—A Cocoon of Terror," *Far Eastern Economic Review* (April 4, 2002). When this report was published, the Bangladesh coalition government went into angry denial mode, calling the report biased and without foundation. Much of the report subsequently appears not to have been without foundation or substance.

39. Common to all these organization was that many of their members had belonged to the Ahle Hadith school, while practically all had at one time or another belonged to the Jamaate Islami, or its student wing, the Islami Chhatra Shibir, and continued to maintain links with their original parent affiliations even while pursuing their separate agenda. Some of these groups, notably the JMB, included Bengali fighters who had fought alongside the Mujahideen in Afghanistan against the Soviet occupation of that country.

40. The Grameen Bank, founded by Mohammed Yunus, pioneered the use of the micro-credit concept for poverty alleviation. The bank and its founder were awarded the Nobel Prize for peace in 2006. BRAC is a local NGO founded immediately after Bangladesh's independence and has transformed into one of the largest NGOs in the world today, delivering non-formal primary education, health care, and agro-extension programs to the rural poor in Bangladesh and elsewhere in the world.

41. "Jamaat link to militants becomes evident," *The Daily Star*, Dhaka, Vol. 5, Num. 471, Thursday, September 22, 2005.

42. *Daily Star*, April 4, 2004.

43. *Daily Star* report, March 3, 2008.

44. Ibid., March 3, 2008.

45. Those forces are strong and deeply entrenched and will resurface with a vengeance if the new elected leaders are unable to deliver what the people crave.

46. The U.S. administration may be tempted or inclined to embrace the same rubric, and priorities, in Bangladesh. At least they appeared to have done so when the BNP-Jamaate Islami coalition was in power.

CHAPTER 6

MUSLIM EXPERIENCE
OF INDIAN DEMOCRACY

Omar Khalidi

ISLAM AND DEMOCRACY: AN INTRODUCTION

Are Islam and democracy compatible? Do Muslim elites embrace
democracy, both its values and institutions? Or do some Muslims view
democratic institutions merely as an instrument to capture political
power? Does Muslim opinion vary from countries where they form the
majority of the national population to countries where they are in the
minority? Given that Muslims are not a monolith—divided as they are
by national boundaries, language, sect, political and ideological orientation, and class—it is unsurprising that there is a variety of Muslim opinion about the precise meaning and experiences of democracy.
Inspired by and building on the Quranic principle of *shura*, consultation, Muslims interpret Islam to be compatible with modern, Western
notions of democracy. Many argue that Islam is inherently democratic

not only because of the principle of consultation but also because of the concepts of *ijtihad*, independent reasoning, and *ijma*, consensus. The attempt to create Islamic forms of democracy is based on a reinterpretation of traditional concepts and historical institutions. Consultation, or political deliberation and community consensus, has been reinterpreted to justify parliamentary democracy, representative elections, and political parties. The Majlis al-shura, the consultative assembly that selected or elected a new caliph in Islamic history, has been transformed and equated with a legislative body. In short, Muslim scholars view their faith as containing democratic precepts and suited to upholding liberal values.[1] Living in the colonial environment of European ideas, Indian Muslim modernists like "Iqbal (1877–1938) saw in the modernized concept of *ijma*, the principle of the consensus of common Muslims and the Muslim elite, and thus the modern principle of democracy,"[2] adapted to specific circumstances with some modifications. Another major thinker, Mawlana Sayyid Abulala Mawdudi (1903–1979), founder of Jamaat-i Islami, held that Islam constitutes its own form of democracy when conceived as a limited form of popular sovereignty directed by divine *sharia*, the Islamic law.[3] He called this form of democracy theo-democracy. Contrary to Muslims' favorable view of their faith's compatibility with democracy, some American scholars find it incompatible with notions of liberal democracy. Samuel Huntington argued famously that Islam and the West comprise two distinct, clashing civilizations, noting the absence of democracy in Muslim-majority countries.[4] Daniel Pipes claimed that Islam fundamentally opposes liberal values and is therefore devoid of democratic spirit.[5] Many academics and journalists find these claims biased, if not bigoted. Some academic studies have been done to explore how Muslims participate in democratic politics and how Muslim-oriented parties operate in Islamic countries, but little work has been done in the case of Muslim minorities' views of, and participation in democratic, non-Muslim states, mainly because the categories of academic and journalistic analysis tend to be within a national framework.

The role of Muslims in public life both potentially and actually differs greatly in countries with only a minority of Muslims in their population versus those with Muslim majorities. A country with a Muslim majority can consider a wide range of alternative roles for Islam in public life, from the Islamization of Iran, Pakistan, and Saudi Arabia to the complete secularization of Kemalist Turkey. But a Muslim minority has a narrower range of choice, constrained by the preferences of the dominant, non-Muslim majority. At a minimum, the Muslim minority would want to safeguard its group interests in a non-Muslim environment within the framework of the nation-state, provided the state does not discriminate among citizens on the basis of religion and respects group identity by granting them autonomy to run religious and cultural institutions to perpetuate self-identity. Of the world's billion-plus Muslims at the dawn of the twenty-first century, roughly one-third live in countries where they are in a minority. Large chunks of Muslim minorities live in non-democratic countries such as China, or in countries that were non-democratic in the recent past, such as the Soviet Union and South Africa. Indian Muslims are unique in some ways, as they live in a country with a durable democracy now two generations old. As I have noted elsewhere, the experience of Indian Muslims has the potential to serve as a guide to Muslim minorities living under conditions of democracy everywhere and therefore merits a study in order to understand the Islamic interface with democracy.[6]

INDIAN MUSLIMS: AN INTRODUCTION

Muslims have lived in India since the eighth century, the earliest days of Islam. Some of the most important sufi lineages are rooted in India. India is redolent with splendors of Islamic architecture; it produced some of the finest examples of Islamic art, scattered in museums at home and abroad. The Indian contribution to Arabic, Persian, and Islamic scholarship has few rivals, as evidenced by the collections in libraries worldwide. From roughly the early thirteenth to the early eighteenth centuries, Muslim elites exercised political and military control over much of the country through the various sultanates and Mogul empire. The Nizams, Southern Moguls, ruled the Deccan right up until the middle of the twentieth century. Under the Moguls and their successor states, a majority of the population remained outside Islam, as Muslims made no attempt to force religious conversation, both because it was forbidden by faith as well as for strategic reasons. The Moguls and their successors incorporated upper-caste Hindu military elites and merchant communities into the state structure through marital alliances and other forms of partnership. Only during and after the colonial era did divisions between Hindu and Muslim elites become salient. The arrival of Europeans and their acquisition of political and military power in the mid-eighteenth century heralded the end of the Muslim elite's dominant position. Now the Muslim elite were reduced to subjects of the British with the rest of the Indians, Hindu and Muslim alike. Until the 1857 Mutiny/Revolt, the Muslim elite nurtured, through memory and nostalgia, a hope for the restoration of Islamic rule. The British East India Company's triumph over the rebels in 1857 shattered that hope forever. Since the British gained formal power from the Muslim elite, the colonial authorities viewed them as seditious, disaffected subjects cherishing a hope for revival of power. Historian William Wilson Hunter's provocatively titled 1871 book, *Indian Musalmans: Are They Bound in Conscience to Revolt Against the Queen*, summed up the colonial fear and distrust of the Muslim elite. Distrusted by the colonial state, divested of lands, deprived of employment, uneducated in modern science and technology through English, the Muslim elite's economic and political condition in the mid-nineteenth century was at its nadir.[7] Unlike Muslims, the Hindu elites eagerly embraced modern scientific education imparted through English. Even though both Muslims and Hindus participated in the Mutiny/Revolt of 1857, the British penalized Muslims more than Hindus. Thus the Muslim elite lacked both state trust as well as modern education. A *modus vivendi* had to be found. A group of modernizing Muslim elites in upper India headed by Sayyid Ahmad Khan took up the cause of modern scientific education. The colonial authorities encouraged Sayyid Ahmad Khan and his colleagues with state funds. In return, the Muslim elite pledged loyalty to the British Raj. Meanwhile, the upper-caste Hindu elite organized an Indian National Congress in

1885. Despite the membership of a handful of Parsis, domiciled Europeans, and an occasional Muslim, the Congress, led by B. G. Tilak and Sardar Patel, remained essentially Hindu in composition and character, often using Hindu icons, idioms, and images in its rhetoric. But from the beginning it also had a left and center-left component—led by Gokhale and Nehru—that was cognizant of and sensitive to India's diverse population. Gandhi stood between the two. The modernizing Muslim elite, still recovering from the shock of political displacement, were reluctant to support the political demands of the Congress for fear of official disapproval. The late-nineteenth and early-twentieth century in Indian history was a crucial period of transition. Constitutional reforms introduced at that time mark the turning point between the frost of the old Raj's monolithic bureaucracy and the gradual relaxation of British power toward parliamentary self-governance through legislative councils chosen in elections. "The thought of elections," according to Percival Spear,

> *sounded the tocsin of alarm in Muslim minds and there began that process by which each constitutional advance was accompanied by a Muslim demand for safeguards. These safeguards took the form of special or 'separate' constituencies for Muslims on the ground that the property qualification proposed would always place them in a minority on account of their poverty compared to the Hindus.*[8]

In 1901 Muslims constituted close to a quarter of the total population, concentrated in what are now Pakistan, Kashmir, and Bangladesh, but were thinly dispersed elsewhere, barring some exceptions. Muhammad Iqbal was probably expressing the assessment of many in the Muslim elite when he declared "the principle of European democracy cannot be applied to India without recognizing the facts of communal groups."[9] Any electoral system, as well as the creation of constituencies, had to be designed in a manner that the Muslim elites' thought would reflect their numbers and "political importance." A representative delegation of Muslim elite assembled from various parts of the country in Simla, the summer capital of the Raj, to meet the Viceroy on October 1, 1906.

Led by His Highness, the Aga Khan, the famous deputation of some thirty-five Muslims presented its address to Lord Minto. Given the character of the Muslim elite, the address was loyalist and supplicating in tone but clearly asserted the community consciousness of its authors. The deputation expressed "a fair share" of any extended representation on councils for the Muslim community. Lord Minto was urged that Muslim representative "status and influence should be commensurate not merely with their numerical strength but also with their political importance and the value of the contribution they make to the defense of the Empire."[10] The deputation underlined their perception of Muslims as a "distinct community...more numerous than the entire population of any first class European power, except Russia."[11] So

> fortified by their sense of a unique identity, the delegation appealed for permission to return their own representatives to all levels of administration, from local boards through the central legislative council. Without separate electorates, they argued, no Muslim truly representative of his community's interest would ever be elected by the Hindu majority.[12]

The Viceroy accepted the deputation's demand for separate electorates, later embodied in the Government of India Act of 1909. Two months after the history-transforming event of 1906, many members of the deputation met in Dacca (now Bangladesh's capital) to form the All India Muslim League. Dismissing the Muslim elites' initiative demanding separate electorates as British inspired, the Hindu-dominated Congress viewed the inception of the new electoral system as a manifestation of the Raj's policy of divide and rule.[13] However, the outbreak of the World War I disrupted the Muslim elites' loyalty to the Raj, as Britain was the Ottoman Empire's enemy in Europe. The war created an alliance between Muslim and Hindu elites when Congress leaders B. G. Tilak and Mohandas Gandhi supported the Khilafat movement in support of the Turks. The alliance culminated in the Lucknow Pact between the Muslim League and Congress in December 1916 in which the latter recognized separate electorates as valid. Congress leader and poet Sarojini

Naidu hailed the Muslim League leader Muhammad Ali Jinnah as the ambassador of Hindu-Muslim unity. But it was a short-lived alliance. It broke apart less than a decade later when a Congress committee headed by Motilal Nehru (father of the Prime Minister) rejected separate electorates in a 1928 report. The Congress had breached the alliance on a question Muslim leaders regarded as "settled facts." Revisiting "these settled facts," wrote Lord Chelmsford, "and any attempt to go back on them would rouse a storm of bitter protest...""[14] It roused more than a storm of protest. Hitherto a party of loyalist landlords and retired civil servants, the Muslim League broadened its social base under the leadership of Muhammad Ali Jinnah, now called Qaid-i Azam, the great leader. But the League's attempt to represent all Muslims did not go unchallenged. In Bengal, Kashmir, Northwest Frontier Provinces, and Punjab there were predominantly Muslim parties who did not share the League ideology. Many were actually aligned with the Congress. In fact, a significant group of traditional scholars, the ulama, organized in Jamiat al-Ulama, opposed the League. In 1935 Jinnah took over the League in preparation for the election of 1937. The Qaid

> announced his willingness to work in coalition with Congress ministries and believed that Congress leaders shared his views. In the elections the League fared only moderately. It was on the Muslim electoral map but by no means exclusively so. The Congress, with assured majorities in six provinces, declined coalitions, offering office to Leaguers only on a personal basis. This was a bitter blow to Jinnah.[15]

Disregarding Muslim economic and cultural interests, the Congress ministries of 1937–1939 further aggravated Hindu-Muslim relations in several provinces, leading the League to demand the creation of Pakistan, an autonomous state or states in Muslim-majority provinces, in 1940. As Ayesha Jalal has persuasively argued, Jinnah's demand for Pakistan sought not separation, but parity for India's Muslims in a larger confederation.[16] "It was," writes Jalal, "Congress that insisted on partition. It was Jinnah who was against partition."[17] The Congress' superior organization, size, and its refusal to accept the British Cabinet Mission proposal for a decentralized India brought about the creation of a vastly truncated and moth-eaten Pakistan at partition and independence in 1947. The Congress emerged triumphant over not only the Muslim League but also over the untouchables, whose leadership it marginalized.[18]

QUESTION OF REPRESENTATION IN POST-INDEPENDENCE INDIA

The partition of India created Pakistan in the Muslim-majority portions of the two provinces of Bengal and Punjab, leaving behind millions of Muslims in the residual Indian provinces. The question of Muslim representation in the national and provincial legislature remained unresolved by partition. Under the terms of the Cabinet Mission statement of May 16, 1947, an advisory committee in the Constituent Assembly was to be established as the principal instrument for considering the minorities' problem. The Advisory Committee and its Minority Rights Subcommittee began work in July 1947. According to Grenville Austin, "sentiment in the Assembly at this time seems to have been in favor of reserving seats for minorities in legislature but strongly against separate electorate."[19] Both congressmen and non-congressmen demanded reservation in legislature for their communities whether Muslims, Sikhs, or Scheduled Castes and Tribes. Voices in favor of separate electorates were few and came from the members of the Muslim League, now confined to Madras province in the south, as the League had disintegrated in the north.[20] Prime Minister Jawaharlal Nehru and his Deputy Sardar Patel, known for his anti-Muslim bias, worked behind the scene to abolish separate electorates. After considering various views and holding prolonged discussions among themselves, the members of the Minorities Sub-Committee rejected separate electorates by 26 votes to 3, and by the same margin accepted the principle of reserved seats for certain minorities, including Muslims, for a ten-year period on July 28, 1947. But barely two years later, the Advisory Committee reversed its decision by denying parliamentary reservations to Muslims, though it granted it to Scheduled Castes—the former untouchables—which explicitly excludes

Muslims via a presidential order of 1950. Thus the abolition of separate electorates, not the partition of 1947, represents the transformative event that crippled the remaining political force of Muslims in independent India.[21] Indian Muslims emerged in the middle of the twentieth century vastly shrunk in numbers and divested of the instrument to exercise their political power as a group. It was time for a fundamental revision of Muslim political strategies in the post-colonial era.

THE POST-COLONIAL CONSTITUTIONAL FRAMEWORK

India's constitution is generally liberal and secular in spirit. Article 14 grants equality to all citizens without discrimination; article 16 gives equal opportunity for public employment; under articles 26–29, minorities are free to manage their own religious affairs; article 30 allows minorities to run educational institutions of their choice. On the downside, a detailed examination of the constitution reveals numerous ambiguities resulting in judicial verdicts negative to minorities' interest, as demonstrated by experience involving cases of Article 30's interpretation.[22] Article 16 (4) provides for reservation for public employment for "backward classes," but excludes Muslims and Christians through a Presidential Order of 1950. By article 44, the state is to endeavor to secure a uniform civil code for all citizens, which Muslims interpret as a license to interfere in the sharia. Article 48 prohibiting cow slaughter imposes a Hindu taboo on beef on all Indians, depriving butchers of employment and restricting the food choice of citizens. With all its limitations, the constitution of India, W. C. Smith observed, offers Muslims, for the first time in history, the opportunity to share power as legal equals with non-Muslims rather than simply to be the rulers or the ruled.[23] S. Abid Husain, an important thinker of the 1960s, had views similar to those of Smith, in fact, even more positive. He remarked:

> The constitution…gives Muslims the right and opportunity to… change anything…in national life which appears to them to be in conflict with Islamic values and to advocate the recognition and adoption of more Islamic values. But…efforts in this direction

can only be effective if they speak...not in religious but secular language and argue their case...not on the basis of religious
authority but on that of observation, experience and reason.[24]

MUSLIM GOALS IN INDIA

What could be the maximum and minimum goals of a minority? Some
Muslims may fantasize that their minority status can be changed into a
majority one by religious conversions, higher birthrates, and immigration from neighboring states of shared beliefs, or even military conquest.
While that may be the fantasy of a few Muslims, it must be the night-
mare of an equally few uninformed Hindus. From around independence
to around the 1970s, Jamaat-i Islami propagated the idea of *iqamat-i
din*, establishment of faith, presumably though conversion to Islam,
but that idea did not earn many converts beyond a tiny segment of the
community.[25] For the most part, the Muslim elites' goal is no more than
closing the gap between the constitutional precept and the actual executive practice to secure for minorities full participation in the polity and
economy. At the same time, the goal is to be met while maintaining and
perpetuating an Islamic identity against the real and perceived threat of
assimilation into Hindu society. The Muslim elite are diverse, ranging
from modernists to maintainers of status quo to revivalists. But they are
united as far as achieving the minimum goal of maintaining a distinctive
identity by participating in the political process.

STRATEGIES

Given the difficulty of keeping a balance between assimilation and inte-
gration, how do Muslims seek to obtain their goals? Two strategies are
widely suggested: one is the total withdrawal from political process as a
group. The other is full participation, either as individuals, as a group, or
both. On the eve of national independence, Mawlana Mawdudi advised
his small number of followers in Jamaat-i Islami to disassociate with
the state and not participate in the political process, deeming it inappropriate in view of the disastrous results of competing Hindu-Muslim

nationalisms and the un-Islamic nature of the state itself.[26] But his party revised the policy in the late 1970s as neither practical nor fruitful. The Tablighi Jamaat, an influential organization dedicated to inculcation of basic Islamic rituals, also stays away from politics, though never actively opposing the political process. Two Muslim sects—the Aga Khani Ismailis and Bohras—consisting mainly of merchants and independent professionals, stay away from formal, visible political process, partly for reasons of security, partly because they do not make any demands on the state other than to be left alone. They are numerically too small to really matter. Leaving the nonparticipants aside, Muslims enthusiastically participate in politics through behavior like voting, membership in various political parties, the formation of political parties based on their own group, competing for electoral office, joining associations of political and civic natures, and the like. The Muslim leaders justify political participation on the grounds that the distribution of material resources and access to public education and employment is largely determined by the political process; in other words, Muslims must be represented in the institutions of governance, legislature in particular. To be represented in the state, there are three political approaches: they can join one of the parties perceived to be most sympathetic to Muslims from the available pool; they can work through a nonpartisan pressure group that would ensure the election of sympathetic individuals regardless of political affiliation; or they can form their own political party or parties and try to extract benefits by holding the balance of power in a coalition government. Indian Muslims have tried all three approaches.

MUSLIMS IN THE DOMINANT POLITICAL PARTY: ALLIANCE WITH CONGRESS

Since the freedom movement, the Congress had been aligned with the Jamiat al-Ulama, the organization of traditional scholars, particularly those based in the seminary at Deoband, U.P. The Jamiat's cooperation with the Congress involved a political bargain, in which the Ulama gave their support to the dominant party on the assumption that mosques, endowments, institutions of religious instruction, and Muslim family laws would be untouched by any state measure. The apparent liberal and secular approach of the Nehruvian, the center wing of Congress, drew to the Congress Muslim politicians of various kinds. In any case, there were no real alternatives in the immediate aftermath of partition. The once-powerful Muslim League had dissolved everywhere except the old Madras state. Consequently, the Congress emerged at the beginning of independence as the natural instrument for Muslim participation in the new political process. Muslim support to the Congress is evident from votes Congress received in the three general—both center and state—elections held in 1952, 1957, and 1962. As a result, a number of Muslims were elected to the parliament on the Congress party ticket, though never in proportion to their numbers in the national population. In the era of Congress dominance, none of the weak opposition parties put a significant number of Muslim candidates in the electoral contests in the first place, so few were elected. Despite the dominance of and nearly unqualified support to Congress everywhere in the nation, Muslims began to be disenchanted with the party due to recurring bouts of anti-Muslim violence, real and perceived discrimination in public employment, and the near-elimination of Urdu as the language of instruction (or even as just one of the many subjects) in government schools in most states. Muslim public opinion, as expressed through the media, perceived fellow Muslim members of parliament and state assemblies elected on the Congress ticket as ineffective in shaping public policy and implementation when it came to the community's issues. After having supported the Congress for two decades, Muslim politicians and community leaders began to ask whether the interests of the community could not be better served by building up a more autonomous position.

POLITICS OF A NONPARTISAN PRESSURE GROUP: MUSHAWARAT AND THE 1967 ELECTION

When Congress party dominance waned in the mid-1960s, the Muslim elite attempted a new strategy. A meeting convened in Lucknow in

August 1964 brought together, for first time in the post-independence era, leaders of various Muslim parties representing several schools of thought, such as the Muslim League, Jamaat-I Islami, and Jamiat al-Ulama together with a significant number of independents. The meeting gave birth to a loosely knit consultative organization, Muslim Majlis-i Mushawarat, or MMM. In preparation for the upcoming general election of 1967, it published a manifesto. Parties and individual candidates signing the manifesto were assured the community's votes in exchange for a promise to support Muslim concerns on security, fairness in education, employment, and cultural matters. A notable feature of this approach was that the MMM supported many Hindu candidates perceived to be sympathetic to the community against perceived ineffective Muslim contestants. Numerous MMM-supported candidates were elected to the parliament in the state assemblies.[27] After the election, the victorious candidates elected with MMM support backed out when the time came for the implementation of the promises made during the electoral fight. The MMM strategy as a nonpartisan pressure group failed because it did not take into account the strong discipline exercised—through "whip"—by the parties over members. The whip prevented sympathetic individual legislators from going against the party line. Like the British, but unlike the American political system where a legislator's loyalty is primarily to the constituents, the Indian system allows the party to exercise great control over the individual legislator. After the decay of the Congress organization in the 1960s and 1970s, many legislators often disregarded party discipline, but more stringent rules now prevent individual legislators from going against the party direction on given issues. After the failure of the 1967 MMM approach, Muslims went back to Congress in the 1972 election, turned away in 1977, and then returned to it in 1980. They supported Congress in 1984, with some variations, but deserted it in 1989. In the four elections of the last decade of the previous century (1991, 1996, 1998, 1999), Muslims voted for a variety of parties—except the Hindu-extremist Bharatya Janata Party and Shiv Sena—and no party could claim the bulk of votes. The same is true of the 2004 election.[28] Still, the Congress and other major parties often view Muslims as a supplicant minority whose wishes can be ignored. It is a measure of the Muslim elites' frustration with Congress that Jamiat al-Ulama, aligned with Congress before independence, seriously contemplated entering electoral politics in 2003, "a desperate measure," according to one observer.[29] Frustrated with the national parties' indifference to Muslim issues, some Muslims formed political parties with membership based solely on their own community in southern India. Thus Majlis-i Ittihad al-Muslimin (MIM) has been functioning in Hyderabad since 1957, but its electoral success and therefore its influence has been limited to the municipal level, though it won 5 out of over 300 seats in the 2004 A.P. state election. Since 1984, the MIM has won only one Lok Sabha seat. In U.P., there has been a Muslim Majlis since 1968, but it is nearly comatose. Only in Kerala has a Muslim party, the League, been successful. Three reasons account for its success. The first is the concentration of Muslims in a single region, Malabar. The second is the diverse, almost evenly balanced, population numbers of Hindus, Christians, and Scheduled Castes, thus preventing the domination of any political party by one religious group and creating space for individuals from any religious group to compete for office. The third reason is Kerala's political fragmentation. No party there has been able to form a government on its own since 1967, which has led to coalitions. The League was a member of every governing coalition from 1967 through 1987, then again in 1991, and from 2001 through 2006. But the League has not been able to expand elsewhere, except briefly in West Bengal in 1971. Like Kerala, Muslims are also concentrated in one region of that state: the two districts of Malda and Murshidabad; however, the Communist Party of India (Marxist) (CPM), as distinct from just Communist Party of India (CPI) (The two parties, originally one, split thus one is called CPI, the other CPM) has successfully prevented League expansion in that region. In summary, an exclusively Muslim party is hindered by the role of religion and caste in the electoral process.

CRITERIA FOR SELECTING CANDIDATES

Religious and caste affiliation has been among the major criteria governing the choices of many voters since the dawn of electoral politics in the twentieth century. Voters focus on various aspects of religion and caste in their political preferences: the religion and caste of individual candidate, the representation of particular castes and religions in the membership and leadership of the parties, the castes with which some parties may explicitly identify themselves, or the extent to which parties address the demands of particular castes. Political parties, including the communist parties, frequently make their selection of candidates based on the caste and community composition of a given constituency. Each political party tries to ensure the solid support of a particular caste or community, and often fields a few fake candidates as vote-splitters. Given the frequent absence of sharp ideological lines between various political parties, selection by caste or community frequently becomes the criteria for winning. In constituencies where no caste or community is dominant, political parties usually select a candidate from the smallest caste in order to neutralize the caste factor. Given such criteria, it is unsurprising that even a leader of Mawlana Abulkalam Azad's stature had to be elected, at the height of Congress domination, from Muslim-majority constituencies in the two post-independence elections of 1952 and 1957. Muslims, like scheduled castes, but unlike scheduled tribes, are scattered in most of the parliamentary constituencies. They are a majority in only a handful of constituencies. The majoritarian character of the electoral system of first-past-the-post tends to exclude minorities. Many Muslim politicians accuse the state of gerrymandering constituencies to split Muslim voting blocs.[30] In addition, several Muslim-majority constituencies are reserved for scheduled castes and tribes, disqualifying Muslims from becoming candidates.[31] In light of the reasons outlined and the caste and community voting preference of the voters, it is no wonder that Muslims have not been elected to the parliament in proportion to their numbers in the national population, as table 6 demonstrates.

TABLE 6. Muslim representation in constituent assembly, 1946–1949, and in Lok Sabha, 1952–2009.

No.	Year	Total Elected Members	Muslims Elected	Muslims expected to be elected on the basis of population	Deprivation %
*	1946		31		
I	1952	489	21	49	57.14
II	1957	494	24	49	51.02
III	1962	494	23	53	56.60
IV	1967	520	29	56	48.21
V	1971	518	30	58	48.28
VI	1977	542	34**	61	44.26
VII	1980	529#1	49**	59	16.95
VIII	1984	542	46****	62	25.81
IX	1989	529#2	33	60	45.00
X	1991	534******	28	65	56.92
XI	1996	543	28	66	57.56
XII	1998	543	29	66	56.06
XIII	1999	543	32	66	51.52
XIV	2004	543	36	66	45.45
XV	2009	543	29	66	56.06
Total			**471**	**836**	**47.12**

Source. * Election to Constituent Assembly, Grenville Austin, *The Indian Constitution: Cornerstone of a Nation* (Oxford: Clarendon Press, 1966), 13.

For Lok Sabha, see Iqbal Ansari, *Political Representation of Muslims in India, 1952–2004* (New Delhi: Manak, 2006), 64.

** Includes Muslims elected through by-elections as well as scheduled, regular election.

#1 Elections not held in Assam (12 seats) and Meghalaya (1 seat).

#2 Elections not held in disputed territory of Jammu and Kashmir (6 seats); 3 seats countermanded—2 in Bihar, one in U.P.

**** Election Commission Office.

The table conclusively demonstrates that Muslims were elected slightly more than their percentage in the national population in the Constituent Assembly because of separate electorates. But if their proportion in the national population is held as the main criteria, they have been consistently underrepresented in parliament since 1952 in Lok Sabha. In the first post–separate electorate parliamentary election of 1952, they constituted 4.4 percent of the total membership, and in the present 2004 parliament they are 6.44 percent, a tiny improvement. No group in India is today as disempowered as Muslims. The Sikhs are powerful because they are concentrated in one state, Punjab, as are the Scheduled Tribes in geographically compact areas. The Scheduled Castes are just as poor as Muslims but are increasingly becoming politically strong, evidenced by the success of their ethnic party—Bahujan Samaj—in U.P.[32] They also have electoral reservation along with the Tribes. Without the political reservation, their parliamentary reservation would go down drastically, as few SC-ST members have been elected from general, nonreserved constituencies.[33] The Indian Christians, increasingly under attack from upper-caste Hindu fanatics in various parts of the country since the 1990s, have some political clout given their church connections in Europe and North America. Only Muslims are politically most deprived, more so now than before given the anti-Muslim phobia in the United States and Europe.

CONSEQUENCES OF POWERLESSNESS

Owing to the consistently lower number of Muslims in parliament, Muslims have been similarly poorly represented in the council of ministers and cabinets since independence.[34] The quality of Muslim representation in cabinets is even worse. Only once in the last six decades has a Muslim held the critical portfolio of home affairs. No Muslim has ever become a minister for defense, finance, or external foreign affairs. The prime ministers have allotted Muslims ministries of little weight or political significance such as sports, tourism, and aviation.[35] What is true of the union—the

TABLE 7. Pogroms against Muslims and Sikhs in India since 1947.

Location	Date/Year	Number of Deaths	Source of info.
Delhi	Late August–Early September 1947	20,000	Vazira F-Y Zamindar
Hyderabad State	September 11–December 15, 1948	Several thousand	Sundarlal/ Abdulghaffar Report
Ahmadabad, Gujarat	September 19, 1969	630	Varshney, p. 220
Nellie, Assam	February 18, 1983	3,300	*India Today*, Feb. 28, 1983; March 15, 1983; Tehelka
Delhi	November 1–3, 1984	5,000 Sikhs killed	Nanavati Commission Report
Bhagalpur, Bihar	October 1989	Nearly 1,000	M. Hasan, p. 256
India, nationwide	December 6–13, 1992	1,200	*Frontline, Sunday, India Today*
Gujarat	February 28– Mid-March 2002	2,000	Human Rights Watch Report

Sources. **Delhi, 1947:** Vazira F-Y Zamindar, *The Long Partition and the Making of Modern South Asia: Refugees, Boundaries, Histories* (New York: Columbia University Press, 2007), p. 21, citing contemporary sources.
Hyderabad State: "A Report on Post-Operation Polo Massacres," in *Hyderabad: After the Fall*, ed. Omar Khalidi (Hyderabad, 1988).
Ahmadabad: Ashutosh Varshney, *Ethnic Conflict and Civic Life* (New Haven, CT: Yale University Press, 2002).
Nellie, Assam: *India Today,* February 28, 1983; *India Today*, March 15, 1983; and Tehelka online at http://www.tehelka.com/story_main19.asp?filename=Ne093006the_horrors.asp.
Delhi, 1984: Nanavati Commission Report online at http://www.carnage84.com/homepage/nancom.htm.
India, nationwide: *Frontline*, January 1, 1993, pp. 105–109; *Sunday*, December 20, 1992, pp. 28–29 and 52–56; *Sunday*, December 27, 1992, pp. 48–50; *India Today*, December 31, 1992, pp. 40–43.
Bombay: *The New York Times*, February 4, 1993: A1.
Gujarat: Human Rights Watch Report, http://www.hrw.org/reports/2002/india/.

federal cabinet—is true at the state level. At the state level, Muslims are typically allocated ministerial portfolios of animal husbandry, jails, small irrigation, and the like (as I have demonstrated through studies of ministerial portfolios for five states during the last five decades[36]). The most serious consequence of Muslim disempowerment is the absence of security of life and property in the population. The community has been the victim of five pogroms and numerous instances of violence, often with the partisan involvement of police and sometimes paramilitary.[37]

Muslims are poorly represented in almost every sector of the economy. Outside of five tiny, ethnic, sectarian groups of Muslims—Bohras, Khojas, Labbais, Maraickars, Memons—only a small number of Muslims own big businesses. Muslims' entrepreneurial ambition has often been curtailed due to the banks' refusal to extend credit.[38] In numerous instances, Muslim businesses have been the prime target of violence and pogroms in which the apparatuses of state are openly involved.[39] Muslims represent a tiny segment of public employment, as persuasively documented by the present writer[40] and a state-appointed panel.[41] The nation's security forces, consisting of the army, air force, navy, paramilitaries, and police have few Muslims, and mostly in subordinate posts.[42] Muslims' educational achievements are also poor compared to Hindus, and under a state policy of homogenization, Urdu is excluded from government schools in Uttar Pradesh.[43] Thus, it is abundantly clear that Muslim grievances are real, acute, and require settlement for the long-term health of Indian democracy. The first order of business is the safety of life and property, followed by measures to improve their economic condition through the acquisition of a modern scientific education. The first is impossible without strong, active state intervention. The second is only partially possible through the mobilization of the community's internal resources—rich endowments, charity, NGOs, and the like. But obtaining an independent political voice through politics alone can bring about change by transforming the bureaucracy on the model of the former untouchables.[44] Transforming the bureaucracy and the police would require political pressure, and for Muslims to acquire that power a series

of changes in the electoral system is required along the principles recommended by Minority Rights Group: ensuring the fair representation
of each minority group; ensuring that different groups will cooperate
and appeals to nationalism will not be unduly rewarded; and ensuring
that designers of electoral systems have a clear understanding of the
situation of all minorities in the country—ethnic/national, religious, and
linguistic—before beginning the redesign. This understanding should
include the numbers of the minorities, their geographical spread, their
levels of literacy (with particular emphasis on minority women), and
languages spoken. In particular, in the Indian case, the delimitation of
constituencies must be rationalized to concentrate, not divide, ethnic
minority groups to increase their electoral chances as well as competition
within minority opinion and the constituencies reserved for Scheduled
Castes and Tribes must either rotate as originally intended to prevent
Muslim-concentration constituencies off-limits to Muslims or the discriminatory clause excluding Muslims and Christians in the category of
Scheduled Castes must be removed.[45]

CONCLUSIONS

Politically mobilized, ethnically concentrated minorities are thought to
threaten the stability of democratic states.[46] Incentives for the minorities to
be absorbed into normalized politics are high if the state wants stability.[47]
Institutional approaches have so far driven attempts at minority incorpora-
tion. The Netherlands has adopted a Consociational approach to its democracy, one which works because ethnic groups are neatly localized within
the country.[48] But the Muslim minority in India is widely dispersed. A new
architecture of democracy is needed to accommodate this large group. One
way would be to introduce proportional representation that permits larger
groups of ethnic-based smaller parties to be represented, as advocated by Syed
Shahabuddin, a former MP and editor of *Muslim India*.[49] This will require
Indian nationalism to make compromises with subnationalisms within
India—through the religious identity of Muslims and Sikhs, or the region/
ethnicity-based subnationalisms in Kashmir and the Northeast. Not doing

so will mean curtailing democracy, as exemplified by the Armed Forces Special Powers Act in force in much of the Northeast and Kashmir since 1958. Political parties based on lower-caste membership have success-fully mobilized in the years since 1980 to capture power in several states and increase their representation in parliament. Indian public opinion hailed it as a qualitative departure from the polity of the past, a strength-ening and deepening of democracy. If and when the electoral system is changed and constituency demarcation rules are modified to permit the creation of Muslim-majority constituencies, and when Muslim-majority constituencies are not reserved for the SCs and STs, then a further qualita-tive change is likely to occur, further deepening democracy. Muslims in India are already enthusiastic supporters of democracy and active partici-pants in the democratic process. The challenge for them is how to make it more efficacious for the community to achieve the goals of gaining physi-cal security, fairness in education, and equal opportunity in employment and the advancement of culture.

Endnotes

1. Khaled Abou Elfadl, "Islam and the Challenge of Democracy," *Boston Review* (April/May 2003). *Boston Review Online*. 25pp. http://bostonreview.net/BR28.2/abou.html. Vall Vakili, "Abdolkarim Soroush and Critical Discourse in Iran," in *Makers of Contemporary Islam*, ed. John L. Esposito and John O. Voll (Oxford: Oxford University Press, 2001), 150–176.
2. Aziz Ahmad, *An Intellectual History of Islam in India* (Edinburgh: Edinburgh University Press, 1969), 14.
3. Sayyid Abulala Mawdudi, *Islamic Law and Constitution*, 9th ed., translated and edited by Khurshid Ahmad (Lahore: Islamic Publications, 1986).
4. Samuel Huntington, *The Clash of Civilizations and the Remaking of World Order* (New York: Simon & Schuster, 1996).
5. Daniel Pipes, "There Are No Moderates: Dealing with Fundamentalist Islam," *National Interest* (fall 1995). DanielPipes.org. 10pp. http://www.danielpipes.org/article/247.
6. Omar Khalidi, "Living as a Muslim in a Pluralistic Society and State: Theory and Experience," chap. 2 in *Muslims' Place in the American Public Square: Hopes, Fears and Aspirations*, ed. Zahid H. Bukhari et al. (Walnut Creek, CA: Altamira Press, 2004).
7. Omar Khalidi, *Muslims in Indian Economy* (New Delhi: Three Essays Collective, 2006).
8. Percival Spear, *A History of India*, Vol. II (New York: Penguin, 1965), p. 226.
9. Muhammad Iqbal, Presidential Address at the Muslim League Session, Allahabad, 1930, published in *Struggle for Independence* (Karachi: 1958).
10. *Report on Indian Constitutional Reforms* (London: HMSO, 1918), 186; full text, 185–188.
11. Ibid.
12. Stanley Wolpert, *Morley and India, 1906–1910* (Berkeley: University of California Press, 1967), 188–189; Stephen E. Koss, "John Morley and the Communal Question," *Journal of Asian Studies* 3 (May 1967): 381–387.
13. "An Official View on Communal Electorates," in *The Partition of India: Causes and Consequences*, ed. T. W. Wellbank (Boston: Heath, 1966), 31–32.
14. *Report on Indian Constitutional Reforms* (London: HMSO, 1918), 186.
15. Percival Spear, *A History of India*, Vol. II (New York: Penguin, 1965), 228.

16. Ayesha Jalal, *The Sole Spokesman: Jinnah, the Muslim League and the Demand for Pakistan* (Cambridge: Cambridge University Press, 1985).
17. Jalal, op. cit., 262.
18. Sekhar Bandopadhyay, "Transfer of Power and the Crises of Dalit Politics in India, 1945–47," *Modern Asian Studies* 34: 4 (2000): 893–942.
19. Grenville Austin, *The Indian Constitution: Cornerstone of a Nation* (Oxford: Clarendon Press, 1966), 149.
20. Mohamed Raza Khan, *What Price Freedom* (Madras: 1969).
21. Details of the Constituent Assembly deliberations on the separate electorates question in my *Indian Muslims Since Independence* (New Delhi: Vikas, 1996), 178–183.
22. Iqbal Ansari, "Minorities and the Politics of Constitution-Making in India," in *Minority Identities and the Nation-State*, ed. D. L. Sheth and Gurpreet Mahajan (New Delhi: Oxford University Press, 1999), 113–137.
23. W. C. Smith, *Islam in Modern History* (Princeton, NJ: Princeton University Press, 1957), 288. My only disagreement with Smith would be his characterization of all Muslims as rulers, when in fact it was only a tiny elite that shared the privilege of ruling. The rest, Muslim or otherwise, were ruled.
24. S. Abid Husain, *The Destiny of Indian Muslims* (Bombay: Asia Publishing House, 1965), 240.
25. Omar Khalidi, *Indian Muslims Since Independence*, op. cit.
26. Omar Khalidi, *Between Muslim Nationalists and Nationalist Muslims: Mawdudi's Thoughts on Indian Muslims* (New Delhi: IOS, 2004).
27. Zaheer Masood Qureshi, "Electoral Strategy of a Minority Pressure Group: The Muslim Majlis-i Mushawarat," *Asian Survey* 8 (December 1968): 976–987.
28. Details in Paul Brass, *The Politics of India Since Independence* (Cambridge: Cambridge University Press, 1994), 189–199; Niraja Gopal Jayal, *Representing India: Ethnic Diversity and the Governance of Public Institutions* (London: Palgrave, 2006), 56–57.
29. Surendra Mohan, "A Desperate Measure," *The Hindu* (March 15, 2003), electronic ed.; justification for entry into electoral politics by Asrarulhaq Qasimi, "A Political Party for Muslims," *The Milli Gazette* (April 1–15, 2003), 24.
30. Iqbal Ansari, *Political Representation of Muslims in India, 1952–2004* (New Delhi: Manak, 2006), 394.
31. Ibid., 393. *Social and Economic Status of the Muslim Community of India: A Report* (New Delhi: Prime Minister's High Level Committee,

2006), 24–25. Retired chief justice of Delhi High Court Rajindar Sachar headed the committee.

32. Kanchan Chandra, *Why Ethnic Parties Succeed: Patronage and Head-counts in India* (Cambridge: Cambridge University Press, 2004).

33. Alistair McMillan, *Standing at the Margins: Representation and Electoral Reservation in India* (New Delhi: Oxford University Press, 2005).

34. Omar Khalidi, "Muslim Ministers in the Union Cabinet: Half a Century of Distrust or Lack of Power," *Radiance* (February 11–17, 2001): 14–15. Niraja Gopal Jayal, *Representing India: Ethnic Diversity and the Governance of Public Institutions* (London: Palgrave, 2006), pp. 147–151.

35. Omar Khalidi, "Muslim Ministers in the Union Cabinet: Half a Century of Distrust or Lack of Power," *Radiance* (February 11–17, 2001): 14–15.

36. Omar Khalidi, "Muslim Ministers in the State Cabinets: The Cases of Karnataka and Andhra Pradesh (1956–2000)," *Radiance* (October 16–27, 2001): 16–17; "Muslim Ministers in the State Cabinets: The Case of Maharashtra," *Radiance* (September 15–21, 2002): 10–11; "Muslim Ministers in the State Cabinets: The Case of Bihar, 1947–2003," *Radiance* (January 4–10, 2004): 10–12; "Muslim Ministers in the State Cabinets: The Case of U.P., 1947–2003," *Radiance* (September 7–13, 2003): 14–16.

37. Omar Khalidi, *Khaki and Ethnic Violence in India* (New Delhi: Three Essays Collective, 2003); Paul Brass, *The Production of Hindu-Muslim Violence in Contemporary India* (Seattle: University of Washington Press, 2003); Ashutosh Varshney, *Ethnic Conflict and Civil Society: Hindus and Muslims in India* (New Haven, CT: Yale University Press, 2002); Steve Wilkinson, *Votes and Violence* (Cambridge: Cambridge University Press, 2004).

38. Omar Khalidi, "Entrepreneurs from Outside the Traditional Mercantile Communities: Muslims in India's Private Sector," *Journal of South Asian and Middle Eastern Studies* 21: 2 (winter 2008): 13–42.

39. Ibid.

40. Omar Khalidi, *Muslims in Indian Economy* (New Delhi: Three Essays Press, 2006).

41. *Social, Economic and Educational Status of the Muslim Community of India: A Report* (New Delhi: Prime Minister's High Level Committee, 2006), 24–25. Retired chief justice of Delhi High Court Rajindar Sachar headed the committee.

42. Omar Khalidi, *Khaki and Ethnic Violence in India*, revised second edition (New Delhi: Three Essays Collective, 2008).

43. Omar Khalidi, "Politics of Official Language Status for Urdu in India," *Journal of South Asian and Middle Eastern Studies* 28: 3 (spring 2004): 53–77.

44. Oliver Mendelssohn and Marika Vicziany, *The Untouchables* (Cambridge: Cambridge University Press, 1998), 224

45. Iqbal Ansari, op.cit. pp. 400–401, has a longer list of recommendations.

46. Robert Dahl, *Polyarchy* (New Haven, CT: Yale University Press, 1971).

47. David Horowitz, *Ethnic Groups in Conflict*, 2nd edition (Berkeley: University of California Press, 2000).

48. Arendt Liphart, *Democracy in Plural Societies: A Comparative Exploration* (New Haven, CT: Yale University Press, 1980).

49. Syed Shahbuddin. See also E. Sridharan, "The Origins of the Electoral System: Rules, Representation and Power-sharing in India's Democracy," in *India's Living Constitution: Ideas, Practices and Controversies*, ed. Zoya Hasan (New Delhi: Permanent Black, 2002), 344–369; Niraja Gopal Jayal, *Representing India: Ethnic Diversity and the Governance of Public Institutions* (London: Palgrave, 2006), 56–57.

PART III

SOUTHEAST ASIA

CHAPTER 7

CHALLENGING DEMOCRACY?

THE ROLE OF POLITICAL ISLAM
IN POST-SUHARTO INDONESIA

Felix Heiduk

INTRODUCTION

More than 80 percent of Indonesia's population of more than 200 million people are Muslim, making Indonesia the biggest Muslim-majority
nation in the world. Since the fall of the authoritarian Suharto regime in
1998, Indonesia has made significant strides toward democracy. Indonesia's democratization featured a general overhaul and the liberalization
of the political system, including the establishment of a multiparty system, freedom of the press, and the first free and fair elections since 1956.
To achieve this, one main task was the strengthening of the country's
weak institutions and the implementation of rule of law. Indonesia's

democratization furthermore encompassed the decentralization of a highly centralized political system in which political power was to a large degree concentrated in the hands of Suharto and channelled through his vast patronage-network. The transition to democracy also saw attempts to reform the powerful military that had backed Suharto's new order and had been the main instrument to oppress any form of opposition movement in the country as well as the reform of the economic system once dubbed as Suharto's "crony capitalism." The latter included, amongst other issues, the fight against endemic corruption and the tackling of the disastrous effects of the Asian crisis on the national economy.

Most reviews of Indonesia's transition to democracy have so far been very positive. It is widely acknowledged that, for the time being, Indonesia does not seem to be in danger of falling back into authoritarian structures. Many researchers (Rieffel 2004, Qodari 2005) as well as international institutions (World Bank, UN, etc.) have described the free, fair, and peaceful elections of 1999 and 2004 as a historic landmark for Indonesia. Meanwhile, the country saw several rotations of government, and legislatures and courts have gained formal independence from the central government. Indonesians also enjoy extensive political freedoms, while countless civil society organizations and other pressure groups try to exercise some sort of a "watchdog function" over the elected governments on the national and local level (Nyman 2006). Along these lines, Indonesia possesses many attributes of a consolidated democratic political system and has remained largely "stable" during the post-Suharto era.

When trying to determine the role political Islam has played in Indonesia's democratization process, the existing theoretical literature largely emphasizes the existence of democratic institutions. Accordingly, free and fair elections, freedom of press, and a multiparty system help to marginalize radicalism by giving radicals an opportunity for political participation. The regime type, democratic or not, therefore obviously seems to determine the strategies and politics implemented by Islamists. In looking at the situation in the Middle East, this hypothesis makes sense, as relaxed autocratic control of certain regimes allowed the participation of radical Islamists. Faced with the opportunity to participate, however, Islamists were ready to adjust former radical positions and in the end became more moderate (Nasr 2005). In a very simplified form, the argument hereby would be: inclusion through participation leads to moderation, exclusion through repression leads to radicalization (Hafez 2003).

How far does this hypothesis carry us with regard to the case of Indonesia? In Indonesia, democratic, or at least reform-oriented, Islamists did—amongst other groups—in fact play a vital part in the ouster of Suharto. They took part in the *reformasi* movement demanding free and fair elections and press freedom, they founded democratic parties and civil society organizations, and so on. But the transition to democracy not only opened up a space for moderate Islamists to participate in electoral politics, it also opened up space for a militant fringe of radical Islam. It seems that political liberalization was a double-edged sword, as it did not prevent the emergence of radical, violent Islamist groups such as the infamous Jemaah Islamiyah terror network or the various Islamist militia groups operating in the country. Thus, the ambiguous role Islamists have played in post-Suharto Indonesia calls into question the aforementioned hypothesis. Democratization not only enabled moderate Islamists to play a reform-oriented role within the electoral politics, but it also weakened the regime's repression of militant groups. This in turn enabled militants to take up an armed struggle for the establishment of an Islamic state in Indonesia. Thus, the correlation between democracy and political Islam seems to be highly ambiguous: the existence of democratic institutions alone cannot obviously be directly equated with Islamist moderation. As we have observed, both radicalization/militancy and moderation followed Indonesia's transition to democracy.

On the other hand, such an observation proves theories of "Muslim exceptionalism" wrong:[1] although a Muslim-majority country, Indonesia did not descend into theocracy after the fall of Suharto. For the time being, it seems safe to state that the majority of the population, as well as the country's political elite, regard the idea of an Islamic state as counterproductive to Indonesia's democratization (Fealy 2004). The 1999, 2004, and 2009 elections did not feature a significant increase in votes for parties with an Islamist agenda. The country has remained on course toward democracy and many (mostly foreign) observers reiterate the importance of a democratic Indonesia as a potential role model for the whole Muslim world, demonstrating the compatibility of Islam and democracy.

My argument hereby is that in order to clarify the ambiguous relationship between democracy and political Islam in Indonesia, we need to go beyond an institution-centered understanding of democracy and look at the configurations of social forces that have determined the shape, scope, and practices of Indonesia's transition to democracy. For this we need to understand the resurgence of political Islam in Indonesia by linking it with a critical examination of the power politics behind the democratic institutions and the free and fair elections. This should bring up a string of questions: What does the democratic practice look like and how much leverage do Islamists really have to achieve their reform agenda? What are alternative policies for those moderate Islamists who have accepted political democracy as the "only game in town" (Linz)? And what role does the violent fringe of the Islamists play? Any examination of the role of political Islam will fall short if it lacks an assessment of the condition of the (democratic) state and politics. Therefore, it is pivotal to contextualize the role of Islamists in the political and economic order they are situated within.

Hence, my understanding of political Islam is one that lacks any clear, theoretical definition of "political Islam." Ayoob has pointed out that "in practice, no two Islamisms are alike" (Ayoob 2004, 1); such observation, in my opinion, stresses the need to contextualize political Islam in its historic, sociopolitical, and economic settings. While common definitions define Islamism as a "form of instrumentalization of Islam by individuals, groups and organizations that pursue political objectives[...]" providing "political responses to today's societal challenges by imagining a future, the foundations of which rest on reappropriating reinvented concepts borrowed from Islamic traditions" (Denoux 2002, 61), such an understanding helps little to take into account the structural context that political Islam is situated in and seems to be reflexive to.

Islamism, like Islam itself, as prominent scholars have pointed out with regard to the heterogeneity of Islam in Asia (Esposito 2008), is not only inherently culture-specific but also shaped by and responsive to the underlying sociopolitical and economic structures. Political Islam in Indonesia, like anywhere else, is therefore to be determined by, and analyzed within, the contexts in which it is situated. Therefore, Achcar (1987) has emphasized that:

> Beneath their agreement on otherworldly matters, beyond their agreement on problems of everyday life[…]and notwithstanding their similar, even identical, denominations and organizational forms, Muslim movements remain essentially political movements. They are thus the expression of specific socio-political interests that are very much from this world.

Without denying the fact that Islamic ideas, symbols, and vocabulary have transcended the boundaries of local communities as well as those of Muslim nations, even these ideas, symbols, and vocabulary are adopted in different ways in response to different contexts and challenges (Ayoob 2004, 2).

Critical positions toward religion in general, as well as toward the rise of Islam, have always followed Marx's critique of religion along two lines: First, they criticize religion as a factor of alienation by the compulsion to respect obligations, which often hamper the full development of the individual, and submit to religious authorities. Second, they critique religious social and political doctrines, all of which are ideological survivals of historical epochs, assisting those in power by offering divine justification for the status quo and thus serving a legitimating function. Marx has described religion as the "false consciousness of the world," but he also made the important observation that religion can also be understood as the "sigh of the oppressed creature, the sentiment of a heartless world, and the soul of soulless conditions"—meaning that religion, while more often than not serving as a tool in the hands of those in power, is at the same time an "expression of real suffering and a protest against real suffering." Thus, religion may provide some sort of compensation (either in material terms or as some sort of a promised utopia for hardships, but only by ultimately accepting a status quo that requires such forms of compensation in the first place (Achcar 2004). I will discuss this further in the later part of the chapter.

In order to proceed with my argument, I will first try to give some insights into the historical relationship between Islam and politics in Indonesia. This is mainly to prevent us from seeing political Islam in Indonesia as a "new" phenomenon. The next section of this chapter will explore the resurgence of political Islam after the ousting of Suharto, following which the specifics and limitations of Indonesia's transition to democracy shall be taken into account. In the last section, I will conclude with an outlook on the prospects and perils of Islamism in Indonesia ten years after *reformasi*.

INDONESIAN ISLAM AND POLITICS IN HISTORICAL PERSPECTIVE

Taking into account Marx's observation of religion serving as the "sigh of the oppressed creature," it is no surprise that Islam as a political ideology came into existence during the colonial era. Demanding liberation from the colonial rule of the Dutch, it competed for mass support during Indonesia's struggle for independence (and beyond) with two other ideological currents: nationalism and communism. Contrary to the history of nationalism, the history of political Islam in Indonesia is "a history crowded with failure" (Fealy 2005, 161). Fealy divides this history into three main periods. The first period—from 1949 until 1959—was shaped by the independence of Indonesia and the country's first experiments with democracy, characterized by relatively free political competition between parties and Indonesia's first free and fair elections. The second period—from 1959 until 1998—was in turn shaped by the faltering of Indonesia's flirtation with democracy. This period consisted of decades of authoritarianism, first under Sukarno's "guided democracy" (1959–1965) and then under Suharto's "new order" (*ordre baru*). Both regimes—with the exception of Indonesia's first experiment with democracy in the 1950s—put tight restrictions on political Islam.

The third period, which began following Suharto's ousting in 1998 and has continued through the present, is being shaped by the country's transition from authoritarianism and its second experiment with democracy (Fealy 2005).

After Indonesia became independent from Dutch colonial rule in 1949, the main political conflict line that ran between Muslim and secular forces concerned the question of whether or not Indonesia should become an Islamic state. The Islamists favored the inclusion of the sharia into the Indonesian constitution and the establishment of a *Negara Islam Indonesia* (Islamic State of Indonesia). Secular forces in turn, amongst them Indonesia's first president, Sukarno, feared that an Islamic constitution could lead to secessionist aspirations among the then mainly Christian eastern provinces of the archipelago and ultimately cause the break-up of Indonesia. These fears of a break-up of the young nation tipped the scales in favor of a constitution that did not include notions of an Islamic state for Indonesia. The constitution that was later adopted was based on the religion-neutral *Pancasila* as the state philosophy.[2] The majority of Islamic actors, although deeply disappointed by Indonesia's "secular" constitution, took comfort in the prospect that the Islamic parties would, if united, certainly win Indonesia's first elections and would then change the constitution. A minority of Islamists even began local uprisings with the goal of establishing an Islamic state (*Negara Islam*) through military force. The so-called Darul Islam movement (House of Islam) eventually managed to establish Islamic government in parts of Sumatra, Java, and Sulawesi, but these were short-lived and eventually crushed by the central government after a decade-long civil war (Dahm 2007, 203).

The first free elections in 1956 provided the Islamist parties with a fierce defeat. Not only was the dream of a politically unified Islam (one Islamic party) made unlikely by various fragmentations between 1949 and 1956, but hopes for a victory in the elections were disappointed when the Islamic parties gained only 43.1 percent of the votes. While from 1956 onwards, Islamic parties took part in the coalition governments under Sukarno, their political influence was often outplayed by the secular nationalism of Sukarno and the PKI (*Partai Kommunis Indonesia*—Communist Party of Indonesia). When Suharto came into power after a military coup in 1965, his first move was directed at the powerful PKI. With the help of Islamic militias and the military, the PKI was de facto liquidated. It is estimated that between 300,000 and one million alleged communists were killed and thousands more imprisoned during the first two years of the new order. But after the consolidation of the *ordre baru*, political Islam, now basically the only potential ideological source of opposition to the regime, was quickly marginalized. This marginalization included a demand for Islamic groups to conform to the state philosophy, restrictions on the use of Islamic symbols and language, and limiting the number of Islamic parties. In 1973 all Islamic parties were forced to merge and form the PPP (*Partai Persatuan Pembangunan*—United Development Party). The name of the party is proof of the nearly complete marginalization of political Islam under the first decades of the new order, as it didn't even bear any reference to Islam anymore. Thus political Islam had very little political influence for decades in Indonesia (Baswedan 2004, 671). The authoritarian politics of the new order were legitimized by the Suharto regime through state-led developmental strategies. These enhanced the legitimacy of the new order by delivering continued high economic growth rates and rising living standards, for which, in the mindset of the architects of the new order, (political) stability was pre-conditional. The latter was achieved through the backing of the new order by the state-security apparatus and massive support from the West. For the West, Suharto was an effective ally to help prevent Indonesia from declining into communism or Islamic theocracy.

As growth rates started to crumble, Suharto—aware of the fact that his (secular) power base had started to become somewhat unstable—began a turn toward Islam in order to further legitimize his authoritarian regime. What followed was a whole bundle of state-led Islamization policies that led to a gradual Islamization of Indonesian society: the appointment of pious Muslims to leading positions in the government and the military, increased support for Islamic teachings in schools and universities, the lifting of the ban on girls wearing the headscarf in school, and expanding the authority of sharia courts, to name only a few. Along with the new policies came the foundation of the IMCI (*Ikatan Cendekiawan Muslim Indonesia*—Muslim Intellectuals Association of Indonesia) as well as the establishment of an Islamic bank and insurance agency. In line with these developments was a change in Suharto's public persona: he took the *hajj* pilgrimage to Mecca, was a guest at Islamic celebrations, and in general showed more commitment to Islam in public than in previous years. During the late 1990s, Suharto even briefly tried to co-opt Islamist forces as a tool against the emerging pro-democratic *reformasi* movement. Within a decade, Islam made the transition from being at the margins of the state to occupying a somewhat favored status within the regime (Singh 2004)—although one must acknowledge that his mainly comprised of the search for an increase in personal piety among the citizens of Indonesia. Political Islam, still largely defined in opposition to the authoritarian and corrupt regime of the new order, was likewise as repressed as any other opposition group.[3]

The Islamization of the late new order, which has influenced the trajectories of Indonesian Islam up until now, is only to be understood against a variety of interconnected factors. First and foremost, tensions between the regime and the military, which had been one of the main pillars of regime stability, drove Suharto to look for other supporters and sources of legitimacy. Second, the mounting divisions within the regime were paralleled by the rapid growth of the traditionally very pious middle classes, caused by the economic boom of the 1970s and 1980s. The middle classes embraced Suharto's gradual renunciation of the military insofar as "they welcomed the opportunity to gain access to senior government positions" (Fealy 2005, 164). Nevertheless, the Suharto regime offered access to power only in exchange for political loyalty. It wasn't until Suharto's retreat from power in the wake of mass demonstrations triggered by the devastating effects of the Asian crisis, that the political liberalization opened up space for a large variety of Islamist actors—ranging from terrorist groups like Jemaah Islamiyah (JI),

Islamist militias, and civil society organizations to various political parties like the PKS. After all, the relationship between political Islam and politics in Indonesia is not easy to pin down: while political Islam was in large part effectively marginalized under Suharto's "new order," the Islamization of Indonesia from the 1980s onward nevertheless must be understood as a social and political process with very strong historical roots. While one cannot fail to notice the growing influence of conservative (*Wahabi*) interpretations of Islam through charitable foundations and other Islamic organizations based in the Arab world from the 1970s onward (Bubalo/ Fealy 2005), the struggle for the establishment of an Islamic state as well as various forms of Islamic militancy can be traced back to before Indonesia's independence.

Hence, the Islamization of Indonesia owes, on the one hand, much to a rising middle class seeking moral orientation and identity in a drastically changing sociopolitical and economic environment. For many, Islam became a reference point, an adamant and consistent element of identification within an ever-changing, modernizing order. On the other hand, the rise of Islam is to some extent intertwined with the Islamization policies implemented by the Suharto regime itself. This is what Ruf (2002, 51) has called an "irony" of the aforementioned macropolitical developments: that "secular" regimes in the Muslim world such as the Suharto regime in Indonesia became promoters of the Islamization process by pushing for the implementation of a wide variety of Islamic policies in an attempt to regain or strengthen their own legitimacy and to control the increasing Islamic political expressions (Hasan 2007, 88). Against this background, the often ambiguous relationship between Islam and politics in post-Suharto Indonesia is to be analyzed. Over and above everything else, the range of historical events described in this chapter question the prominent image of Indonesian Islam as being inherently tolerant and moderate. However biased such an image has been, it most certainly (unintentionally) reflected the fact that Islam as a political force had for decades been marginalized or even repressed under the new order. With the ousting of Suharto, this was about to change drastically.

THE RESURGENCE OF POLITICAL ISLAM
IN POST-SUHARTO INDONESIA

The end of the new order, which happened in the wake of the Asian crisis, led to the opening of the political sphere for a great variety of Islamic actors.[4] Moderate Muslim intellectuals were active in the pro-democratic reform movements that took to the streets in 1997 and early 1998 and demanded Suharto's resignation. While playing a vital role in the immediate events that led to the downfall of Suharto, the "movement for a democratic Muslim politics in Indonesia" (Hefner 2005, 274) was soon effectively marginalized by a rising conservative (and often militant) spectrum of Islamist actors, ranging from transnational, pan-Islamic terrorist networks like Jemaah Islamiyah (JI) to Islamist militias to regular Islamist political parties. The aforementioned displayed a heterogeneous array of organizational structures, goals, applied strategies, and relationships with the state.

Closely following the opening of the political system was an outbreak of inter-communal violence between Muslims and Christians, as well as the establishment of Islamist militia groups and the attacks by the terror network Jemaah Islamiyah on Christian churches (2000), nightclubs in Bali (2002 and 2005), the Australian embassy (2004), and the Marriott Hotel (2003).[5] Shortly after the ousting of Suharto, nominal Christian paramilitaries sprung up attacking what happened to be nominal Muslim communities in Poso (Sulawesi), Central Kalimantan, and the Moluccas. While the roots of these conflicts—all of which had been effectively suppressed by the iron rule of Suharto—were to be found in competition over political and economic power, local leaders effectively mobilized support amongst "their" constituencies by portraying the conflicts in religious rather than in political-economic terms (van Klinken 2007). The sectarian violence between Christians and Muslims in the three provinces has cost more than 12,000 lives so far. The outbreak of sectarian violence in 1998–1999, paralleled by the intensification of long-running separatist conflicts in the provinces of Aceh, West Papua, and East Timor, led many analysts to the assumption that a break-up of

Indonesia (often termed "balkanization") could very well be underway (Wanandi 2002; Mally 2003).

Even more worrying, the escalation of violence in Ambon (Moluccas) owed a great deal to the establishment and deployment of Islamist militia groups such as the at-present-disbanded Laskar Jihad (Jihad militia), which was reportedly involved to a large extent in the killings between Muslims and Christians on the Moluccas. Besides the LJ, the Front Pembela Islam (Defenders of Islam-Front), another Islamist militia, made headlines by patrolling the streets of Jakarta and other cities in order to prevent what their members perceived as "vice" (e.g., massage parlors, nightclubs, the selling of "nudist" literature, etc.). Furthermore, the FPI conducted raids during Ramadan, targeting businesses and individuals who were deemed disrespectful to the holy month. In April of 2006 the organization attacked the then newly founded office of the Indonesian edition of *Playboy*, as well as organized gatherings and demonstrations against newly founded left-wing Papernas party in 2007, accusing the party of spreading "communist ideals."[6] The various militia groups were often backed in these activities by political elites as well as businessmen. The Laskar Jihad, for example, was reportedly armed and trained by members of the Indonesian military. The FPI attacks on leftist gatherings and bookstores were backed by local elites in order to suppress "un-Islamic" democracy activists. As long as their existence and "street politics" were of any use to the power politics of various elites, they often gained significant support from such sources.

The resurgence of militant Islamist groups only seemed to highlight the country's growing problem with a radicalizing Islam and especially with its militant fringe. In addition, some political observers claimed that Jemaah Islamiyah had close ties with the international terror-network Al Qaeda (Abuza 2003). Although the empirical evidence behind such assessments has turned out to be scarce, to say the least (Hamilton-Hart 2005), they led to concerns among many security analysts over the threat posed by radical Islam in post-Suharto Indonesia. Some even mentioned the possibility of a destabilization of the country's course toward democracy as a consequence of the rise of radical Islam.

Apart from the "uncivil society" (Hefner), another striking feature of the resurgence of political Islam in Indonesia is the remarkable rise of the Muslim Brotherhood–inspired PKS party during the national elections in 2004 and 2009. The PKS, a party that gained less than two percent of the votes in Indonesia's first free and fair elections in 1999, managed to win more than seven percent in 2004 and 2009. As a result, the PKS became Indonesia's seventh-strongest political party and joined the ruling coalition of President Susilo Bambang Yudhoyono. The PKS even saw its leader, Hidiyat Nur Wahid, chosen as speaker of the Indonesian parliament. Analysis of the 2004 elections has shown that PKS won many votes through its somewhat "secular agenda" (i.e., by demanding a reform of the welfare system and by pushing for stronger anti-corruption policies).[7] It has differed from other Islamist groups by not openly demanding the establishment of sharia law and mainly sticking to governance issues.

Attempts by other Islamist groups to include the sharia in the constitution have so far failed due to a majority of the members of parliament voting against the implementation of Islamic law. Nevertheless, such attempts have been increasingly successful on the local level through the establishment of local sharia-style bylaws in currently over 10 percent of Indonesia's districts and provinces (Hasan 2007b). But then, such policies are often implemented with the support of non-Islamist parties like the former Suharto-party Golkar. This shows that the adoption of sharia-style bylaws has become a strategy used by local politicians to mobilize and to gain political support. Parties that support the adoption of sharia regulations are often seen by their constituencies as more likely to deliver services and good governance according to the principles of Islam (Assyaukanie 2007).

It seems clear that Indonesia's democratization has opened up space for a great variety of Islamist actors, who in turn have catalyzed the political importance of Islam in general. Democratization encompassed the establishment of a multiparty system, a lifting of the ban on the freedom of press, and an enormous decentralization process that has allowed Islamists to spread their ideas legally through wide communication networks. It also enabled the return of Islamist parties to the political arena. Furthermore, the decentralization process made possible the implementation of local sharia-style bylaws because the regional autonomy law from 1999 states that local governments at the district level are entitled to implement their own regional regulations. As a result of the alleviated repression of oppositional groups, the establishment of various Islamic civil society organizations became possible. Amongst those were moderate, liberal organizations, but also what Hefner has termed the "uncivil society." While post-Suharto Indonesia certainly proves the hypothesis that democratic institutions automatically facilitate Islamist moderation wrong, realities on the ground have also brought into question an alternative "the state versus the Islamists" perception. Especially Islamist militias have often acted in a grey zone between repression and cooptation and therefore have largely remained with impunity. The varying relationship between the state and Islamist actors—ranging from inclusion, to cooption, to repression—only emphasizes that political Islam is an instrument of specific social forces used to foster specific sociopolitical interests. Hence, neither the Islamist actors nor the Indonesian state can be considered to be like a "monolithic bloc"; rather, it is a stark characteristic of post-Suharto Indonesia that the relationship between the state and Islamist actors has lost its cohesion. The ambivalent relationship between political elites and the "uncivil society," as well as the rise of the PKS in the 2004 elections, again must be understood within the wider context of Indonesia's transition to what Hadiz has termed "illiberal democracy" (Hadiz 2003).

CONTEXTUALIZING POLITICAL ISLAM IN POST-SUHARTO INDONESIA: THE OLIGARCHIC CONTINUUM

When analyzing the end of the new order and Indonesia's transition to democracy, the aforementioned positive reviews of the democratization process mainly refer to factors such as elite choices, leadership, and the importance of political institutions to the course and outcome of the democratization process (O'Donnell and Schmitter 1986). Following these tracks, the crafting of democratic rules and institutions, combined with democratic forms of governance and the existence of a pro-democratic, enlightened civil society serving as a "watchdog" of the government, is equated with the consolidation of democracy (Rieffel 2004). While such new institutional arrangements may be pivotal for the establishment of a democratic political system, they largely exclude the constellations of social forces (or classes) that "determine the parameters of possible outcomes in any given situation...the direction of political change following the end of authoritarian rule is primarily the product of contests between these competing social forces" (Hadiz 2003, 592; see also Bellin 2000). Bellin has pointed out that, therefore, capital and labor are "contingent, not consistent, democrats"—that is, support for democracy or the authoritarian state depends on whether these specific social forces see their political and economic interests served by the respective form of rule or not. When political and economic conditions change, interests may change, too. Thus social forces might see the need to redefine their position toward the respective regime (Bellin 2000).

The change of the political and economic conditions in Indonesia was brought about by the Asian Crisis in 1997. With the new order descend-ing into a vast economic crisis, more than one third of the population slid under the poverty line, living standards of large parts of the popula-tion declined, and economic growth rates amounted to less than zero. Once legitimized by high economic growth rates and rising living stan-dards, the new order regime, personalized at large by Suharto—who was often referred to as *Pak Pembangunan* (Father of Development)—saw itself confronted with a looming political and economic crisis. As Suharto proved to be incapable of solving the crisis and hundreds of thousands demanded reforms, the minions withdrew their loyalty and forced Suharto to step down (Smith 2003).

The fall of Suharto and the institutional reforms that followed are not to be equated with the establishment of a democracy and a "free" market economy. Yet they did change the "balance of power" and the "terms of conflict" (Robinson 2001, 120): the formerly dominant politico-business oligarchs and bureaucrats lost the powerful centralized state apparatus that had guaranteed their privileged positions and had secured their interests. A new and more open political system came into place, one in which politics was not exclusively rendered vertically through the state apparatus and Suharto's cronies anymore, but increasingly through parties and the parliament. The "diffusion of politics" after the fall of Suharto made it necessary for the old power-holders to adapt to the politics of reform and consequently to engage in wider and more horizontal alliances in order to be able to protect their own resources of political and economic power (Slater 2006, 208). A coalition of moderate reformers and old elites under the leadership of Suharto's deputy Bacharuddin Jusuf Habibie took over power and initiated moderate democratic political reforms—effectively marginalizing those social forces that had demanded more radical reforms. At the same time, the system of collusion, corruption, and nepotism amongst officials and politico-business oligarchs did not cease to exist. Due to the de facto elimination of any mass-based opposition during the "new order" there simply were no social forces strong enough to break up the old power structures.

Therefore, while the political institutions were widely reformed, the socioeconomic power structures of the new order (i.e., the vast, informal patronage networks of the elites) remained largely unaffected through this quasi-"evolutionary," elite-driven transition process. The result was what Slater (2004) has called the construction of a "political cartel." Although elections are formally competitive, the cartel of political elites protected those in power from outside competition. Slater (2006, 208) has even made the point that the political cartel has made Indonesia's oligarchy "practically irremovable through the electoral process, even though elections themselves have been commendably free and fair." Coming from such an assessment it is not surprising that corruption, political violence, collusion, and nepotism—"old" phenomena associated with the new order—are still common in Indonesia. According to the Bertelsmann Transformation Index, while "electoral democratic institutions seem to be working in Indonesia, the political system is still constrained by a high level of corruption, patronage politics and other informal institutions."[8]

Fueling the "money politics" is a party system in which political parties have not emerged out of "broad-based social interests" and therefore with the backing of different, often competing social forces—this wasn't possible due to the elite-controlled transition process—but instead exist mainly as "patronage machines" of elite factions. While according to democracy theories the constituents of the political parties should nominate party leaders to run as their candidates for local and national elections, in reality these decisions are made in favor of the candidate with the highest bid. One example is the backing of former deputy governor Fauzi Bowo by the Indonesian Democratic Party of Struggle (PDI-P) during the 2007 local elections in Jakarta. This decision, which was made only weeks before the elections, came as a surprise to the PDI-P party chapters and the public, as Bowo had previously been registered with former Suharto-party Golkar. Despite his lack of roots within his new party, and although other candidates had already been selected, Bowo was immediately given a chance to register as an independent candidate for PDI-P. Disappointed party members as well as political analysts described this as a "political ploy played by the elite," who hold the tickets to enter the race for lucrative and sought-after posts within the local and national government. These tickets are usually sold to the highest bidder, which effectively marginalizes democratic decision-making processes inside the parties.[9]

Voter buying is common in all districts of Indonesia, with more than 7,000 election violations reported—including multiple vote-buying incidents—during the 2004 parliamentary elections. During the presidential elections of 2004 the NGOs Indonesian Corruption Watch (ICW) and Transparency International Indonesia (TII) suspected nearly all presidential candidates of vote buying. All of this left an Australian journalist to wonder whether corruption is running so rampant that it fully undermines democracy:

> Democracy is a good thing. But what is the point of it when the state apparatus is so corrupt that most laws are subverted to the point of irrelevancy? Who cares whether this or that leader is

elected when corruption will mean that their policy platforms are
unlikely to be implemented, and certainly not in the way that they
would intend?[10]

Indonesia today is still among the thirty most corrupt nations according
to Transparency International's annual Corruption Index. Corruption is
so endemic, that, for example, an estimated 85 percent of judges[11] and
60 percent of all police officers are believed to be corrupt (Webber 2006,
408) and companies working in Indonesia are believed to use about
10 percent of their overall budgets to "smooth" business operations
(Henderson/ Kuncoro 2004).

While collusion and nepotism were largely directed through Suharto's
patronage networks under the new order, nowadays the political democratic parties serve as patronage vehicles of Indonesia's "new" elites.
Although distinct from illegal corruption practices, the fact that many
government officials, from the local to the national level, either hold
positions of have holdings in private-sector businesses, further adds
up to the lack of public scrutiny of and accountability for the political
elites.[12] In a country in which, according to the common poverty definition of the World Bank (less than two U.S. dollars per day), more than
50 percent of the population continues to live below the poverty line,[13]
the practice of money politics severely restricts political decision making to competing wealthy elite factions. Hence the workers and farmers
who make up the majority of Indonesia's population have no de facto
political representation (Hillman 2006, 27).

Thus Robinson/Hadiz (2004) have described Indonesia's transition
process as the "oligarchization" of democracy. Within the democratic
oligarchy, as opposed to the authoritarian new order of Suharto, the once
extremely centralized state apparatus has lost its cohesion. It therefore
cannot be understood as a monolithic bloc, but rather as a focal point of
competing social forces. Against this background must be understood
not only the deployment of Islamist militias serving as instruments in
the hands of competing elite factions, but also the success of the Islamist
PKS. Against what is perceived by many Indonesians as the "old,"

ineffective, and corrupt political establishment, the PKS presented itself as an "anti-establishment" party with a political agenda mainly focusing on anti-corruption policies and socioeconomic reforms. The success of the "clean and caring" message during the 2004 elections was a result of the many shortcomings of the "new" democratic order.

CONCLUSION: THE PROSPECTS AND PERILS OF POLITICAL ISLAM TEN YEARS AFTER *REFORMASI*

The analysis of the substance of democracy as well as the realities of "democratic" practices in post-Suharto Indonesia have shown a widening gap between the formal aspects of democracy (e.g., free elections, democratic institutions) and the democratic rhetoric of elected elites on the one hand, and the realities on the ground. The growing importance of political Islam in Indonesia must be interpreted as a response to this gap. Some groups decided to choose militancy, sometimes even with a pan-Islamic agenda (Jemaah Islamiyah), while others chose to engage in political parties. Within this context, PKS managed to mobilize the votes of many disappointed members of the middle-class through its commitment to clean government and social reforms.

Thus, PKS and others have so far tried ineffectively to put through their reformist agenda by forming alliances with the predatory elites. But "realpolitik" has provided the PKS with some serious blowbacks throughout the last few years. By being a part of the Yudhoyono government, the party had to carry some of the responsibility for "tough" policies such as the cuts on fuel subsidies. More damage to the party's "clean and care" image was done through corruption charges against PKS members serving in regional governments. Ironically, the "clean and care" campaign that gained the PKS many votes during the 2004 elections could not be successfully transformed into realpolitik under the Yudhoyono government, and thus currently has the party in a state of decline.

While Islamist parties like the PKS managed to gain electoral success with an agenda focused on governance issues, it seems rather hard for them to deliver. Public opinion polls seem to provide further evidence for this lesson, as they've recently shown flagging support for political Islam in general. Only 9 percent of the population—versus 20 percent in 2004—currently support a larger role for Islam in government. PKS support in polls at the national level also declined from 8 percent in 2004 to just 2.5 percent currently.[14] Another poll showed that whereas 43 percent of Indonesians would vote for secular parties in the upcoming elections, only 5 percent would vote for Islamist parties. The rest of the population would opt for moderate Muslim parties.[15] In the absence of a political program able to tackle these issues and mobilize voters other than their middle-class core constituency, the party continues to lack a mass base among the farmers and workers. To a large extent, political Islam has therefore remained an urban, middle-class phenomenon.

Consequently, the party lost the local elections in Jakarta in August of 2007. According to many observers, the reason for the loss[16] was the fear of many voters that the PKS, if it was to win, might establish sharia-style bylaws in the city. Its inability to push through the "clean and care" reform agenda had in turn led to a switch to moral policing. This was shown through the participation of the PKS in bringing forward the controversial "anti-pornography bill" in 2006, which would have banned bikinis and the Hindu minority's traditional dances, as well as its suppor of the implementation of local sharia-style bylaws. The public outcry that followed the proposal of the "anti-pornography" bill didcost the party many voters. Plus, in a society that has been in a process of Islamization for nearly two decades now, attempts to increase political legitimacy through moral policing are not the sole domain of the Islamists, as local sharia laws have been implemented by "normal" Muslim and even "secular" parties, too.

At the same time, the government managed to crackdown on the militant, pan-Islamic fringe of political Islam. The *amir* (leader) of JI and the organization's military commander were both arrested, amongst other members, during the spring and summer of 2007. During these operations, large caches of weapons and explosives were found by the police, further weakening JI's military capabilities. This came months after a split within JI had occurred: Noorhaidin Mohammed Top, the mastermind behind JI's various attacks between 2002 and 2005, is believed to have left JI due to differing viewpoints about future tactics. He is also believed to now run a JI splinter group that is planning further attacks on Western targets, while JI is now in the midst of recruiting new members and restructuring itself (ICG 2007, 5). Besides JI, the security apparatus has also cracked down on many other local and national militant groups (such as Laskar Jihad), many of whom it once had forged tactical alliances with (i.e., to silence democracy activists) in the past. Again, this must be understood in the context of the post-9/11 (and post-Bali) politics: the crackdowns have served the military well to polish its damaged image and to present itself once again as the guardian of the nation. This has even led to the re-installment of military relations with the United States, European Union, and Australia—all of which had abandoned military relations with Indonesia in the aftermath of the East Timor massacres.

Of course, this does not mean that the decline of political Islam in Indonesia is not irreversible. The continuum of predatory interests, graft-ridden political institutions, rampant poverty, and unemployment still—despite high economic growth rates—make political Islam seem like a credible alternative for many. Yet the oligarchic character of Indonesia's "democracy" has minimized the positive effects of moderate Islamist parties to a large extent. The real challenge ahead of Indonesia's democracy, therefore, is not political Islam per se, but rather the appropriation of the democratization process by the power politics of predatory elites. With many Indonesians feeling disappointed with the limits of democratic reforms as well as with the at-least-partial cooptation of the PKS through the SBY government, militant groups could in the future regain some of their strength.

ENDNOTES

1. The theorem of "Muslim exceptionalism" is backed by the rather general findings of authors such as Huntington (1997, 1991), Lipset (1994), or Gellner (1994), who see Islam as responsible for the absence of democracy or, if democracy has been introduced to a Muslim state, as at least responsible for the aforementioned challenges of a democratic consolidation in Muslim states. Underlying this is the belief in a "unique relationship between religion and politics in Islam that precludes the separation of the religious and political spheres" (Ayoob 2006, 2). This is to say that political thought and political action in the Muslim world are mainly driven by religious goals, or at least by religious convictions.

2. The *Pancasila*, literally translated as "the five principles," was formulated by Sukarno as the *desar negara* (state philosophy) in 1945. It comprised the belief in one god (whereas the Islamists wanted a formulation where the religion of Indonesia is Islam), humanitarianism, nationalism, democracy, and social justice.

3. One example of this is the event known as the "Tanjung Priok massacre." On September 12, 1984, an anti-government demonstration against the imposition of a law which required all organizations to adopt the sole ideology of the state, the Pancasila, took place in the Tanjung Priok harbor area of north Jakarta. The protests followed the arrests of several individuals who were accused of giving anti-government sermons at Tanjung Priok Rawa Badak Mosque. They were encircled by security forces, which opened fire on the demonstrators. Survivors claimed that several hundred people were killed during the incident.

4. While the impact of 9/11 and its aftermath is not part of this analysis, it needs to be noted that the ramifications of 9/11, the "war on terror," and the invasion of Iraq certainly had implications on the resurgence of political Islam in post-Suharto Indonesia. Von der Mehden (2008) argues that these events reinforced a sense of Islamic identity amongst Indonesia's Muslims while at the same time amplifying perceptions of a clash between the "West" and the "Muslim world." Furthermore, 9/11 and its aftermath helped to facilitate the radicalization of elements within Indonesia's Muslim community and it increased support for the goals and actions of these radicalized elements. The general public as well as the majority of the political elites, while initially condemning the 9/11 terrorist attacks, reacted very negatively to the "war on terror" and the invasion of Iraq, leading

to an increased negative perception of the United States and their allies amongst Indonesia's Muslims.

5. Timothy Mapes, "For Indonesia, Security Woes Persist," *Asian Wall Street Journal*, May 30, 2005, p. A1

6. Prodita Sabarini, "Militants Attack New Leftist Party," *The Jakarta Post* (online), March 30, 2007.

7. Jusuf Wanandi, "Legislative Elections and Indonesia's Future," *The Jakarta Post* (online), May 21, 2004.

8. Bertelsmann Transformation Index 2008, Country Report Indonesia, online at http://www.bertelsmann-transformation-index.de/fileadmin/pdf/Gutachten_BTI_2008/ASO/Indonesia.pdf (accessed February 20, 2008).

9. Prodita Sabarini, "Party Nomination Process Blasted as Undemocratic," *The Jakarta Post* (online), March 21, 2007.

10. Michael Backmann, "Bribery and Corruption on the Election Trail," *The Age* (online), April 9, 2004.

11. Frans H. Winarta, "Judicial Corruption Not Only Rampant but Also Shameful," *The Jakarta Post* (online), October 31, 2005.

12. Kristian Tamtomo, "Conflicts of Interest a Source of Corruption," *The Jakarta Post* (online), August 27, 2007.

13. Urip Hudiono, "Poverty Numbers Down 'Slightly'," *The Jakarta Post* (online), July 3, 2007.

14. "Islam and Politics in Indonesia," *The Wall Street Journal* (online), October 24, 2006.

15. Ary Hermawan, "Gloomy Outlook for Islamist Parties," *The Jakarta Post* (online), October 16, 2006.

16. The term "loss" does not precisely reflect the outcome of the local elections in Jakarta in August 2007 because the PKS, while opposing a twenty-party-strong coalition comprised of nearly all other political parties, still managed to win more than 40 percent of all votes. Notwithstanding this, it did not succeed in providing Jakarta's next governor.

Bibliography

Abuza, Zachary. 2003. *Militant Islam in Southeast Asia: Crucible of Terror*. Boulder and London: Lynne Rienner.

Achcar, Gilbert. 1987. Eleven Theses on the Resurgence of Islamic Fundamentalism. *International Marxist Review* 2, no. 3. Online at http://www.internationalviewpoint.org/spip.php?article1132 (accessed January 3, 2008).

———. 2004. Marxism and religion—Yesterday and Today. International Viewpoint (online), no. 365, March 2005). Online at http://www.internationalviewpoint.org/spip.php?article622 (accessed January 3, 2008).

Anderson, Benedict. 1990. Old State, New Society: Indonesia's New Order in Comparative Perspective. In Language and Power—Exploring Political Cultures in Indonesia, edited by Benedict Anderson, 94–120. Ithaca, NY: Cornell University Press.

Assyaukanie, Luthfi. 2007. The Rise of Religious Bylaws in Indonesia. *RSIS Commentaries* 22. Singapore: S. Rajaratnam School of International Studies.

Bawedan, Anies Rasyid. 2004. Political Islam in Indonesia—Present and Future Trajectory. *Asian Survey* 44 (5): 669–690.

Bellin, Eva. 2000. Contingent Democrats: Industrialists, Labor, and Democratization in Late-Developing Countries. *World Politics* 52:175–205.

Bubalo, Anthony, and Greg Fealy. 2005. Joining the Caravan? The Middle East, Islamism and Indonesia. Lowy Institute Paper 05, Lowy Institute for International Policy. Alexandria: Longueville.

Dahm, Bernhard. 2007. Radikalisierung des Islam in Indonesien. In *Antje Missbach: Indonesia—The Presence of the Past*, edited by Eva Streifeneder. Berlin: regiospectra.

Denoeux, Guilain. 2002. The Forgotten Swamp: Navigating Political Islam. *Middle East Policy* 9 (2): 56–81.

Esposito, John L. 2008. Islam in Asia in the Twenty-First Century. In *Asian Islam in the 21st Century*, edited by John L. Esposito, John O. Voll, and Osman Bakar, 3–10. Oxford: Oxford University Press.

Fealy, Greg. 2004. Islamic Radicalism in Indonesia: The Faltering Revival? In *Southeast Asian Affairs 2004*, edited by ISEAS. Singapore: ISEAS.

―――. 2005. Islamisation and Politics in Southeast Asia: The Contrasting Cases of Malaysia and Indonesia. In *Islam in World Politics*, edited by Nelly Lahoud and Anthony H. Johns, 152–169. London: Routledge.

Hadiz, Vedi R. 2003. Reorganizing Political Power in Indonesia: a Reconsideration of So-called 'Democratic Transitions.' *The Pacific Review* 16 (4): 591–611.

Hafez, Mohammed M. 2003. *Why Muslims Rebel: Repression and Resistance in the Islamic World*. Boulder and London: Lynne Rienner.

Hamilton-Hart, Natasha. 2005. Terrorism in Southeast Asia: Expert Analysis, Myopia and Fantasy. *The Pacific Review* 18 (3): 303–325.

Hasan, Noorhaidi. 2007a. The Salafi Movement in Indonesia: Transnational Dynamics and Local Development. *Comparative Studies of South Asia, Africa and the Middle East* 27 (1): 83–94.

―――. 2007b. Islamic Militancy, Sharia, and Democratic Consolidation in Post-Suharto

Hefner, Robert W. 2005. Muslim Democrats and Islamist Violence in Post-Soeharto Indonesia. In *Remaking Muslim Politics: Pluralism, Contestation, Democratization*, edited by Robert W. Hefner, 273–301. Princeton, NJ: Princeton University Press.

Henderson, J. Vernon, and Ari Kuncoro. 2004. Corruption in Indonesia. NBER Working Paper Series 10674, August 2004, available online at http://www.nber.org/papers/w10674 (accessed January 5, 2008).

Hillman, Ben. 2006. New Elections, Old Politics. *Far Eastern Economic Review* (January/February): 26–29.

Indonesia. Working Paper 143, S. Rajaratnam School of International Studies, Singapore.

International Crisis Group (ICG). 2007. Indonesia: Jemaah Islamiyah's Current Status. Asia Briefing No. 63, Jakarta/Brussels, May 3, 5.

Kramer, Martin. 2003. Coming to Terms: Fundamentalists or Islamists? *Middle East Quarterly* 10, no. 2. Online at http://www.meforum.org/article/541 (accessed December 20, 2007).

Malley, Michael. 2003. Indonesia: The Erosion of State Capacity. In *State Failure and State Weakness in a Time of Terror*, edited by Robert I. Rotberg, 183–218. Washington, DC: Brookings Institution Press.

Nasr, Vali. 2005. The Rise of "Muslim Democracy." *Journal of Democracy* 16 (2): 13–27.

Nyman, Mikaela. 2006. Democratising Indonesia—The Challenges of Civil Society in the Era of Reformasi. NIAS Reports 49, Copenhagen.

O'Donnell, Guillermo, Philippe C. Schmitter, and Laurence Whitehead, eds. 1986. *Transitions from Authoritarian Rule—Prospects for Democracy*. Baltimore and London: Johns Hopkins University Press.

Qodari, Muhammad. 2005. Indonesia's Quest for Accountable Governance. *Journal of Democracy* 16 (2): 73–87.

Rieffel, Lex. 2004. Indonesia's Quiet Revolution. *Foreign Affairs 83, no. 5. Online at http://www.foreignaffairs.org/20040901faessay83509/lex-rieffel/indonesia-s-quiet-revolution.html* (accessed May 10, 2005).

Robinson, Richard. 2001. Indonesia: Crisis, Oligarchy, and Reform. In *The Political Economy of Southeast Asia: Conflicts, Crises, and Change*, edited by Garry Rodan, Kevin Hewison, and Richard Robinson, 104–137. Oxford: Oxford University Press.

Robinson, Richard, and Vedi R. Hadiz. 2004. *Reorganising Power in Indonesia: The Politics of Oligarchy in an Age of Markets*. London: Routledge.

Ruf, Werner. 2002. Islam: A New Challenge to the Security of the Western World. In *Islam and the West—Judgements, Prejudices, Political Perspectives*, edited by Werner Ruf, 41–54. Münster: LIT.

Singh, Bilveer. 2004. The Challenge of Militant Islam and Terrorism in Indonesia. *Australian Journal of International Affairs* 58 (1): 47–68.

Slater, Dan. 2004. Indonesia's Accountability Trap: Party Cartels and Presidential Power after Democratic Transition. *Indonesia*, no. 78:61–92.

———. 2006. The Ironies of Instability in Indonesia. *Social Analysis* 50 (1): 208–213.

Smith, Benjamin. 2003. "If I Do These Things, They Will Throw Me Out": Economic Reform and the Collapse of Indonesia's New Order. *Journal of International Affairs* 1: 113–128.

Van Klinken, Gerry. 2007. *Communal Violence and Democratization in Indonesia*. London: Routledge.

Von der Mehden, Fred. 2008. Islam in Indonesia in the Twenty-First Century. In *Asian Islam in the 21st Century*, edited by John L. Esposito, John O. Voll, and Osman Bakar, 11–30. Oxford: Oxford University Press.

Wanandi, Jusuf. 2002. Indonesia: A Failed State? *The Washington Quarterly* 25 (3): 135–46.

Webber, Douglas. 2006. A Consolidated Patrimonial Democracy? Democratization in Post-Suharto Indonesia. *Democratization* 13 (3): 396–420.

CHAPTER 8

ISLAM AND DEMOCRACY
IN MALAYSIA

THE AMBIGUITIES OF ISLAMIC(ATE) POLITICS

Naveed S. Sheikh

The study of political Islam, as the phenomenon finds expression within the Middle and Far East, has often been approached by policymakers and analysts alike with an underlying assumption that the political mobilization of religious norms and identities has historically functioned as a riposte to illiberal secularism. This is to say that Islam becomes salient as a political expression of protest vis-à-vis political models that are nominally secular, but short of liberal. Yet, in many cases, residual forms of Islamism (defined as a discourse which pairs the Islamic religion and state politics) were default dispositions within post-colonial nations that had, after all, frequently agitated for independence

within composite discursive formations, one element of which was positing the faithful, albeit downtrodden, masses against the infidel mas-
ters who owed their political dominance in part to moral caprice and in
part to technological capacity. Such residual Islamism, which we may
refer to as "banal Islamism," was perpetuated in society in the forms
of collective memory, narratives, and symbols in key institutions of
(exo-)socialization.[1] Whilst serving to insulate the state from charges
of being, to borrow Jalal Al-e Ahmed's parlance, "Westoxified,"[2] banal
Islamism also had the effect of sustaining Islam as a political discourse, thus also a political program, among constituencies that sought
the implementation of social, political, or economic models alternative to those emanating from the bipolar centers of geopolitical power.
Nowhere was this ambiguity of political Islam more pertinent than in
the case of Malaysia.

The single definatory issue for the political past as well as the political future of Malaysia, as for much of the Muslim world, remains the
relationship between Islam and the political system. Islam, to be certain,
is to be understood both as a community of believers (a *Gemeinschaft*), a
society with certain normative codices and practices (a *Gesellschaft*), and
a thought-complex with certain ontological delineations (otherworldly as
well as this-worldly). The political system, on the other hand, entails not
only the mechanics of representative bodies, the bureaucracy, and other
elements of the executive, but equally ideational structures that underlie
the national narratives about the selfhood (*ipseity*) and the ultimate interests and purpose (teleology) of the nation. Methodologically, therefore,
Islamicate politics is best approached with a triangular model in mind,
consisting of structure, agency, and event.[3] The structure is material as
well as ideational, and informs the context of behavior (eschewing, however, both reductionism and determinism). Agency belongs to political
and religious actors, official as well as unofficial, whereas "the event"
signifies the flow of historical happenings (what Machiavelli referred
to as *fortuna*) that may lead to a certain path-dependency, or at the very
least, constrain choices for political actors. With this triangular analytic
model, the present chapter will seek to analyze the changing contours

and ramifications of Islam, as a social construct, within the political life of Malaysia and the Malay nation.

THE (RE)MAKING OF MALAY ISLAM

Situated at the crossroads of Southeast Asia's ancient trade routes, the Malay peninsula has, by design or default, been home to varied religious and cultural influences. Mercantile activity from India, Arabia, and China, and colonial imposition from Portugal, the Netherlands, Japan, and Britain brought unto Malay shores nearly all world civilizations and their respective religious manifestations—from Hinduism, to Buddhism, to Sikhism, to Confucianism, to Taoism, to Islam and Christianity—producing a rich but neither uncontested nor unproblematic religio-cultural fabric. In the formative period, the two most pervasive cultural influences were of course the Indic, followed from the fourteenth century onward by the Islamic, as Muslim merchants and Sufi mystics from Arabia and Muslim India persuaded rulers and subjects throughout Southeast Asia to embrace the Islamic credo.

Regicide of the Hindu Maharaja Dewa Shah in the year 1446 made Islam the palace religion. From the outset, thus, Islam was not without implication for both social and political change, being both catalyst and consequence. Governance (*hukūma*) and politics (*siyāsa*) soon were to be judged against the parameters laid down in Islamic ethical codes and, to a lesser extent, Islamic legal codes—a distinction that is said to be quintessential for the ethos of Malay Islam. Thus, too, the sultanate found its source of legitimacy in the Islamic—or properly speaking, quasi-Islamic—outlook; for the head of state became the defender of faith, the guardian of Islam, only slightly short of the prince of the believers.

For the lay Malay, too, Islam was quintessential in terms of identity. As a core element in Malay identity, Islam tied together the family, the community, and the polity with an integrated spatio-temporal cosmology that rendered meaning to rituals, quotidian practices, traditions, and institutions. To be Malay was to be Muslim—and vice versa. Indeed, conversion to Islam was seen as taking on Malay attributes, in a sense becoming Malay (*masuk Melayu*), an idea that permeated social understandings of the interface between ethnicity and religiosity.[4]

Being syncretic, albeit less so than its Javanese counterpart, Malay religious culture had co-opted local rites and customs of animist, spiritist, Hindu, and Buddhist pedigree, embracing them fully as part of the Shariatic legal code under the juristic category of *'urf* (customary praxis) or *'adat* (local social praxis).[5] Such hybridity, however, did not negate the "aura of religious sanctity" that undergirded the polity, for it was not insisted that all aspects of government be "derived from religious sources," merely that a supernatural ethic inform the ethos of community life.[6] In this sense, Malay Islam was less about "the law" and more about "the way."

Yet, British colonialism's attempt to bring about a clear distinction between governance (now state) and custom (here religion) changed this to some extent. The British quest for order, paradoxically, accorded the Malay sultans with bureaucratic and legal machineries to implement their directives in a more systematic and invasive manner than was thitherto the case. Yet, once subjugation to political colonialism had become a reality, the social technology of identity politics made the Shariatic courts—the only symbolic power left with the sultanates—the most salient expression for cultural autarky. Thus the courts began to apply a stricter, or purer, legislative code relative to that applied prior to colonial times and, in the final instance, the austere application of the Islamic penal code became a manifestation of defiance against Western subjugation and imposition. As such, the Malayan experience pertaining to the revitalization of religious norms and institutions in the modern era replays a familiar theme from the wider Muslim world: Once colonialism had sought to curtail the role of religion in public life, the empowerment of the sacred became a resistance strategy, or indeed a liberation strategy, against institutions and mores considered repressive.

Of course the articulation, and perpetual re-articulation, of social identity remains always a function of collective memory, which is itself invariably selective—mired in myopia, closures, and silences. It was therefore conveniently forgotten that Mecca was always distant: Malay Muslims had always been in the Islamic hinterland, and Malay Islam had always had its own social complexion, not least because of the composite nature of its history, culture, and demography.

ISLAM AND THE (IMPOSSIBLE) CONSTITUTIONAL BARGAIN

A diverse federation, equally multi-ethnic and multi-religious, modern Malaysia has struggled to develop a coherent national identity that would simultaneously inform the self-image of the population and provide the foundation for the legitimacy of the state. At the heart of Malay nationalism is the notional nativism of the *bumiputra* (Sanskrit for "son of the soil"), a designation that denotes Malays, the largest ethnic group (fifty-four percent of the twenty-four million strong contemporary population), in addition to non-Malayan but equally indigenous ethnicities, such as the Javanese, Bugis, Minang, and tribal aboriginals. The Chinese and Indians, who constitute respectively about twenty-six and eight percent of the populace, were initially economic migrants under British colonial rule and are thus not considered native children of the soil, even six generations later.

As the stillborn Malayan Union (1946) gave way to the Federation of Malaya Agreement (1948)—courtesy of the non-cooperation of the Malayan nationalist movement—the attempts to build a unitary body politic of the diverse denizens of the Malayas revealed nearly unbridgeable fissures along ethno-cultural lines in what was to be a future Malaysian nation. The federal constitution came to reflect a "tortuous forging of acceptable terms and compromises among the various racial components of the Malaysian society."[7] The historic attempt to build a consensus relied on give-and-take negotiations, but all understood that what was at stake was the very soul and character of the national polity and the concomitant distribution of rights and obligations of the various ethnic communities.

In the end, the 1957 constitution accorded the *bumiputra* groups privileges in business, employment, education, and land ownership.

It thus went against what the British had envisioned as a centralized Malay Union with equal citizenship and instead perpetuated, by way of legal codification, the special status of Malays, of Islam, and of the sultans. In exchange for the adoption of the generic principle that citizenship was not to be determined by ancestry—a principle that largely, if not perfectly, extended citizenship rights to Chinese and Indian communities[8]—the Malays retained state-sanctioned economic and linguistic privileges, flowing less from a majoritarian argument than an ethno-national imagination which insisted that the *bumiputra* ought to determine the final cultural contours of the composite nation. In short, the Malaysian nation was to be a unified but differentiated populace, the heart of which would be the Malay ethnicity, its lifeblood Malay identity. If anyone was in doubt, they simply needed to look at the national flag (much later dubbed *Jalur Gemilang*), where the crescent prominently displayed the ownership of the nation.

The ethno-linguistic divides were augmented by a policy of religious differentiation; hence a political demand for Malay supremacy (*Ketuanan Melayu*) implied also the privileging of Islam as topos. Islam was thus deemed a distinctive and essential feature of the Malay people, as religious affiliation was conflated with communitarian self-identity. Article 3(1) of the federal Constitution insisted that "Islam is the [official] religion of the Federation," thus subscribing to the (anthropomorphic) assumption that institutions embody a value-system (or personality). The fact that this was an exercise in identity politics, rather than a bona fide attempt at formulating civil or criminal law on the sly, seemed to have been recognized by the British as well as the non-Muslim minorities, even as, for good measure, it was insisted that Article 3 be confined to jurisprudential domains pertaining to personal and customary law only. Conversely, the autonomy of the Shari'a courts was sealed with the adoption of Article 121(1a), in the 1988 amendment of the federal Constitution, and thenceforth it was clear that High Courts were to "have no jurisdiction in respect of any matter within the jurisdiction of the Syariah Courts."[9] This was, of course, an attempt to pre-empt the paradox of dual law on singular subjects, but also functioned as a means of ethno-legal primacy within a system of differentiated citizenship. Uniquely, thus, being subject to Shariatic law became a privilege. While Art. 3 had added that "all other religions may be practised in peace and harmony in any part of the Federation," this allowance, in effect, seemed conditional upon not disturbing the "peace and harmony" of the faith groups by evangelical or missionary activity.

As national identity and religion were used interchangeably in the discourse of Malay nationalism, Malay equaled Muslim, even as not all Muslims were Malays.[10] In Art. 160 of the federal Constitution, a Malay was defined as a person who "professes the religion of Islam, habitually speaks the Malay language, conforms to Malay customs [however defined] and is the child of at least one parent who was born within the Federation of Malaysia before independence of Malaya."[11] Being Muslim, thereby, was a necessary, albeit insufficient, condition for being Malay. This merger of ethnic and religious identity was iterated by apostasy laws, prohibiting lapsed Muslims from changing religious affiliation, but thereby also politicizing faith in a context where ethnic identity had implications for the balance of power and the distribution of rights.[12]

There were of course historical reasons for the attempt to build structural biases within the polity and governance: The Chinese were seen to have been the main beneficiaries of British colonialism, having amassed considerable economic wealth and entrepreneurial dominance, even as many were initially recruited from Hong Kong and the mainland to work in the mines and the tropical forests. An inbuilt bias in the system would, it was argued, restore the equilibrium and thus "affirmative" and "preferential" arrangements, typically utilized for minority communities, were here envisioned and elaborated as the redemptive strategy of the majority community.

Ethno-Political Cleavages and Modern Malaysia
Antedating independence in August of 1957, Malaysian politics has continually been characterized by inter-racial, ethno-national cleavages, embodied in the three ethno-nationalist political parties that have

dominated the political landscape, namely the United Malays National Organization (UMNO), the Malaysian Chinese Association (MCA), and the Malaysian Indian Congress (MIC). While serving distinct ethnic and economic interests, the ebb and flow of national as well as international power configurations have often proffered considerations requiring the coupling of partisan rhetoric with pragmatic alignment patterns. In addition, common foes—from colonialists to communists—have prompted broad-based bandwagoning as exemplified, for instance, in the common front against the Malayan Communist Party during the five years of the emergency rule (1948–1953).

In the global security architecture of the Cold War, Britain's concern to envelop Malaysia in an iron curtain—as part of the Western containment policy—necessitated that the communities work together to prevent Malaysia from falling as part of the Communist domino. Moreover, to defeat the Socialist insurgents, it was necessary to develop a relatively unified and coherent vision of the political good (even if only as a mirror image of the political bad), in the mold of the trans-ethnic multi-party alliance, which was forged between UMNO, MCA, and later MIC to contest the first federal elections for seats in the new Federal Legislative Council.[13]

Not all sections of Malay-Muslim were happy with a joint national front, however; and certainly not those who subscribed to rural Malay traditionalism. Even as the emergence of Islamist opposition parties is a recent (and urban) phenomenon in much of the Middle East, among Malays, Islamic political opposition existed vis-à-vis the dominant UMNO party well before Malaysian independence. The pan-Malayan Islamic Party (PMIP) was formed in 1951 by defectors from UMNO to combat any attempt to form a polity that would not safeguard the role of Islam (and thus Malays) in the constitutional arrangements between Malay and non-Muslim ethnicities.

From the outset, this organization (which later took the name *Partai Islam Se-Malaysia*, or PAS[14]) promoted a more uncompromising line toward non-Malay culture and a greater commitment to Islam as definatory for not only Malay identity but also the Malaysian political system. Unlike the typical revivalist movement, PAS was led and supported by the *'ulama*, giving it both vertical and horizontal legitimacy via the Islamic institutions of learning and preaching. At once embodying religio-cultural activism and political partisanship, PAS could benefit from religious institutions to run an ongoing campaign, irrespective of electoral season, with perpetual leitmotifs being the denunciations of economic greed, cultural laxity, and moral corruption. The natural base of PAS was conservative and rural, and unlike UMNO, PAS had little investment in the multi-racial project that was Malaysia and could freely play the jingoistic card.

With the events of May 13, 1969, which horrified the nation with bloody Sino-Malay race riots in Kuala Lumpur and subsequently saw a declaration of national emergency, came PAS's moment in history. In the wake of the riots, identity became insatiably politicized; who you were was to determine what you got. UMNO's decade-long act of balancing opposing pressures had entailed a need to offset its own role as the epitome of Malay nationalism with the reality of Malaysian multi-ethnic pluralism. After 1969, grassroot pressures prompted a reappraisal of UMNO's relatively inconspicuous public symbolry and a greater emphasis was now placed on Malay-Muslim concerns, economic as well as cultural. In 1971 a twenty-year development plan under the name of New Economic Policy (NEP) was launched, aiming to redress socio-economic imbalances between the relatively affluent elites (often of minority extraction) and the underdeveloped Malay majority (which owned less than 2.5% of the national assets and had rural poverty rates of nearly 60%).[15] A byproduct of this attempt at social engineering, however, was the continued preoccupation with ethno-cultural identity. In the Malaysian social contract, it appeared, Malay "special rights" went hand in hand with a subscription to the notion of rightful ownership of Malays (*ketuanan Melayu*). The new affirmative action, thus, was not charity; it was returning to the owners what was rightfully theirs.

The *Dakwah* Revival of Societal Islam

In the period that followed the 1969 trauma, the quest for Malay identity produced the growth of movements dedicated to instilling Islamic consciousness in society. Styling themselves as awakening movements—a form of Islamic Babtism—and taking their cues from the broader developments in the wider Muslim world, they were referred to as the *Dakwah* movements (from the Arabic *da'wa*, meaning call or invitation to faith). Less concerned with spreading the Message to the uninitiated (viz. the uncircumcised), protagonists of the *Dakwah* sought to inculcate Islamic mores in what increasingly appeared to be a wayward Malay nation in need of redemption. Key tropes were the ancient, but not ancestral, ones: The Text (*Qur'an*) and the Prophetic Archetype (*Sunna*) were to form the compass with which to return the nation back unto the Straight Path (*al-Sirat al-Mustaqim*) from whence it had strayed. Islam, it was argued, had to be understood not only as an identity, but as a way of life—a *deen*—which by necessity had to permeate the individual, the family, society, and the polity at large.

The *Dakwah* took place against a backdrop of rapid urbanization, which had brought into the metropolises young generations of erstwhile rural Malays, with concomitant feelings of dislocation in urban landscapes that lacked the familiarity, and possibly piety, of the village miliuex. Cathartically, perhaps, a romantic notion surrounding "the true Islamic life" emerged, oftentimes contrasted with (post-)modern life in the urban jungle. Islam thus became salient as not only an identity marker but as a provider of comfort in a time of rapid social mobility and demographic change.

Still, the *Dakwah* could be no unified program of action, but remained rather a cluster of movements tied together by a sense of commitment to "Islam," however defined. Among them were those who spoke of avoiding spiritual vices—from immodest dress and inter-gender social life, to lewd music and nightclubs, to the consumption of alcohol and drugs. But there were those, too, who extended this separatist call to socio-political systems, thus ideologizing faith identity, similar to Ayatollah Khomeini's dictum, "Neither East nor West: Islam is the best!"

Indeed, in addition to emerging in a period of national self-doubt, the Dakwatic turn in the religio-political history of Malay Islam was a beneficiary also of the increased globalization of Islamic self-assertion on the world scene. In the Middle East, the inter-Arab Cold War between secular nationalism (led by Gamal Abdel Nasser) and con-servative Islam-legitimized monarchism (exemplified in the Saudi kingdom) was irrevocably tilting toward the latter. With the failure of secular pan-Arabism in the 1967 Six-Day War, in which the Nasser-ites and Ba'athists lost face as well as land, Islam had been decisively propelled to provide "answers" to the woes of the Muslim condition (even as the questions remained unclear). Over the next decade, in the shadow of a string of dramatic global events—the Iranian Revolu-tion, the military coup in Pakistan under Zia-ul-Haq, the Afghan jihad against the Soviets, the spread of the Muslim Brotherhood, Jaafar Numayri's takeover of the Sudan, and Wahhabism's global ascen-dancy—political Islam became the currency of the day. It was not that the call to Islam was an atavistic craving, but that the collapse of secular and nationalist movements had discredited political ideologies that were tainted by mimicking alien powers—indeed, powers that had previously been (more directly) imperial. In Malaysia, as in much of the Muslim world, it was clear to the public that the political future had to be self-made.

The *Dakwah* revivalism, whilst non-partisan, spurred political pres-sure, naturally most readily onto UMNO, which could no longer dodge the question of Islam proper (as opposed to Malay identity) for the fear of alienating non-Muslim/non-Malay groups. Rather than moving in the direction of pan-national reconciliation, UMNO now had to be seen as being more vocal in the defense of Muslim faith–based privileges and Malay socio-economic rights. It also had to be seen as being more asser-tive in demarcating the Malay-Muslim cultural sphere vis-à-vis both Western and Sinic ("yellow") encroachment.

THE NEW WAVE OF ISLAMICATE POLITICS

The call for self-reliance notwithstanding, Malay graduates of foreign universities were instrumental in adding to the *Dakwah* momentum—both when the foreign universities were Islamic, in which case graduates returned with a repository of normative and actional discourses from the Muslim mainland, and in cases where the foreign universities were Western, in which case graduates brought home organizational skills, a renewed sense of commitment to the nation, and ideas about the non-governmental movements as agents of social change.[16]

But more important than either of these groups were the growing number of student activists at Malaysian university and college campuses. Among all *Dakwah* movements of the 1970s, the Islamic Youth Movement of Malaysia (*Angkatan Belia Islam Malaysia*, or ABIM), under the dynamic leadership of Anwar Ibrahim, soon became the dominant force. ABIM attracted the young, the modern-educated, the (in theory) socially mobile, who sought to make Islam a viable vehicle for social and political reform. Denouncing corruption, malfeasance, poverty, misappropriation of resources, maldistribution of wealth, violation of human and civil rights, nepotism and lacking transparency, the growing decadence of popular culture, and a host of other social ills, ABIM became quintessential in shaping a discourse of Islam as a resource for building a better society and improved state.

Positing a global paradigm of Islam as the autarkic third way between capitalism and communism, ABIM did not subscribe to the equation in which Islam equaled Malay nationalism. Rather it denounced the *bumiputra* affirmative action as bribing Muslims to remain complacent in the face of an exploitative, unjust, ergo un-Islamic, system. It also saw in the ethnic politics of UNMO a racial component that was anathema to the non-racial call of Islam. ABIM argued instead for a progressive social conception of the sacred: More Islam would mean less discrimination, more Islam would mean more democracy, more Islam would mean more equality. Indeed, far from binary opposites, in ABIM's discourses, Islam and democracy were interchangeable. Hardly unambitious, Anwar

Ibrahim's futuristic vision for Malaysia was at once Islamic, democratic, and multicultural:

> The future society should be more committed and have a better understanding of the Islamic struggle, with the aim of creating a fair society, one that respects human rights [...] a national policy that guarantees real justice for all. [...] Islam places high regard for the rights of minority groups, the freedom of worship [and] a just economic system that will abolish class distinctions, and wipe out narrow communal feelings.[17]

To ABIM, Islam was thus about progress, not identity; about movement, not stasis; about tomorrow, not yesterday. In contrast to PAS, ABIM's natural constituency was the urban youth, who saw modernity not as a challenge to Islam but instead saw Islam as a vehicle for modernity. In this sense, ABIM complemented PAS, though ABIM's dynamism also illustrated how PAS's moribund discourses of yesteryear could neither galvanize Malaysian youth nor capture the imagination of the Malaysian nation as a whole. Given this contrast, ABIM became a catalyst for a generational change within PAS, whose old-guard leadership was challenged by younger activists (the so-called "Young Turks"), many of whom had simultaneous affiliations with ABIM.[18]

ABIM itself was not to enter electoral politics, except on the student level. Sweeping student union elections in 1974, ABIM became a force to be reckoned with, a fact that did not go unnoted in UMNO headquarters. The cult-status of Anwar Ibrahim—bright, good-looking, and articulate—combined with his status as an early martyr and his palpable organizational talents made him embody the aspirations of the emerging middle class, a position that could decisively alter the intra-Malay balance of power between UMNO and PAS, should he decide to openly support PAS (or worse, seek to take over its leadership).[19] UMNO itself was in flux, as a new contender, Tun Dr Mahathir bin Mohamad, took over leadership in 1981 with a promise of stability and economic advancement.

Mahathir's invitation to Anwar to join the government in 1982 was as remarkable as it was unexpected. On both sides of the ideological divide, this marriage of convenience was denounced—either because it meant cooptation into unjust structures (the critique emanating from the PAS opposition who felt cheated of their closest ally), or because it would allow an anti-system Islamist access to state resources (the critique from the UMNO rank-and-file). As it happened, Ibrahim turned out to be a capable politician and administrator, rapidly working his way up the hierarchies of power. In just over a decade, from 1983 to 1993, he held several key cabinet positions, namely minister of culture, youth, and sports (1983), of agriculture (1984), of education (1986), of finance (1991), and finally (from 1993 until his fall from grace in September 1998), deputy prime minister.

The Mahathir-Anwar symbiosis proved a winning formula for the government, which moved on to score significant electoral victories in national elections—now being able to claim the mantle of the defenders, indeed implementers, of Islam. Under the Mahathir-Anwar duo, Malaysia expanded the role of Islam in the national curriculum, established a new International Islamic University, expanded Islamic studies in existing universities, increased funding for mosques and Islamic centers, increased *Dakwah* outreach, and convened international conferences on Islamic themes. It also increased its involvement in international Islamic organizations, from the Organization of the Islamic Conference, to the World Assembly of Muslim Youth, to the Regional Dawa Council of Southeast Asia and the Pacific, to Asia Pacific Mosque Council.[20]

UMNO, furthermore, established several national committees to address law, education, economics, science, and technology as they pertained to an "Islamic concept of development." Other clear policy shifts included a declaration to restructure Malaysia's economic system according to Islamic principles, with the establishment of Islamic economic institutions like the Islamic Bank and Islamic Economic Foundation. Islamic content on radio and television was increased, and, in time, private morality became a public issue. Encroaching thus on PAS territory, UMNO had the unintended effect of moving the spectrum, as PAS radicalized its positions, in particular with respect to the application of Shariatic law. An Islamic modernist, Mahathir had prevented PAS from implementing the *hudud* (Islamic criminal penalties for severe offenses) in the state of Kelantan, a state under PAS rule, arguing that Malaysia's federal laws were already in complete conformity with Islam; indeed, Malaysia was already fully Islamic.[21]

Still, coinciding with the global revival of Muslim pride (epitomized in the 1973 oil embargo) and the globalization of Muslim consciousness (often courtesy of Saudi oil wealth), the top-down enactment of Islamization did not have the intended effect of stalling the bottom-up agitation for more Islam in politics. In fact, short of Anwar as leader, the ABIM crumbled under the weight of more radical voices emanating from the likes of the Islamic Republic Group, whilst ABIM operatives increasingly followed in Anwar's footsteps and "defected" to the government. More confrontational and uncompromising than ABIM, the Islamic Republic Group took over university campuses with a pronounced ideological purism (akin to Islamist Trotskyism): the system rather than individual policies was to be at the heart of reconstruction. The anti-traditionalist Islamists opposed not only the government but also the sultans, arguing for a new normative Islamic republicanism (a remaking of the *kaum muda*, or "new nation," strand in Malay political thought which had equated the sultanates and the old guards of *kaum tua* with stagnation).[22]

Within PAS quarters, the influx of graduates from Cairo's al-Azhar or Medina's Islamic University functioned as a viaduct of *étatist* ideas about Islam. To products of the Islamic academies in the Middle East, it appeared that Malaysia was wholly inadequate when it came to the Islamic credentials of its state and society. Democracy, they learned, was hypocrisy, and no Islamic movement worth its salt could agitate in favor of such a mirage. As the political thought of Egypt's *Ikhwan al-Muslimin* and Pakistan's *Jama'at-e Islami* became globalized in the 1980s, many Malay activists also wanted the Islam-on-steroids political form that had threatened the status quo elsewhere in the Muslim world.[23] Malay expats and students in Britain, moreover, had organized more radical organizations, such as the UK-origined *Suara Islam* (Voice of Islam), which on return to Malaysia inducted a more radical stream of members into the PAS mainstream. Uncompromising, the new crop sought to drive PAS in the direction of Sudanese-style Islamic government in Malaysia, and certainly were not amenable to settling for anything less than a Shari'a-abiding Islamic state in Malaysia.

Still, at critical junctures, PAS remained faithful to the operative principles of the Malaysian system. With the exception of momentary lapses, there was no call for revolution, for abrogating the constitutional rights of minorities, for annulling the federal system, for replacing the premier with a caliph. Instead, PAS channeled its energies into more limited policy areas pertaining to culture, education, and civil law. Having had its national aspirations somewhat curtailed by the runaway success of the Mahathir-Anwar partnership, it also seemed content with a deeper civil society engagement in more circumscribed territories in eastern states of Malaysia.

On the other hand, UMNO was not afraid of flexing its Islamic muscles, almost to signal its determination not to be outbid in the Islamization game. While the post-Dakwah period saw a myriad of local, regional, national, and international organizations express visions, utopian or otherwise, of revitalized Islam, with the case of the Dar al-Arqam organization it became clear that UMNO would not allow a religious free market. Here was a millennial movement, led by the charismatic Sufi leader Ashaari Muhammad, whose social and economic activities were tied into a broader eschatology in which the movement itself would be the forebear of the coming of al-Mahdi, the awaited Imam before the Apocalypse. But Malays were not quite ready for the end of times. By 1994, the authorities made an example of Dar al-Arqam, banning the organization for allegedly embracing and spreading "heterodoxy," their centers forcefully closed down and their leader placed under arrest.[24] With this action, the government, having used the Islamic Council (*Pusat Islam*), could claim not only to have safeguarded Islam as a community but also Islam as a doctrine—a role historically reserved for the trans-Muslim Caliph.

(DE)CONSTRUCTING DEMOCRACY: RIVAL INTERPRETATIONS

By the 1990s, Malaysia's leader Dr Mahathir bin Mohamad placed UMNO on a decisively more Islamic orientation with a emphatic shift in rhetorical policy, if less so in operational policy, within both domestic and international arenas. Islam was now to be employed as a strategy of legitimization vis-à-vis domestic challenges from PAS and internationally vis-à-vis increased scrutiny from the West. It was here that Mahathir could develop an idiosyncratic theory of governance and development in the form of the "Asian values" paradigm. As a double-edged sword, Mahathir could on the one hand combat Western critiques with reference to the limited applicability of Western notions of democracy and political accountability; and, on the other hand, he could speak to PAS and the new Islamists about "Arab Islam" not being suitable for a Malaysian context.

Whilst Mahathir insisted that democracy was a valued ideal for all, not only some, societies, he equally insisted that democracy came in multiple shapes: "[I]s there only one form of democracy and only one high priest to interpret it?" he provocatively asked.[25] Of democracy, Mahathir warned that it was a strong medicine, which had to be administered in small doses to avoid ill effects. He argued that the pursuit of democracy could lead to disruption and anarchy, destroying an otherwise stable and prosperous society.[26] As a true skeptic, Mahathir cautioned:

> Indeed democracy causes a great deal of instability in many countries. Political parties mushroom and use bribery, corruption, threats and economic disruptions in order to fight each other. Development cannot take place as everything is politicized. The energy and the wealth of the whole nation is wasted in political infighting between numerous political parties set up for nothing more than the furtherance of the political ambitions of various aspirants for the highest post in the country.[27]

In short, what could be better than a benign benefactor—a wise, enlightened leader, who knew what the nation needed and could deliver the goods accordingly? If the West was unhappy with this alternative model of governance—this paradigm of "good governance"[28] rather than democracy—it was only because good leaders would not be wimps or sell-outs. In fact, Mahathir argued, Western nations had habitually used democracy and human rights as tools to engulf parts of Asia in a new informal dominion:

> They speak eloquently of the rule of law, human rights, democracy or the voice of the majority, without taking [into] account the existence of certain man-made laws that are unfair, excessive human rights, and unwise majority voices. Hence, the laws in the West place too much priority on the individual's right that allow him to do anything he pleases even though his actions may threaten the pace and security of the society.[29]

There is, of course, a clear structuralist bias in Mahathir's thought, which revolves around the binary between the (imperial) hegemon and the (nominally postcolonial) subaltern. True to Marx's maxim that in every epoch the thoughts of the ruling elite are the ruling thoughts, the central trope remains that, in the absence of either isolation or equilibrium, the ideas of the hegemonic states become the hegemonic ideas. As such, democratization remains a strategy of domination.

To attain a modicum of autonomy in the face of the ideational onslaught of the West, Mahathir shifted Malaysia's traditional pro-West outlook to a "Look East" policy that sought horizontal South-South relations of friendship, rather than vertical North-South relations of clientship. This policy initiative fitted well with UMNO's domestic position to the extent that it would bring together, exactly as suggested by Samuel Huntington, the Confucian and Islamic civilizations in a new alliance.[30] As a world system theorist, Mahathir's building blocks were world civilizations but his etiology was decidedly materialist. Ostentatious megaprojects, including the world's tallest twin buildings—Kuala Lumpur's Petronas towers—would cement, rather literally, the new Malaysia, a symbol of the compatibility between Islam and progress.[31]

If Mahathir's understanding of democracy was idiosyncratic, his definition of Islam was no less so. Mahathir's discursive construction of

Islam rested on a parallel to the Weberian argument about the Protestant ethic as foundational for the flourishing of capitalism.[32] Islam, to Mahathir, equaled hard work, honesty, discipline, and therefore cumulatively, national progress. From Islam, Mahathir wanted not otherworldly salvation, but this-worldly success; not truth in the Hereafter but triumph in the here-and-now,; not premodern piety but postmodern productivity. In short, Islam was good if could support national development, science, technology, literacy, industry, and economic uplift. Social and economic development was Mahathir's top priority and Islam was good only to the extent that it helped serve this objective. In the context of this developmentalism, democracy too was a potential means, not an end.

In clear contrast, Anwar had, since his days as ABIM chair, relatively consistently argued for openness, accountability, representation, rule of law, and equal rights for all. The quest for Islam with a human face had brought to Malaysia *mutatis mutandis*, notions similar to *glasnost* and *perestroika* in the face of an illiberal state. As such, Anwar brought an Islamic worldview to bear on a project of liberalization.

> Only the autocrats and authoritarian leaders seem to create a perception that democracy is something alien, as a Western agenda, imposed by the administration in Washington [...] But the desire to be free is universal. It's neither East nor West; Islam[ic] nor Christian [...] Pluralism and diversity has its own legitimacy within Islam. It's a tradition attributed to the Prophet Muhammad that divergence of opinion among the scholars is a *rahma*; a blessing.[33]

Islam, Anwar argued, was not merely compatible with democracy, nor was it that Islam was only conducive to democracy. Properly conceived, Islam *was* democracy. Nor was it the case that one could subscribe to hyphenated democracy (under the pretext of safeguarding distinctly Asian or Islamic values).[34] Democracy was indivisible, and autocracy indefensible.

Anwar Ibrahim's sudden dismissal and arrest in September 1998 on what were widely believed to be spurious charges of corruption and

sexual misconduct manifested the increasing alienation between the disciplinarian and the reformer—an alienation that was augmented by the
differing positions on the Asian financial crisis of 1997–1998.[35] As the
Mahathir-Anwar marriage of convenience ended in divorce, the ensuing economic-cum-political crisis led to the formation of a middle-class
protest movement, the *reformasi*, which sought to transform the political
agenda. Led from the helm by Wan Azizah Wan Ismail, the stoic spouse
of the imprisoned Anwar, a new People's Justice Party (*Parti Keadilan
Rakyat*) sought to initiate a great public debate about Islam, justice, and
legitimacy. Democratization could no longer be so easily dismissed as
a "Western" preoccupation. It had become the most important issue in
Malaysian politics, for Muslims and minorities alike.

ON THE *VIA MEDIA*: ISLAM HADHARI

Against the backdrop of Mahathir's idiosyncratic reading of Islam in
the context of state-building and development, and the opposed liberal
instigations of Anwar's Muslim (social) democracy, the new premier
Abdullah Ahmad Badawi (in office 2003–2009) sought to induct a new
discourse in Malaysian Islam. A descendent of prominent scholars of
religion, and in more modest terms himself possessor of religious where-
withal, Badawi had some credentials in this regard. Driven by the dual
considerations of developing an Islamic form which would simultaneously satisfy the demand of Islamic authenticity and be non-threatening
to non-Malay minorities, Badawi made himself spokesperson for what
he termed *Islam Hadhari*, or civilizational Islam (presumably in contradistinction to political Islam, ideological Islam, liberal Islam, fundamentalist Islam, etc.).

Islam Hadhari was to be understood as a comprehensive translation
of Islam as a social (life) force and thus provide a moderate, but meaningful, blueprint for national life in a world of states. Written as a laun-
dry list of ten desirable characteristics, the Hadhari paradigm of Islam
included not only faith as a pillar, but also a just and trustworthy government, a free and independent people, the acquisition of knowledge,

balanced economic development, protection of minority rights, cultural and moral integrity, protection of the environment, and (curiously) strong national defenses.[36] Inclusive, even if contradictory, progressive ideas of economic, social, and political capacity-building were included in Islam Hadhari, which also defined unity, universality, and tolerance as key virtues for the Islamically aware politician—in no small measure a hint to PAS positions. In Badawi's template, Islam was not simply an attendant to Western democracy, nor an obstinate civilizational opposition to liberalism, but instead Islam entailed a wholesome and universal appeal to a benevolent "governmentality," understood as a technology of control, direction, and governance.[37]

Although more systematic than Mahathir's ruminations on Islamic developmentalism, Islam Hadhari was an attempt to use Islam as a resource for material development, progress, and stability. At the same time, however, the new civic Islam was to be communally inclusive, as well as spiritually authentic. Borrowing from the intellectual precursors in Islamic intellectual history (in particular, the notion of the *maqasid al-Shari'a*, or the objectives rather than the manifestations of the Shari'a), Badawi sought to develop a new optic through which the Islamicity of a nation could be gauged. If Malaysia fulfilled the ten cardinal principles of Islam Hadhari, it was *ipso facto* an Islamic domain—an acknowledgement that would render PAS-like agitation somewhat redundant. Exactly as the cultural critic Farish Ahmad-Noor sensed "a state-sanctioned and state-sponsored exercise in social engineering," it was increasingly clear that Islam Hardari was a thinly veiled attempt to control the discourse and appropriate from non- or anti-governmental voices the prerogative to define what Islam was, or ought to be, in a social context.[38]

Nonetheless, while Mahathir's last years in office (he retired in October 2003) had seen the national leader rely more on the political support of Chinese and Indian Malaysians—as a result of the post-Anwar alienation of the Malay vote—Badawi brought back the overwhelming majority of Muslim-Malays to the UMNO fold. The 2004 general election, Badawi's first election as the incumbent prime minister, not only delivered a stunning victory for the *Barisan Nasional* coalition by winning 198 out of 220 seats in parliament, but also wrested control of the Terengganu state government back from the PAS opposition, as well as coming close to capturing the traditional PAS stronghold of Kelantan. The victory was widely regarded as an approval of his rethinking on the role of Islam in the Malaysian polity.

CONCLUDING REFLECTIONS: ISLAM AS ASCENDING AND DESCENDING IMPERATIVES

Historically, Islam has been integral to Malay social identity and thus, too, to Malaysian political history. The presence of significant non-Malay population groups, courtesy of imperial immigration policies, brought Islam to the forefront both as a corrective discourse vis-à-vis the domination of intruding capital and as a vision for the reestablishment of Malay autonomy. Because Islam was pervasive as a construct, it was also contested along several axes—vertically among Malay nationalists as well as horizontally between Malay and non-Malay ethnicities. For UMNO, Islam was tantamount to one element in the whole package that described "Malayness": race, culture, language, customs and, to this extent only, religion. PAS, on the other hand, had insisted on an ideological reading of Islam as an action program, which would not only assert Malay-Muslim dominance within an environment of plural population groups and conflicting claims, but also, eventually, usher in an Islamic state. The constitution—upholding Malay special rights and the role of sultans and Shari'a courts within a federated political structure—gave equal weight to both views, but thereby also legitimized religio-political constructions in Malaysian politics.

Mahathir bin Mohamad's Islamization drive was distinct from any model familiar in the Middle East or South Asia. Islam was here synonymous with material determination, industrial direction and, building thereupon, cultural pride and self-sufficiency in a globalizing world. It was the postcolonial manifestation of *swadeshism*. ABIM entered the scene only to develop a new dialectic between UMNO and PAS.

Initially an asset for PAS as a galvanizing partner against governmental corruption and authoritarianism, ABIM also lent itself to appropriation by UMNO to the extent that it provided a base of young, modern-educated Malay urbanites whose rallying cry was religion *qua* reform. In the political history of Malaysia, ABIM thus made Islam and democracy interchangeable, eschewing both the ethnic pride of UMNO and the religious chauvinism of PAS.

A historical reading of the five decades of Malaysian independence reveals that Malay Islamism has been Janus-faced. It has fluctuated between being a legal and principled opposition, being non-partisan and grassroot-driven, being the controlling force in state politics, and being a means of controlling and constraining the opposition. In addition, Islam has functioned as an ever-changing ideal: at times progressive, at other times reactionary; at times urban, at other times rural; at times pro-regime, at other times anti-regime; at times from above, at other times from below. In this sense, Islam has been a constant, yet a variable, in the socio-political landscape of the nation.

Critically, though, the key characteristic of Malay political Islam has been its commitment to operate within the constitutive rules of the political system, rather than delegitimizing the system or seeking a revolutionary change. In short, Malaysian political Islam has been anti-regime, rather than anti-system, and as a consequence has typically, though not consistently, been allowed to operate relatively unobstructed by governmental interference. Conversely, this ability to be part of the system has—in contradistinction to the situation in many Middle East states—reinforced, both as a cause and an effect, a pragmatic non-radicalism that successive governments (all centered around UMNO as the hegemonic political force) could accept, albeit grudgingly. Futhermore, central political voices could lift pages from the Islamic manifestos and make the discourse of political Islam their own in an attempt to defuse any challenge to power. Such policy of discursive appropriation was coupled with a policy of cooptation of key agents of the Islamist movement, most notably, of course, the case of Anwar Ibrahim.

Cumulatively, thus, three characteristics of political Islam in Malaysia are salient. First, the common theme in Malaysian political Islam has been its respect for the constitutive and regulatory rules of the system. Those who seemed to challenge this were met with persecution and ferocious crackdown—even if they belonged to a wayward Sufi movement called Darul Arqam rather than any militant anarcho-Islamist cell. A second, and related, feature was the emphasis on pragmatism: UMNO would not denounce the call for more Islam as fundamentalism, ABIM would not eschew an invitation for power sharing, and PAS would not reject modernization and generational change. The inability of any individual (a grand ayatollah, for instance) or any party (like Hizbullah, the "Party of God") to have exclusive access to Islam as a policy resource augmented this pragmatism, as no single political center could monopolize the discourse. A third recurrent feature of Malaysia's Islamic religio-politics was the insistence that Malaysia could not simply replicate the Saudi, Iranian, or Pakistani models. Without imported roadmaps, Malaysia had to find its own way, even if by trial and error. The challenge in this attempt to chart its own waters lay in the strong postcolonial ethno-national component of Islamist agitators and the simultaneous realization that Islam was only one among many religions within the composite nation. In this conflation of Islam and communitarian identity, the history of Malaysian Islamism is conspicuous, although not unique.

In sum, in Malaysia, Islam has been used both as a top-down strategy of legitimization (a descending imperative) by the state, and a bottom-up strategy of delegitimization (an ascending imperative) by partisans seeking to challenge, and ultimately capture, state power. In addition, Islam has been used horizontally, as social capital, to bind together a racial (in)group vis-à-vis minority (out)groups in the pursuit of distributive privileges. Finally, Islam has been used as a civic resource for nation and institution building. Ubiquitous, the constructs of "Islam," "Islamic," and "Muslim" have nonetheless historically been almost infinitely malleable. The upshot, in turn, is two-fold. First, for the foreseeable future,

Islam is bound to remain a constant, if contested, feature in the Malaysian political landscape. Second, the presence of the Islamic discourse alone bears no predictable correlation with either the preference formation of the public or the policy choices of political actors. In the final calculation, in Malaysia too, God remains transcendent.

ENDNOTES

1. Exo-socialization, a term introduced by Ernest Gellner, refers to the modern phenomenon of communal identities derived from modern institutions of socialization outside the familial relationships. See E. Gellner, *Nations and Nationalism* (Oxford: Blackwell), 37.
2. In the cultural milieu leading up to the Islamic revolution in Iran, Jalal Al-e Ahmed's book on *Gharbzadegi* (or Westoxification) epitomized the popular resistance toward the Shah's modernization drive. Ali Shariati and Ayatollah Khomeini used this concept to denote Western-orientated governance, lacking Islamic authenticity.
3. I am here modifying the trinitarian approach to the study of religio-political phenomena developed by Scott Appleby and others. See G. A. Almond, S. Appleby, and E. Sivan, *Strong Religion: The Rise of Fundamentalisms around the World* (Chicago: University of Chicago Press, 2003).
4. J. L. Esposito and J. O. Voll, *Islam and Democracy* (Oxford: Oxford University Press), 125.
5. For instance, multiple religious functionaries (imams, bomohs, pawangs, etc.) coexisted in the same locale, often providing spiritual services according to a contingent mixture of Islamic norm and local magical-spiritist custom. Even as the sultans were simultaneously faith leaders, royal services, too, brought together the pluralism of traditions, Islamic and non-Islamic. See. G. P. Means, "The Role of Islam in the Political Development of Malaysia," *Comparative Politics* 1:2 (1969): 267–269.
6. F. R. von der Mehden, "Islamic Resurgence in Malaysia," in *Islam and Development: Religion and Socio-Political Change*, ed. J. L. Esposito (Syracuse, NY: Syracuse University Press, 1980), 164.
7. H. P. Lee, "Constitutional Amendments in Malaysia," *Malaya Law Review* 18 (1976): 59, cited in J. Ling-Chien Neo, "Malay Nationalism, Islamic Supremacy and the Constitutional Bargain in the Multi-Ethnic Composition of Malaysia," *International Journal on Minority and Group Rights* 13:2 (2006): 96, fn 3.
8. The citizenship laws entailed that Malays, who were the subjects of any of the nine sultans, as well as British subjects in the Penang and Melaka became federal citizens with no other qualification, while other communities were able to acquire citizenship only by application and only under the condition that they were born within the designated territory and had been resident there for eight years, or were born outside the territory but had

remained resident there for a minimum of fifteen years. Thus, in effect, a large number of domiciled emigrant communities were denied citizenship. See J. M. Fernando, "The Making of the Malayan Constitution," *MBRAS Monographs* 31 (2002): 73.

9. J. Ling-Chien Neo, op. cit., p. 101.

10. Though all Malays are, by constitutional definition, Muslims, additional Islamic faith groups render the total figure of Muslims to sixty percent of the population according to the 2000 census. As Malay fertility rates are higher than non-Muslim rates, this figure may have moved by one or two percentage points in the interim. See, for example, V. T. Palan and Y. T. Takeshita, "The Pattern of Fertility Among the Malay Chinese," in *Fertility Transition of the East Asian Populations*, ed. L. J. Cho and K. Kobayashi (Honolulu: University Press of Hawaii, 1979), 198–221.

11. See "Constitution of Malaysia," online at http://confinder.richmond.edu/admin/docs/malaysia.pdf (accessed August 4, 2009).

12. The much-publicized case of the conversion of Lina Joy (born Azlina Jailani) from Islam to Christianity, and the High and Federal Courts' rejections of her appeal to change her religious identification on her national identity card, illustrates the practical impediments in a legal context where ethnicity and religious affiliation are fused. See Timo Kortteinen, "Islamic Resurgence and the Ethnization of the Malaysian State: The Case of Lina Joy," *Journal of Social Issues in Southeast Asia* 23:2 (2008): 216–233, and "Lina Joy's Despair," *The Economist*, June 2, 2007.

13. J. Ling-Chien Neo, op. cit., 99.

14. The PAS acronym reflected the "Jawi" or Arabic script letters *Pa-Alif-Sin*, rather than the English, subtly hinting at the orientation of the party.

15. Certain policies, as a means of affirmative action for *bumiputras*, were implemented in the New Economic Policy, including quotas for the following: admission to government educational institutions, qualification for public scholarships, positions in government, and ownership in business. Specifically, the NEP's target was to uplift the *bumiputra* economy such that it would go from an equity share of 2.4 percent in 1970 to 30 percent by 1990. Contemporary figures differ, but analysts agree that this benchmark was far from attained in the target period of two decades.

16. Among the Malaysia expatriate organizations was the Malaysian Islamic Study Group, founded in Illinois in 1976. See http://www.misgonline.com/ (accessed August 2, 2009).

17. Cited in von der Mehden, op. cit., 174–175.

18. D.K. Mauzi and R.S. Milne, *Malaysian Politics under Mahathir* (London: Routledge, 1999), 82.
19. Anwar's early martyr status derived from his 1974 arrest during student protests against rural poverty and hunger. He was imprisoned under the draconian Internal Security Act, which allows for detention without trial, and spent twenty months in the Kamunting Detention Center.
20. Esposito and Voll, op. cit., 138.
21. J. Stark, "Constructing an Islamic Model in Two Malaysian States: PAS Rule in Kelantan and Terengganu," *Sojourn: Journal of Social Issues in Southeast Asia* 19 (2004).
22. David Wright-Neville, "Dangerous Dynamics: Activists, Militants and Terrorists in Southeast Asia," *Pacific Review* 17, no. 1 (2004): 32–33. See also R. A. Abd Rahim, "Traditionalism and Reformism Polemic in Malay-Muslim Religious Literature," *Islam and Christian-Muslim Relations* 17, no. 1 (2006): 93–104.
23. On the influence of Jama'at-e Islami's founder on Malaysia and neighboring states, see M. Kamal Hassan, "The Influence of Mawdudi's Thought on Muslims in Southeast Asia: A Brief Survey," *Muslim World* 93, no. 3/4 (2003): 429–464.
24. A. F. Abdul Hamid, "The Futuristic Thought of Ustaz Ashaari Muhammad of Malaysia," in *Blackwell Companion to Contemporary Islamic Thought*, ed. I. Abu-Rabi (Oxford: Blackwell Reference, 2009).
25. Esposito and Voll, op. cit., 141.
26. BBC News, "Mahathir Warns against Too Much Democracy," July 27, 2000.
27. Gulf News, "Mahathir Rejects 'Western Democracy'," online at http://makepeace.ca/respublica/my-text.html (accessed July 31, 2009).
28. S. Subramaniam, "The Dual Narrative of 'Good Governance': Lessons for Understanding Political and Social Change in Malaysia and Singapore," *Contemporary Southeast Asia* 23, no. 1 (2001): 65–80.
29. Cited in Esposito and Voll, 140–141.
30. Samuel P. Huntington's seminal *The Clash of Civilizations and the Remaking of World Order* (New York: Simon and Schuster, 1996) anticipated an Islamo-Confucian axis vis-à-vis the Western world.
31. Measuring nearly 452 meters, the Petronas Twin Towers were the tallest buildings in the world until Taipei 101 was built, and remain the tallest twin buildings in the world. The towers' eighty-eight floors are constructed largely of reinforced concrete, with a steel and glass facade designed to resemble motifs found in Islamic art.

32. M. Weber, *The Protestant Ethic and the Spirit of Capitalism*, 2nd ed. (London: Routledge, 2001 [1905]). Weber, needless to say, did not agree that Islam was conducive to economic rationality.

33. A. Ibrahim, "The Future of Muslim Democracy," remarks at the New York Democracy Forum, December 1, 2005. Online at http://www.ned.org/nydf/anwarIbrahim05.pdf (accessed August 3, 2009).

34. M. R. Thompson, "Whatever Happened to 'Asian Values'?" *Journal of Democracy* 12, no. 4 (2001): 154–165.

35. On the significant difference in fiscal policy between Mahathir and Anwar, see Amy L. Freedman, "Economic Crises and Political Change: Indonesia, South Korea, and Malaysia," *Asian Affairs* 31, no. 4 (2005): 244–246.

36. The ten cardinal principles, or objectives, of Islam Hadhari have been listed as follows: 1) faith and piety in Allah, 2) a just and trustworthy government, 3) a free and independent people, 4) mastery of [religious and secular] knowledge, 5) a balanced and comprehensive economic development, 6) a good quality of life for all, 7) the protection of the rights of minority groups and women, 8) a cultural and moral integrity, 9) protection of the environment, and 10) a strong defense policy.

37. Michel Foucault used the concept of "governmentality" to denote the way governments try to produce citizens best suited to fulfill government policies as well as the technologies and practices through which subjects are governed. See, for example, M. Dean, *Governmentality: Power and Rule in Modern Society* (London: Sage, 1999). In the Foucaldian sense, thus, Islam Hadhari can be said to be a form of govenmentality.

38. See F. Ahmad-Noor, "The Future of Islam Hadari" http://www.mysinchew.com/node/17105 (accessed July 31, 2009). See also I. Gatsiounis, "Islam Hadhari in Malaysia," *Current Trends in Islamist Ideology* 3 (2006), and M. H. Hassan, "Islam Hadhari: Abdullah's Vision for Malaysia?" *IDSS Commentaries* 53 (2004).

PART IV

CENTRAL ASIA

CHAPTER 9

TALIBAN AND AL QAEDA SUICIDE BOMBERS IN AFGHANISTAN

TRACING THE EMERGENCE OF A TERROR TACTIC

Brian Glyn Williams

GARDEZ, TRIBAL AREA OF EASTERN AFGHANISTAN, MAY 2007

On an unusually warm spring day, my Afghan driver drove me out of Kabul and we made our way down a road known as "IED alley" that leads to the Pakistani border.[1] On the way, he pointed out several sites where Taliban suicide bombers had recently detonated themselves next to U.S. and NATO convoys. With a grin that concealed his fears, he informed me that a Taliban bomber had also hit a civilian SUV much like our own on this very stretch of road just a few weeks earlier. For this reason we tried to maintain a low profile as we joined the dusty line of brightly decorated "jingly" cargo trucks, packed buses, beat-up Toyota Corollas, and Afghan army vehicles disgorging from the capital.

Having made our way out of the city, we soon left the main road and turned south. There we found ourselves on a newly built tarmac road that wound its way through clay-walled villages, dry fields, and barren mountains to the Pashtun tribal lands. But for all their stark beauty, the provinces we were driving through were among Afghanistan's most dangerous and had recently been labeled a no-go "red zone" by most foreign NGOs and the UN. This point was driven home by the Afghan National Police soldiers who stopped us at several checkpoints along the way. At the last one, Kalashnikov-toting paramilitaries warned us to turn back, as Taliban insurgents operating in the area had just attacked a UN vehicle.[2]

Sadly, such attacks were becoming increasingly common in this region. Since 2005, the Taliban had been making inroads into the Pashtun territories of the south-east and the province we were aiming for, Khost, had become a hotbed for insurgent activity. Alarmingly, the tiny border province of Khost had also become the number-two target (after the Taliban's spiritual capital of Kandahar) for *fedayeen*, the dreaded Taliban suicide bombers. And truth be told, it was my research on Afghanistan's suicide bombers that had drawn me from the safety of my own world to the Pashtun tribal regions that straddled the Pakistani-Afghan border. For this reason I opted to press onward and hoped that our low profile kept us out of harm's way.

But we did not need to go all the way to Khost to study the toll the Taliban suicide bombers were taking on the Afghan people. As we pulled into the provincial capital of Gardez, we passed an Afghan National Army base entrance that had just been hit by a suicide bomber. While the bodies of the victims had already been taken away, the blackened detritus of the bombing was still plainly visible from the road. Just hours before, a Taliban terrorist had approached the entrance and blown himself and those around him to bits in a tactic that had come to define the Taliban insurgency.

When I interviewed locals—who were still traumatized by the attack—I began to understand the impact that a single bombing has on a community. As I talked to bewildered villagers who cursed the bombers as "bad Muslims who pervert Islam" or "enemies of Afghanistan," their shock and fear were palpable. It reminded me of the fear that had struck America when the so-called Beltway Sniper roamed the Washington, D.C., area in 2002 killing his innocent victims at random.

But that comparison only went so far because the Beltway Sniper had "only" killed ten people and had had a relatively brief run. In Afghanistan, hundreds of bombers have now detonated themselves seemingly at random in the midst of average Afghans going about their daily lives. There seemed to be no pattern to the killing, or so I thought when I first began my study. Hundreds were dying in the bloody carnage that seemed to be part of a cruel effort to destroy the very optimism that the war-weary Afghans have begun to tentatively build since 2001.

As I interviewed the angry and fearful people of Gardez, one old, turbaned elder asked me,

> How could this evil have come to us? What sort of humans blow themselves up among people trying to go about their lives? We never had these things before. Not even when the Soviets occupied our lands. What are these killers trying to achieve?

While I did not have the answer to his question of what motivated the suicide bombers or how this alien tactic had arrived in this land, I told the elder that *inshallah* (God willing) one day I would. The following is the result of my U.S. government–sponsored study to understand the mysterious origins, overall strategy, impact, and distinct Afghan trajectories of this deadly phenomenon. Among other things, this study points to one of the first examples of the so-called "Iraq effect" (i.e., the transfer of terror tactics from the Iraqi theater of action to other zones) and to a uniquely Afghan bombing campaign that, for all its Iraqi origins and inspiration, has its own distinctly Afghan targeting patterns.

"THE IRAQ EFFECT" COMES TO THE "FORGOTTEN WAR" IN AFGHANISTAN

Prior to the summer of 2005, conventional wisdom held that Afghanistan was "tamed" and that the Taliban fighters who were carrying out random terror attacks in the southern Pashtun tribal regions were "dead-enders." Having toppled the Taliban Emirate of Afghanistan in 2001 with a minimum of casualties, the victorious Americans could be forgiven for believing that the Taliban's days were over. And besides, all eyes were on Iraq. It was there that the "real" war on terror was unfolding. By 2005 the "Forgotten War" in Afghanistan had been relegated to Central Command's back burner as the U.S. military focused on the suppression of a surprisingly vicious insurgency in Iraq's Sunni Triangle.[3]

But in a demonstration of the law of unintended consequences, the Taliban, who had found refuge in the Pashtun tribal areas of neighboring Pakistan, took heart from the successes of their Iraqi counterparts. Al Qaeda operatives who made their way to the mountains of Pakistan's tribal zones from the deserts of Iraq's Anbar Province brought inspirational tales of the feats of Abu Musab Zarqawi's American-hunting Iraqi insurgents. Far from being invincible, they argued that the American "kafirs" (infidels) who had so disheartened the Taliban with their satellite-guided bombs, close air support, and "Beeping Joe Dos" (B-52s in the local dialect) could be beaten.

But the Al Qaeda emissaries warned that Afghanistan's "infidel occupiers" could not be beaten via frontal "swarm" attacks or traditional guerilla warfare of the sort favored by the Pashtun tribes who made up the majority of the Taliban.[4] The Taliban needed an equalizer, much as the anti-Soviet mujahideen had had with their Stinger ground-to-air-missiles in the 1980s. If the Taliban wanted to resist the might of the *Amriki* (Americans) they needed to use terrorism to level the playing field.

And nothing, the Arabs argued, was as effective in the pursuit of this goal as *fedayeen* (martyrdom) operations. The way to defeat the seemingly invincible American occupiers was by sending young men strapped with bombs into police stations, crowded markets, military checkpoints, police recruitment centers, and military convoys. The Al Qaeda Arabs claimed that these human "guided missiles" could infiltrate enemy positions and shred the fabric of the very society the Americans and their "*munafiq*" (apostate) "stooge puppets" were trying to build.

While the Arabs realized that the local Taliban had deep-seated taboos against suicide and such "un-manly" forms of warfare (the Taliban were predominately Pashtun tribesmen who had a well-defined code of honor and pride in their ability to wage frontal combat), this would have to change. The Arabs argued that those who engaged in martyrdom operations were not condemned to hell as "craven suicides." On the contrary, they were Allah's warriors, they were the true *gazis* (fighters of jihad) and their heroic actions were not only effective, they were sanctioned by the holy Qu'ran.

While the Taliban's reclusive spiritual head, Mullah Omar, was initially opposed to the employment of this "sinful" foreign tactic, many of his mid-level commanders, such as Mullah Dadullah, were willing to adopt it. They were especially willing after they were shown graphic DVDs of Iraqi insurgents using suicide bombings to kill Iraqi "collaborators" and Coalition troops in places like Baghdad, Baquba, and the Anbar Province.

By 2005, the first wave of Arab volunteers had infiltrated Afghanistan and had begun to strike at Coalition and Afghan government targets in an effort to teach their Afghan hosts *istishhad* (suicide) tactics. The lesson they taught was that even a few suicide bombings could have a profound destabilizing effect.

While the Arab bombers (and the first few Afghans) carried out no more than twenty-two attacks that first year, the impact these bombings had on the Afghans—who had never seen anything like it before—was tremendous. By killing International Security and Assistance Force (ISAF) troops, Afghan National Army soldiers, and even the police chief of Kabul, the bombers showed that no one who worked with the "infidel occupation" forces was safe.[5] As Western NGOs pulled out of areas that had been hit by suicide bombs and Coalition troops became skittish when on patrol, the Taliban celebrated the deaths of their enemies caused by what would ironically enough become known as "Mullah Omar's missiles."[6]

In response, by 2006 the Deobandi school of Islam practiced by the Taliban appears to have endorsed the previously forbidden tactic of suicide bombing. Soon thereafter scores of indigenous Afghans began to blow themselves up to kill "traitors," "infidels," "occupiers," "stooges," and most importantly, hundreds of innocent Afghans who were near these targets at the time of the attacks. Astoundingly, by year's end, the Taliban and their Al Qaeda allies had unleashed 139 suicide bombers on targets across Afghanistan. By 2007, the number would rise to 160. In just one year Afghanistan had gone from being a land that had never had a tradition of suicide bombings to being surpassed only by Iraq in sheer number of suicide attacks.[7]

This chapter is the result of my field research analyzing the process whereby Iraqi-style suicide bombing came to Afghanistan and took on uniquely Afghan features that sharply delineated it from the Iraqi bombing campaign. To understand this story, one must trace the gradual efforts by Al Qaeda in Iraq and Al Qaeda Central (the core group around Bin Laden in Pakistan) to graft this tactic and ideology onto the Taliban insurgency.

THE GATHERING STORM, 2002–2004

In the aftermath of the U.S.–led Coalition's overwhelmingly victory in 2001's Operation Enduring Freedom, much of the so-called "village Taliban" was destroyed or simply melted into the Afghan countryside. The hardcore Taliban, however, withdrew over the border into the Pashtun tribal regions of Pakistan to regroup. It was at this time that Mullah Dadullah, a Taliban hard-liner, Jalaladin Haqqani, a former mujahideen extremist, and several second-tier commanders, such as Nek Muhammad and Baitullah Mehsud, gradually took the lead in re-unifying the Taliban in the Federally Administered Tribal Agencies of Pakistan.[8]

In a short time, the Taliban had established *shuras* (councils) in Quetta, Baluchistan and Wana, Waziristan (a Pakistani Pashtun tribal agency) and given command of local operations to a variety of Taliban commanders. As in the earlier jihad against the Soviets, Arabs once again became a major source of funding for the jihad against the Coalition forces. Only on this occasion, the Arabs appear to have played a greater role as trainers and propaganda activists as well.[9] Both the Taliban and the Arabs shared a common goal of waging jihad against the infidel occupiers, even though the local Talibs were often taken aback by the Arab fighters' willingness to die.

In light of the symbolic importance Arabs place on Afghanistan, the land where Bin Laden and the first Arab mujahideen unit had their baptism of fire in the 1987 Battle of Jaji (Paktia Province), it is not surprising that they chose to assist the Taliban in resisting the formation of the pro-Western Karzai "puppet" government. That Al Qaeda chose suicide bombings as a tactical response to their joint defeat is even less surprising, considering the failures of the Taliban and allied Al Qaeda fighters (the so-called *Ansars* or "Supporters") to hold ground in frontal combat with Coalition forces. Both the Taliban and Al Qaeda had seen the devastating effect of U.S. close air support.

Al Qaeda's response to their enemies' overwhelming military superiority was to rely upon a tactic that was central to its overall strategy and ideology, *istishhad* (self-sacrifice). Stressing the premise that "we cherish death more than you cherish life," Al Qaeda began to promote the idea that it was the true Muslims' willingness to sacrifice themselves that gave them an advantage over the "weak-willed infidels." Yoram Schweitzer and Sari Goldstein Ferber have aptly summed up the importance of suicide attacks to Bin Laden's organization as follows:

> In Al-Qaeda, the sacrifice of life is a supreme value, the symbolic importance of which is equal to if not greater than its tactical importance. The organization adopted suicide as the supreme embodiment of global jihad and raised Islamic martyrdom (al shehada) to the status of a principle of faith. Al Qaeda leaders cultivated the spirit of the organization, constructing its ethos around a commitment to self-sacrifice and the implementation of this idea through suicide attacks. Readiness for self-sacrifice was one of

the most important characteristics to imbue in veteran members and new recruits.[10]

Despite initial reluctance from Taliban chief Mullah Omar, Al Qaeda had no problem in finding support among such increasingly important operational Taliban commanders as Dadullah and Haqqani for a campaign based on these Arab principles. By 2003, the Taliban field commanders were clearly interested in *any* strategy or tactic that allowed them to undermine the U.S.–backed Karzai government's claims to bring security to the long-suffering people of Afghanistan.

But there seems to be little evidence that the rank-and-file Pashtun-Taliban were willing recruits to suicide terrorism at this early stage. It would be up to Al Qaeda to legitimize the tactic and demonstrate the effectiveness of a taboo act that was as-yet alien to Pashtun.

Al Qaeda's 2002 Afghan suicide-bombing campaign began in the symbolically important capital of Kabul with two failed attempts on Afghan government targets. Al Qaeda subsequently launched three suicide attacks in 2003 against two government targets and a busload of German NATO troops. They followed this up with three attacks in 2004 against NATO troops.

I was in Kabul around the time of the attack on the German NATO troops in 2003, which killed six soldiers, and I remember it having an unsettling impact on both Afghans and foreigners in Afghanistan. But most people I met passed it off as the work of "die-hards" who could not halt the general trend of rebuilding. And from the Taliban's perspective there was actually still little at this stage to suggest that the suicide tactics most closely associated with the underdog Palestinians and Chechens resulted in any tangible benefits. On the contrary, suicide bombing seemed only to lead to more repression. Most recently it had actually cost Al Qaeda its state-within-a-state in Afghanistan following the 9/11 suicide attack.

But this perception would eventually change as a result of external factors related to another zone where suicide bombers were to subsequently demonstrate suicide bombing's effectiveness. Most notably, it was changed by developments in distant Iraq, a country that had by that time become a magnet for jihadi extremists across the Middle East.

THE IRAQI THEATER OF ACTION: TERRORISM'S NEW TESTING GROUND

As Al Qaeda's initial suicide-bombing campaign of 2002–2004 was tentatively playing out in Afghanistan, foreign fighters in Iraq (many of them linked to Abu Musab Zarqawi's group Tawid wal Jihad/Al Qaeda in Iraq) launched an insurgency that many counter-terrorism analysts felt had the potential to destabilize surrounding regions.[11] Afghan specialists in particular feared that the Iraqi jihadi incubator might undermine the progress in Afghanistan, a country that had become a showcase for the Bush administration.

Concerns increased when it became obvious that the Iraqi insurgents were intent on disseminating their cult of carnage to other zones where their "Muslim brothers" were fighting "unbelievers." It was known that many of the foreign jihadis in Iraq had direct ties to the core Al Qaeda group hiding out in Pakistan. It was also widely suspected that Al Qaeda operatives had begun to pass between these two theaters of action, sharing information, funds, strategies, and tactical information. And it soon became evident that Al Qaeda in Iraq had a lot to teach the defeated Taliban about insurgent tactics.

By the fall of 2003 the Iraqi insurgents had, for example, begun to employ suicide bombing on a scale and with a lethality not seen before in the Middle East. While the Coalition had proven unbeatable on the field of battle, there was little the Americans and their allies could do by 2004 to prevent suicide bombers from attacking a wide range of targets such as: a top UN representative in Baghdad, over a hundred Shiites and their leader Grand Ayatollah al-Hakim, U.S. intelligence headquarters in Irbil, the Turkish Embassy, the Red Cross, Kurdish party headquarters, U.S. military bases (including the headquarters of the 82nd Airborne Division in Ramadi), police stations, and an Italian compound in Nasariya.

The widespread calls for the withdrawal of Italian troops from Iraq that took place in Italy following the last-mentioned attack vividly demonstrated the impact that even one bombing could have on a weak Coalition government. Clearly this terror tactic worked from both a tactical perspective (as a leveler or equalizer) and a strategic viewpoint (as a powerful societal destabilizer and means to mobilize anti-war sentiment in Coalition countries).

And lest these lessons were lost on others, Zarqawi and his associates in Iraq launched an unprecedented media blitz, which saturated the Internet with "snuff" images of improvised explosive device (IED) and suicide bombing attacks on U.S. military targets that were previously deemed impregnable.[12] For extremists everywhere, Zarqawi's DVDs and online video images were electrifying and the era of the cyber-jihad began.

By the summer of 2004, jihad videos from Iraq that had been dubbed into Pashtun were readily available in the tribal areas of Pakistan. These kill DVDs were often spliced (presumably by techno-savvy Al Qaeda operatives) with scenes from Guantanamo Bay and images of U.S. "collateral damage" in Afghanistan. For the Taliban, who had been stunned by their horrific losses against a seemingly invincible enemy in 2001, the images of U.S. and Coalition targets being blown apart by Iraqi IEDs and suicide bombers in such DVDs as "Slaughter of the Americans in Iraq" were nothing if not inspirational.[13]

But the Taliban needed more "theater specific" videos with local content to inspire their followers to engage in the previously forbidden tactic of suicide bombing. To answer this need, an Al Qaeda operative named Abu Yahya al Libbi began producing jihad videos for Afghanistan based on the Iraqi models. These came to include such "hits" as "Holocaust of the Americans in Afghanistan," "Pyre for the Americans in Afghanistan," and "The Winds of Paradise."[14] The online versions of these videos soon came to include all the hallmarks of Iraqi DVDs, including images of Afghan bombers reading their last testaments and wills before blowing themselves up.

Another indicator of the borrowing of Iraqi horror tactics by the Taliban began to appear in the form of videotaped beheadings of the sort that had become Zarqawi's stock and trade. While the Taliban had banned the Internet from the Islamic Emirate of Afghanistan as recently as August 25, 2001, Al Qaeda had always been more media savvy and willing to use the Internet to broadcast its message.[15] By 2004, Al Libbi had convinced the Taliban to use this useful propaganda medium as Internet cafes sprung up in post-Taliban Afghanistan and the tribal areas of Pakistan.

In September of 2004, a Taliban Internet site known as Labaik posted a video of a gruesome beheading of a "Crusader spy" that appeared to be an imitation of Zarqawi's videotaped beheadings in Iraq. One commentator writing at the time wrote, "This latest video reveals how the practice of decapitation initiated by al-Zarqawi and, in the early days, resisted by the leadership of al-Qaeda, has reached Afghanistan."[16] This Iraqi-inspired trend eventually led to the unbearably gruesome 2007 beheading of an "infidel spy" by a twelve-year-old boy trained by Mullah Dadullah.[17]

Coalition forces also noticed an increase in the use of Iraqi-style IEDs in Afghanistan at this time. A Western military analyst claimed,

> The insurgency in Afghanistan has been very carefully studying the lessons learned by the insurgents in Iraq...We're starting to see more organized ambushes in Afghanistan and starting to see the sort of roadside bombs that previously we were just seeing in Iraq.[18]

Clearly the exiled Taliban government was morphing into a brutal terror group under the impact of a particularly virulent form of terrorism emanating from Iraq that was so bloody that even Ayman al Zawaheri (Al Qaeda Central's number two) originally resisted its macabre emphasis on butchery. And certainly the question of the destabilizing impact that the invasion of Iraq has had on the "Other War" in Afghanistan is one that is politically loaded in the United States.

Not surprisingly, many Afghans whose country was suffering from the bombing campaign shared this perspective. As one Afghan National Directorate of Security official put it to me in Kabul, "Had the Americans not invaded Iraq and created a jihadi training ground there, we would never have had these bombers here. This all comes to us as a result of America's war against [Saddam] Hussein."[19] The implication was that the U.S. invasion of Iraq directly contributed to the destabilization of his own country.

For this reason, members of the U.S. military whom I spoke with, including Lieutenant General Karl Eikenberry, commander of Combined Forces Command-Afghanistan, were loath to acknowledge any *direct* link between suicide bombing in Iraq and Afghanistan. In May of 2006, Eikenberry went so far as to claim, "We have not seen conclusive evidence that there has been any migration from Iraq to Afghanistan of foreign fighters that are bringing with them skills or capabilities."[20]

Up until 2007, many sources in the media unquestioningly parroted the U.S. military's agnostic approach, which continued to be that they had seen "no direct evidence of links between the insurgents in Iraq and in Afghanistan."[21] Radio Free Europe, for example, refuted the notion that there were any direct ties between Iraqi and Afghan insurgents claiming, "While the neo-Taliban have acknowledged that there are foreign fighters among their ranks, there is no evidence to suggest concerted co-operation between Al-Qaeda and neo-Taliban."[22]

But the rather coy words of the extremist Taliban commander, Mullah Dadullah, given in a subsequent interview to Al Jazeera, tell a different story. In light of their importance in pointing to *direct operational ties* between Iraqi insurgents—who perfected suicide bombing techniques by 2003—and those in Afghanistan who had never used this tactic, I have included Dadullah's interview here:[23]

> MULLAH DADULLAH: We like the Al-Qaeda organization. We consider it a friendly and brotherly organization, which shares our ideology and concepts. We have close ties and constant contacts with it. Our cooperation is ideal.

INTERVIEWER: Do you coordinate with them in military
                        operations in Afghanistan?
MULLAH DADULLAH: Yes, when we need them, we ask for their
                        help. For example, the bombings we carry
                        out—*we learned it from them* [emphasis
                        mine]. We learn other types of operations
                        from them as well. We have "give and take"
                        relations with the mujahideen of Iraq. We
                        cooperate and help each other.
INTERVIEWER: Did Arabs from Al-Qaeda participate in the
                        recent operations in south Afghanistan?
MULLAH DADULLAH: Some may have participated in the bombing
                        operations.
MULLAH DADULLAH: We may have sent our people to Iraq, and
                        [the Iraqis] may have sent their friends to
                        us. We have continuous contacts with them,
                        whether by phone or by other means. Some
                        of our brothers may have met them, and they
                        may have met with us too.
INTERVIEWER: Yes. Do you send people for training, for
                        example, do they come here for training,
                        or do you maintain contact through the
                        Internet?
MULLAH DADULLAH: We have training centers here in Afghani-
                        stan, and, as you know, they have their own
                        centers there. If we discover anything new,
                        they come here to learn it, and if they dis-
                        cover anything new, our friends go to learn it
                        from them.[24]

Pakistani journalist Syed Saleem Shahzad provided a more detailed
account of one such *direct* meeting between Al Qaeda in Iraq fighters
and Mullah Dadullah that took place in 2005:

In March a three-man delegation was sent by Abu Musab al-
Zarqawi (al-Qaeda's leader in Iraq) to Afghanistan, where they
met Osama bin Laden, Ayman Zawahiri and Mullah Omar...The
delegation brought audio and video material justifying suicide
attacks. There was no precedent for this in conservative, observant

Afghanistan: suicide is strictly prohibited in Islam. There had recently been a few suicide operations, but they were isolated incidents and never turned into an effective strategy.

Dadullah set out to win hearts and minds in order to develop an organized strategy of suicide attacks for the 2006 offensive. He showed audio and video material from the Iraqi resistance which explained that suicide attacks were permitted and demonstrated how the Iraqis used them as their most effective weapon. He managed to convince groups from Uzbekistan, Tajikistan and Pakistan, as well as Waziristan. A first group of 450 recruits came from the Kunar Valley...That was just the tip of the iceberg.[25]

While the U.S. military continued to deny that there was any evidence that Afghan bombers might be getting direct assistance or inspiration from their Iraqi counterparts, a *Newsweek* reporter managed to uncover the following proof of such ties during the following interview:

Mohammad Daud (a Taliban commander in the contested province of Ghazni) launches into a glowing account of where he spent the first few months of this year and what he's done since his return.

"I'm explaining to my fighters every day the lessons I learned and my experience in Iraq, I want to copy in Afghanistan the tactics and spirit of the glorious Iraqi resistance."

Daud and other Taliban leaders tell NEWSWEEK that the Afghan conflict is entering a new phase, with help from Iraq. According to them, Osama bin Laden has opened an underground railroad to and from jihadist training camps in the Sunni Triangle. Self-described graduates of the program say they've come home to Afghanistan with more-effective killing techniques and renewed enthusiasm for the war against the West. Daud says he's been communicating a "new momentum and spirit" to the 300 fighters under his command.

Worse yet, he says, there are "strong indications" that Al Qaeda has brought in a team of Arab instructors from Iraq to teach the latest insurgent techniques to the Taliban. "We have information that the Taliban have received new weapons and explosive devices," says a European diplomat who didn't want to be named because of the sensitivity of the subject, "most probably because of increased financial support from abroad and some traffic between Iraq and Afghanistan through Iran."

One beneficiary of Al Qaeda's renewed interest in Afghanistan is Hamza Sangari, a Taliban commander from Khost province... Sangari spent his time in Iraq being escorted to guerrilla bases in towns like Fallujah and Ramadi, and in remote desert regions. He says he was welcomed wherever he went. "I've never been so well received," he says. He was impressed with what he saw. "The Iraqi mujahedin are better armed, organized and trained than we are," he says. He stayed four weeks at a remote training camp called Ashaq al Hoor, he says, *where he saw adolescent boys being trained as suicide bombers* [emphasis mine].

The big worry is that studying Iraqi tactics will make the Afghan resistance significantly stronger and more lethal. During a recent sweep of pro-Taliban sites along the Afghan frontier in north Waziristan, Pakistani troops collected a mound of Arabic-language training manuals, apparently copies of the ones used by insurgents in Iraq. Sangari says he was impressed by way Iraqi insurgents created combat videos to help fund-raising and recruiting efforts; now similar videos of Taliban attacks are showing up in bazaars along the Pakistani border.[26]

Around this time, Dadullah was said to have issued bottles of holy *zamzam* water from Mecca to purify bombers and "transport them to paradise." A Taliban commander named Mullah Haq Yar, who had been dispatched to Iraq by Mullah Omar to learn the Iraqi insurgents' tactics, also returned at this time and began to carry out an insurgency strategy that resembled that of the Iraqis.[27]

The pieces were slowly being put into place for the indigenous Afghan militants to begin a campaign that would deploy "human guided missiles" against "infidel" targets across Afghanistan. In one of the most unexpected turns of the war on terror, far from acting as a catalyst for democratization, Iraq had become a disseminator for new forms of insurgent terrorism that were about to make their impact felt in the "Forgotten War."

2005: THE CAMPAIGN BEGINS

While the 2005 campaign started out tentatively with an attempt to kill the horse-riding Northern Alliance Uzbek warlord General Rashid Dostum with a suicide attack, Afghanistan suffered its first Iraqi-style mass casualty bombing on June 1. That bombing, which killed twenty-one people (including the Kabul police chief) in a mosque in the Taliban's spiritual capital of Kandahar, stunned average Afghans. Many considered the fact that the bombing had happened in a place of worship to be blasphemous. One of my Kandahari sources described it as "an obscenity, an insult to Islam."

Perhaps as a result of this negative reaction, the Taliban denied involvement in the blast.[28] While it is impossible to say whether the Taliban approved of this particular mosque bombing (which might have been carried out by Al Qaeda), it proudly took credit for the bombing spree that shook the country in the following months. Space does not permit an analysis of all the subsequent bombings of 2005, but my study shows that suicide bombers struck Afghan government targets nine times and foreign troops eight times before the year was over. Government targets included provincial governors, a polling station, an election oversight body in Kabul, a local police commander, and the parliament building in western Kabul. In other words, exactly the same sort of targets being hit by suicide bombers in Iraq. *But with one notable exception.* Apart from the Kandahar mosque bombing (which local officials believed was carried out by an Arab), there were no targeted killings of crowds of innocent civilians of the sort that had begun to shred the fabric of society in Iraq (e.g., bombings of crowded bazaars, schools, bread-lines, religious festivals, etc.).

It was the comparatively low number of civilian targets that first led me to conclude that Taliban suicide bombers were acting on a completely different set of targeting principles than their Iraqi counterparts. It became increasingly apparent that, for some reason, the Taliban suicide bombers were more selective in their targeting patterns than the Iraq-based bombers. Far from going for "soft" civilian targets, the Taliban seemed to going for more difficult "hard" military targets.

When I pointed this trend out to Pashtun colleagues they explained that this targeting was more emblematic of the Pashtuns' martial code (known as Pashtunwali), which does not condone the killing of civilians. The Taliban's Pashtun-style attacks on hard targets included bombing strikes on U.S. convoys in Helmand and Kandahar provinces, Afghan National Army (ANA) convoys in Kandahar, and a NATO convoy in Kabul.

But for all the fear they inspired, the bombings of 2005 were clearly a means to test the waters and perfect the technique. It was not until 2006 that the Taliban were finally prepared to unleash a full-scale bombing offensive that would see waves of "human guided missiles" go after an increasing array of targets. In the process, Afghans would begin to die in the hundreds as the "collateral damage" of a bloody campaign that impacted Afghans of all walks of life in an increasingly broad swath of Afghan territory in the south-east.

2006: THE *ANNUS HORRIBILIS*

The new year began with a failed suicide bombing in Kandahar (January 5), which was followed by a suicide-bombing assassination attempt on the U.S. ambassador during a visit to local leaders in Tirin Kot, Uruzgan Province. Proving the maxim that suicide bombing usually results in more civilian than military deaths despite the "best" of intentions, on this occasion the suicide bomber missed his target but *killed ten civilians* and wounded fifty. But at least the Taliban were able to claim that they were trying to kill a high-ranking American, not civilians.

No such claim could be made of the attack on a wrestling match in the Pakistani-Afghan border town of Spin Boldak, Kandahar Province on January 16, 2006. This bloody bombing proved to be Afghanistan's worst attack in terms of civilian casualties thus far. What made this attack so "un-Afghan" is that the suicide bomber seemingly targeted a crowd of innocent civilians with no government or military targets in the immediate vicinity. For all intents and purposes, the Spin Boldak massacre, which killed twenty-three innocent spectators watching a traditional Afghan wrestling match, had all the hallmarks of an Iraqi-style suicide bombing.

The response of the local Afghans to this bloody outrage seemed to catch the Taliban by surprise. Local Afghans closed their stores and marched to protest the slaughter of so many of their countrymen who were engaged in one of Afghanistan's most beloved pastimes. The attack, which led marchers in Spin Boldak to chant "Death to Pakistan, Death to Al Qaeda, Death to the Taliban," was clearly a public relations disaster for the Taliban/Al Qaeda in a tribal region where chants of "Death to America" were more the norm.[29]

While the Taliban initially claimed responsibility for the bombing (as they had with all previous bombings in Kandahar Province), it is noteworthy that they subsequently denied involvement in this unpopular attack. Although one can see the Taliban's denial of responsibility as damage control, the fact that the nature of the target differed so drastically from the Taliban's *modus operandi* (i.e., a tendency to go after hard military/government targets) might lend some credence to their claim. My study clearly shows that the Taliban had avoided this sort of bombing for fear of losing support among fellow Afghans who might be "on the fence." It is probable, therefore, that the suicide bomber who struck in Spin Boldak was not an indigenous Afghan (i.e., someone who would have qualms about killing so many of his countrymen). Rather, he was a foreign Arab-Salafite extremist who would have found an "un-Islamic" activity like a traditional wrestling match to be an affront to his puritan beliefs. I have attended these sorts of events in Afghanistan and have found that local Afghans usually bet on the outcome. Strict Wahhabi fundamentalists from the Arab Gulf States consider any form of gambling to be *haram* (religiously forbidden) and viscerally dislike such "sinful" activities.

For their part many locals speculated that the horrific bombing had to be the work of outsiders. One source claimed, "I think suicide bombings across Afghanistan are the work mainly of Arabs...At times they are accompanied by Pakistanis." Another Afghan claimed that, "regardless of their nationality, suicide bombers should be condemned as cowards...if suicide bombers were 'real men,' they would come out and fight openly."[30]

Clearly chastised by the widespread disgust that the bombing had called forth, the Taliban appeared to have learned their lesson from the Spin Boldak incident. While my study shows that there were a stunning 139 suicide bombings in Afghanistan for the year 2006, *there was only one suicide bombing against what patently appeared to be civilian targets that year*. All the other bombings in the terrible campaign of 2006 were against hard military-government targets.

That is not, however, to say that the Taliban did not kill scores of innocent bystanders as "collateral damage." On the contrary, my studies show that for all their efforts to avoid civilian casualties, *it is innocent Afghans who indisputably suffered the most deaths from the 2006 suicide bombing campaign* (only fourteen foreign soldiers were killed by suicide bombers in 2006).

This high rate of "collateral damage" stems in part from stepped-up defensive procedures on the part of the Coalition troops and Afghan government. While I was able to photograph "soft skinned" (i.e., unarmored) U.S. Humvees on the roads of Afghanistan in the summer of 2003, by the summer of 2005 I noticed that they had begun to be replaced by heavily armored versions. Having learned the terrible lessons of Iraq, where 80 percent of U.S. casualties came from IEDs, Coalition forces in Afghanistan had begun to deploy heavily armored LAVs (light armored vehicles) by the time the Afghan suicide bombing campaign began.

Such armored vehicles were able to deflect much of the blast power of suicide bombings and allow those inside to survive many attacks (especially those carried out by bombers on foot who carry far less explosives than vehicle-borne improvised explosive devices [VBIEDs]). But the civilians in the vicinity of the attacks had no such protection. In numerous instances suicide bombers driving VBIEDs plowed into Coalition convoys on crowded streets and the explosion, shrapnel, or burning car ricocheted off their armor into bystanders. On other occasions, suicide bombers on foot trying to infiltrate Afghan government targets were caught up in stepped-up security procedures. When they were apprehended, they blew themselves up in lines of civilian workers trying to enter through checkpoints.

An analysis of the major bombings for 2006 clearly reveals the outlines of this trend: On August 3, a suicide bomber drove his car into a Canadian ISAF convoy killing six soldiers and *nineteen civilians* (Kandahar). Then on August 28, a BBIED (body borne improvised explosive device) bomber blew himself up next to a former police chief and killed the chief and *sixteen civilians* and wounded forty-seven more (Lashkar Gah, Helmand). On September 8, a suicide bomber blew himself up next to a U.S. convoy and killed two U.S. soldiers and *sixteen civilians* (Kabul). On September 18, a suicide bomber struck at a U.S. convoy and killed two policemen and *thirteen civilians* (Kabul). On the very same day, a suicide bomber tried assassinating the Deputy Head of Police for Herat and succeeded in killing four policemen and *seven civilians* (Herat).

As the rampage year continued, on September 26 a suicide bomber aiming for the governor of Helmand killed nine soldiers and *nine civilians* (Lashkar Gah). Finally, on September 29 a suicide bomber who was noticed by guards in a line of workers as he attempted to infiltrate the Interior Ministry set off his bomb prematurely and killed *twelve civilians* (Kabul). The mayhem continued on October 13 as a suicide bomber who hit a U.S. convoy killed one ISAF soldier and *eight civilians*. The year ended on December 7 when a suicide bomber bounced off a U.S. military convoy, killing no U.S. soldiers, but slaughtering *fourteen civilians*.[31]

When I broke down the civilian-to-military death ratio from bombings for 2006, I found that Afghan suicide bombers, *who were targeting government or military targets in every one of these incidents,* actually succeeded in killing 114 civilians and only 25 government-military targets (i.e., 4.6 civilians for every military-government target).

But clearly there was more to the Taliban's terrible success rate than the logistic difficulties involved in trying to take out hard military targets that were protected by armor, sandbags, and blast barriers. In fact, by 2006 another tendency became noticeable as well. My study found a bizarre trend wherein dozens of Taliban suicide bombers (in some months the majority) succeeded in killing only themselves! The high rate of victimless bombings led me to question whether or not the suicide bombers were engaging in suicide bombing...*or suicide?*[32]

TALIBAN FEDAYEEN: THE WORLD'S WORST SUICIDE BOMBERS?

As I analyzed the circumstances behind each and every suicide bombing for 2001–2007, I noticed that time and again Taliban suicide bombers exploded their bombs prematurely and killed themselves and no one else. This trend was to culminate in the first weeks of 2007, when I recorded nineteen bombings from January to the end of February.[33] Astoundingly, of these nineteen bombings, the suicide bomber was apprehended or killed in three instances and *on twelve other occasions succeeded in killing only himself.* In two bombings the bomber killed only one person other than himself, and in only two bombings out of nineteen did the suicide bomber kill more than one victim. Hardly an inspiring kill ratio.

Such underwhelming statistics stood in stark contrast to Iraq, where the kill ratio was much higher (it is common for Iraqi suicide bombers to kill more than sixty people per bombing). These statistics also beg the question that I asked Afghan National Directorate of Security (NDS) leader, Yama Karzai: "Why are Afghanistan's suicide bombers so uniquely incapable of hitting their targets....with *bombs?*"

Mr. Karzai and several Afghan National Police (ANP) commanders whom I interviewed offered a most unexpected explanation that seemed to account for much of the Afghan suicide bombing failures. ANP commanders whom I interviewed spoke of arresting bombers who were often mentally unsound, deranged, or retarded.[34] Western journalists and observers have similarly written of a suicide attack by a disabled man whose only motivation was the promise of payments for his family in exchange for mounting an attack. This was also the case of bombers who were invalids and one who was blind and an amputee.[35]

Far from being elite, "white-collar" terrorists like the 9/11 hijacking team, one Afghan official has claimed that, "at least three of every five [Afghan] bombers suffer from a physical ailment or disability. Adding those who suffer from mental illnesses, the number of sick and disabled bombers climbs to more than 80 percent."[36]

My own findings backed these sorts of claims. While I was initially skeptical of the NDS' claims (all too often victims of suicide bombing are prone to dismiss the bombers as "deranged," "fanatical," "on drugs," or "brainwashed"), I found overwhelming evidence to support the theory that Afghanistan's bombers were uniquely "challenged."[37]

While it is increasingly accepted by the intelligence community that suicide bombers are not brainwashed dupes, but rather intelligent self-conscious actors like the 9/11 suicide team commander Mohammad Atta, my field work in the Afghan theater points to an entirely different paradigm. This Afghan paradigm points to the existence of a poor quality of bomber that are in a much lower class than bombers found in other Islamic zones where bombing campaigns have taken place.

One source from the U.S. military stationed at Bagram Air Base described an incident that exemplifies this trend. He shared his story of a case where a teenaged suicide bomber threw his explosive-filled bomb vest at a U.S. patrol, wrongly assuming it would explode on impact. Afghan National Police sources say they have had several calls where concerned citizens had discovered abandoned suicide vests on the streets of Kabul, perhaps indicating a last-minute change of heart in potential suicide bombers.

In a similar incident, Craig Harrison, head of security for the UN mission in Afghanistan, told me of an instance where an Afghan employee came to him saying he had noticed strange wiring in a car that had run out of gas on his way to work. He grew suspicious after helping the car's driver push the car for a while and came to warn his UN employers. When the police arrived on the scene with guns drawn they found the suicide car bomber *pushing* his car toward his target![38]

In another case that was widely reported as the second of its kind in a week, a suicide bomber on his way to his target stumbled leaving his house and set off his bomb prematurely, killing himself and wounding two passersby.[39] But the most interesting case involved a group of five terrorists who were preparing their VBIED when it accidentally went off, killing them all in January of 2008.[40] Another story I heard from a UN source involves a suicide bomber who pulled up to a gas station driving a VBIED. When the gas station attendant saw a strange device in the car, he and another worker tackled the bomber, fought with him to prevent him from detonating his device in a packed gas station, and eventually subdued him. In this instance the bomber failed simply because he forgot to fill his car up with gas in advance. U.S. military and ISAF seem to agree that Afghan suicide bombers are far more incompetent than their Iraqi counterparts who have effectively used elaborate bombs to kill over a hundred people on many occasions. The fact that the Taliban are deliberately using those who are mentally unsound or of limited intelligence might help explain this phenomenon.

What follows is a typical military account that highlights the Afghan suicide bombers' strange failures:

> When an 18-year-old from Pakistan dismounted his bicycle a couple of kilometers outside the eastern town of Khost, his clothes flapped up, revealing a suicide vest to an alert farmer nearby. Police soon surrounded the teenager and ordered him to remove his vest. He refused, grew increasingly agitated and eventually blew himself up, said Yaqoub Khan, police criminal director for Khost province. No one else was hurt.

> [On another occasion] a suicide attacker waited on a roadside in eastern Paktika province, apparently biding his time for a target to appear. When an Afghan army convoy approached, the bomber blew himself up—several meters ahead of the vehicles, said Gov. Mohammad Akram Akhpelwak. He caused no injuries or damage.

> The nature of these two would-be suicide bombers' deaths is strikingly common in Afghanistan. Maj. Luke Knittig, a spokesman for NATO's International Security Assistance Force, said NATO commanders have noticed how often suicide attacks in Afghanistan fail. "We have certainly noticed that there have been

a fair number that are pretty poorly executed and bungled, and of course they're all ill-conceived," he said.

A U.S. military spokesman, Lt. Col. Paul Fitzpatrick, said that commanders do see trained, planned maneuvers in the field, but that many Taliban attacks fail because of a lack of experience. "Certainly there are a fair number of failed attempts, and that's OK," he said. "I hope they don't get better."[41]

When combined with a propensity to go after hard targets, such as fast-moving, heavily armored convoys or guarded installations, the unskilled nature of the Taliban bombers have led to a comparatively ineffective bombing campaign. But I found something even more disturbing that accounted for much of the shocking ineptitude in Afghanistan's bombers—namely the Taliban's reliance on boys as young as six years old to carry out their "martyrdom operations."

AFGHANISTAN'S CHILD BOMBERS

My work in the Pashtun areas east of Kabul led me to the conclusion that many young Afghan boys go to Pakistan for *madrassa* (seminary) training, often without their parents' permission. There they join young Pashtun lads from the Pakistani tribal regions in search of adventure, a sense of religious mission, and prestige. They are also taught to emulate those who die in the fight for the faith and to reject what few pleasures they do have in this world for the pleasures of the next. Fed on a diet of jihad, hatred for the infidels, and DVDs depicting the horrors of the foreign invasion of Afghanistan, these poor young men provide the perfect human material for "Mullah Omar's missiles."

Those who are "honored" by being chosen for suicide bombing missions are isolated from their peers and indoctrinated, then transported to their target. They are told that their family will receive a reward of up to $15,000 for their "martyrdom." Added incentive comes in the form of "passes to paradise" that Dadullah was filmed handing out to suicide bombers-in-waiting in a cave in Pakistan.[42]

The following case of two young Pakistani Pashtuns who left school without their parents' permission to become suicide bombers sheds light on the recruitment process for Afghan suicide bombers and might help explain why they yield such poor results on hard targets:

> "We were told to fight against Israel, America and non-Muslims," said Muhammed Bakhtiar, 17, explaining why he wanted to become a suicide bomber. "We are so unhappy with our lives here. We have nothing," he said.
>
> "We read about jihad in books and wanted to join," said Ahmad. "We wanted to go to the Muridke madrassa so we would have a better life in the hereafter."
>
> "We were told it is our choice to become a freedom fighter or a suicide bomber," explained Ahmad, who had a neat beard and wore a white Muslim prayer cap. "But we should never fight against Pakistan."
>
> "The jihadi man who brought us to Muridke told us we would become great by fighting jihad," said the clean-shaven Bakhtiar. "We knew we could never become great if we stayed in Buner. I wanted to become great."
>
> [But] the tribal elders intervened and now Bakhtiar and Ahmad are back in school in Buner. "My brother and my uncle found me in Lahore," said Bakhtiar. "The people at Muridke let us leave and said we could come back after we finished our exams at home," he said. But we asked them, "Do you want to go back and learn jihad?" "I don't know," said Bakhtiar. "Maybe, maybe." Ahmad agreed. "There is nothing for us here. Nothing."[43]

I heard a similar story while meeting with UN officials in Gardez, Paktia Province in the aftermath of the bombing (described at the beginning of this chapter) that had taken place just a few hours earlier. Local Pashtun villagers told me that young men had been disappearing in neighboring Khost Province after receiving funding from the Taliban to fight against Coalition troops. The parents had little recourse in getting their sons back. On the contrary, they often came to hear that their sons had been killed only when the Taliban arrived at their house with money to congratulate them on the "martyrdom" of their boys. In one tragic case, a mother found out that her son had returned from a *madrassa* in Pakistan with the intent of becoming a suicide bomber (his family would have received $3,600). When she desperately fought with him to prevent him from carrying out his mission, his bomb went off, killing her and three of his siblings.[44]

While Mullah Nazir, a powerful Taliban leader in Pakistan's Waziristan provinces recently made an unprecedented request for the Taliban to stop recruiting children, a video of a suicide bomber ceremony in the region would seem to indicate that his appeal has been honored in the breach. In the video that was obtained by ABC, boys as young as twelve are shown "graduating" from a suicide bombing camp run by Mullah Dadullah Mansour, the successor to Mullah Dadullah, who was killed in May 2007.

As disturbing as this video is, it pales in comparison to the discovery Afghan security officials recently made in eastern Afghanistan. In an incident that caused tears of fury among local villagers, a six-year-old street urchin approached an Afghan security checkpoint and claimed that he had been cornered by the Taliban and fitted with a suicide bomber vest. They had told him to walk up to a U.S. patrol and press a button on the vest that would "spray flowers." Fortunately, the quick-thinking boy instead asked for help, and the suicide bomb vest was subsequently removed.

While this case is obviously an extreme example, it fits the trend and certainly goes a long way in helping to explain why almost half of Taliban suicide bombers succeed in killing only themselves. Many Taliban bombers come from small backwater villages and have to be taught how to drive on strange roads, travel beyond their locale or country, and hit fast-moving, armored coalition convoys with improvised explosives. Even at the best of times, suicide bombing is a task that involves considerable resolve, determination, focus, and a degree of intelligence. Clearly, such vital ingredients are often missing in the Afghan context, where many of the bombers appear to be as much victims as perpetrators.

This sort of tragedy has created a certain level of tension between the Taliban and local tribes. On one occasion a local chieftain in Khost threatened to attack the Taliban with his entire tribe when he discovered that Taliban commander Jalaludin Haqqani had taken his son for a suicide mission. Bloodshed was averted only when the chieftain's son was returned with the admonishment that his father had denied him the chance to become a martyr.[45]

I collected many such stories and it seems that the Taliban have been actively preying on young men who are brought to *madrassas* and convinced that suicide bombing offers them a route to honor and the pleasures of paradise. Although the Taliban claims to have "hundreds" if not "thousands" of suicide bombers prepared to attack "infidels" in Afghanistan are exaggerated, they do seem to have a large recruitment pool made up of impressionable Pashtun youth on both sides of the border.

But I suspect that many of these young indoctrinated Pashtuns might have qualms about killing innocent fellow Afghan Muslims, especially if they are carrying out the bombings with the aim of acquiring much needed financial payments for their impoverished families. This might help explain why so many Afghan suicide bombers detonate their bombs prematurely and succeed in killing only themselves.

In one case that would seem to exemplify this trend, a suicide bomber with a bomb strapped on his waist approached security officials and asked for help in removing it.[46] As he tried to take his bomb off, it detonated, killing him. One can extrapolate from such tragedies and infer that many of the suicide bombers who kill only themselves are doing so not just because they are incompetent or up against hard military targets, but because they are genuinely reluctant to kill others.

All these factors work to mitigate a bombing campaign that could have been far worse and taken on the proportions found in Iraq, where thousands of civilians have been deliberately targeted by suicide bombers. For all the havoc the Afghan bombers indisputably wreak, it seems that (through incompetence or choice) they are not taking the same toll on innocent civilians that their Iraqi counterparts have been. While the bombing inspiration and training clearly came from Iraq, the Taliban campaign reflects the unique culture of the Pashtuns, which has strict taboos on killing innocents.

Or so my findings led me to believe by the time I finished up my field research in fifteen of Afghanistan's provinces in May of 2007. As I ended my expedition, which had been timed to coincide with the Taliban's much touted spring offensive, I was confident that my findings had highlighted a little-noticed facet of the Taliban campaign that sharply delineated it from the Iraqi campaign.

But in the month after I left, this paradigm began to shift. It was at this time that the Taliban appeared to shed their concerns about killing civilians and began to unleash a new wave of mass-casualty bombings. The little comfort I and countless average Afghans had previously taken from the fact that the Taliban bombers were not setting out to deliberately kill unarmed civilians was to be taken away.

IRAQI-STYLE MASS BOMBING COMES TO AFGHANISTAN

The first signal of an increasingly deadly campaign came in June 2007 when a Taliban bomber boarded a bus carrying policemen in Kabul and detonated an unprecedentedly powerful explosive. The ensuing explosion tore the bus apart and killed thirty-five policemen on board.[47] While there had previously been a couple of bombings in Afghanistan that had surpassed twenty deaths (most notably the bombing of the wrestling match in Spin Boldak and the attack on Baghram Air Base during Vice President Cheney's visit), this was the first bombing to kill over thirty.

This attack was followed by a similarly powerful attack on a bus carrying Afghan soldiers in Kabul in September of 2007 that left thirty dead. These two unexpectedly powerful attacks left the Afghans reeling, but at least they fit the earlier Taliban pattern of hitting hard military targets.

But this pattern too was to change decisively with a deadly Iraqi-style bombing on a civilian-packed event held in the town of Baghlan, northern Afghanistan, in December 2007. This bombing massacre was carried out at the inaugural opening of a sugar plant attended by scores of local students, parliamentarians, and workers. Between ninety and one hundred people were killed in a bombing that left dozens of its victims, including six parliamentarians, dead.[48] Tragically, the vast majority of the victims were actually schoolboys who had come to the event with their teachers, five of whom were also killed in the explosion. Many of these innocents were killed by the bomb, which was packed with hundreds of ball-bearings, a tactic that was previously rare in Afghanistan. The sickening carnage caused nationwide mourning and seemed to demonstrate that the Taliban were losing their sensitivity to the issue of collateral damage. Clearly the Taliban had decided that the destabilizing effects of mega-bombings outweighed the negative publicity that came from such slaughters.

This point was vividly driven home when the Taliban launched another mass-casualty suicide bombing attack in a crowd of spectators gathered to watch a dog fight in Kandahar in February 2008. As many as 100 were killed in this attack, which appeared to be aimed at a pro-Karzai militia commander. Once again many of the victims were innocent spectators (although the militia commander and thirty-five of his followers were also killed in the horrific explosion). The following day, a Taliban bomber crashed into a Canadian ISAF convoy in Kandahar and killed thirty-eight bystanders with another unusually powerful explosive. The Taliban, it seemed, had taken off the gloves and were now waging full-scale Iraqi-style suicide bombing warfare in Afghanistan.

The rising death toll was caused in part by the Taliban's decision to use much more powerful bombs. Explosives experts attributed the increasing carnage not just to such improvisations as adding ball bearings and other forms of shrapnel to the bombs, but to the terrorists' use of a highly explosive C-4 compound. At the time, a Taliban spokesman hinted at more carnage to come when he proclaimed, "All these bombs are stronger than before, this is because of the growing experience of our jihadi fighters…We will continue to make these kinds of bombs to attack our enemies with."[49] Fearful Afghans seemed to realize that the Taliban were now increasing the lethality of their bombs and putting aside concerns about the negative fall-out from their attacks. One Afghan professor claimed,

The attacks show that the enemies of Afghanistan are changing their tactics. Now they are not thinking about civilians at all. They wanted to cause such big casualties in these attacks to weaken the morale of the government and the international community, to show the world the Afghan government is too weak to prevent them.[50]

Further large-casualty civilian attacks included the January 14, 2008, suicide bombing attack on the Serena Hotel in Kabul and the July 7, 2008, Indian Embassy bombing, also in Kabul, which killed fifty-eight. The second bombing seems to have been organized by the Taliban with the help of Pakistan's notorious Inter Services Intelligence and may point to a Pakistani hand in the increased suicide-bombing violence.

But it was not just Afghanistan that began to suffer from a savage new wave of Taliban suicide bombings. By 2007, Pakistan, a country that had like its Afghan neighbor been largely spared from this scourge, began to experience a bloody wave of bombings. These appeared to be directed for the most part by a Taliban commander named Baitullah Mehsud who had close ties to Al Qaeda. And if anything the bombings in Pakistan have been deadlier than those in Afghanistan.

By year's end Pakistan had suffered as many as fifty suicide-bombing attacks, including a massive attack on former Prime Minister Benazir Bhutto's convoy that killed approximately 150 but missed its primary target, and a later one that succeeded in killing her. The suicide bombers in Pakistan seemed to have had less compunction about killing civilians and struck at political rallies, religious festivals, hotels, funerals, *jirgas* (tribal meetings), and other soft targets. This especially holds true for Shiite civilian targets, which were hit in large numbers from 2002 to 2006. But still, the overall trend I have noticed in Pakistan is (the Shiite targeting and attacks on Bhutto and the recent Marriott bombing aside) a tendency to aim for hard army, police, or government targets, just not as pronounced as in Afghanistan. The Pakistani bombers also have a higher death rate from their bombings than their Afghan counterparts.

As in neighboring Afghanistan, the Pakistani bombings demonstrate that *fedayeen* suicide tactics have entered the military culture of the

Pakistani Taliban extremists and have become a weapon of choice for destabilizing the government. For Al Qaeda and the radical wing of the Taliban, which coalesced around such extremists as Mullah Dadullah and Baitullah Mehsud's Pakistani Taliban Movement, these developments represent a clear victory over the Taliban moderates. And this development has unsettling ramifications for a region that is home to nuclear weapons, thousands of Taliban fighters, and Bin Laden's Al Qaeda Central.

As a new generation of Taliban insurgents puts aside their cultural compunctions against killing innocent civilians, the inroads made by the Iraqi-inspired terrorists become more permanent and may one day threaten the West. Each and every one of "Mullah Omar's missiles" sends the message that the Taliban have not forgotten the "Forgotten War" in Afghanistan nor the new war in Pakistan. Before his May 2007 death, Mullah Dadullah showed that he was all too aware of the long-term strategic implications of the Taliban's adoption of "martyrdom" tactics when he triumphantly proclaimed, "The Americans have sown a seed. They will reap the crop for quite a long time."[51]

ENDNOTES

1. IED (improvised explosive device).
2. For photographs from this and other journeys in Afghanistan, see my Web site at www.brianglynwilliams.com (under "Field Research").
3. The U.S. had shipped Predator drones, elite special forces, and other resources to Iraq, leaving a small force of U.S. soldiers in Afghanistan, a Texas-sized, mountainous country that is considerably larger than Iraq.
4. The Taliban insurgents took huge losses from 2004–2006 when they attempted to wage frontal combat with the technologically superior Coalition forces.
5. The Taliban and Al Qaeda subsequently tried to launch terror attacks against Spanish targets (Taliban commander Baitullah Mahsud) and German targets to punish them for providing troops to NATO in Afghanistan. See: "Was Baitullah Mahsud Behind the Spanish Terror Operation?" and "German Intelligence Describes a 'New Quality' in Jihadi Threats," *Terrorism Monitor* 5, no. 7 (February 20, 2008).
6. Mulah Omar continued to publicly make calls for the Taliban to avoid killing civilians, but he seems to have come to the conclusion that suicide bombings' benefits outweighed its drawbacks.
7. Iraq continued to surpass Afghanistan in total numbers of attacks and actually reached sixty-seven in one month. "One Month's Toll in Iraq: 67 Suicide Bombers," *Guardian*, May 12, 2005.
8. This mountainous Pashtun region had never been incorporated as a proper part of Pakistan. Rather, it was run by government-appointed agents who acted as intermediaries with the largely autonomous Pashtun tribes.
9. Brian Glyn Williams. "The Return of the Arabs. Al Qa'ida's Military Role in the Afghan Insurgency," *West Point Combating Terrorism Center Sentinel* 1, no. 3 (February 2008).
10. Yoram Schweitzer and Sari Goldstein Ferber. *Al Qaeda and the Internationalization of Suicide Terrorism*, The Jaffee Center for Strategic Studies, Tel Aviv, Memorandum no. 78 (November 2005): 26.
11. For the destabilizing impact of Iraq, see Brian Glyn Williams, "The Failure of al Qaeda Basing Projects from Afghanistan to Iraq," in *Denial of Sanctuary. Understanding Terrorist Safe Havens*, ed. Michael Innes (London: Praeger, 2007).
12. One has only to go to www.youtube.com and type in the words "jihad Iraq" to see how effective the Iraqi insurgents have been in exploiting this medium.

13. "Underground Jihad Videos in Pakistan Thrive on Beheadings, Hangings," *Vital Perspective*, http://vitalperspective.typepad.com/vital_perspective_clarity/2006/05/underground_jih.html.

14. See Al Qaida al Jihad's surprisingly sophisticated Afghan video at http://www.liveleak.com/view?i=184_1201720200.

15. "Taliban Enlist Video in Fight for Afghanistan," National Public Radio, *All Things Considered*, November 2, 2006. Online at http://www.npr.org/templates/story/story.php?storyId=6423946. For the Taliban bomber's testimony, see Hekmat Karzai, "The Logic of Afghan Suicide Bombing," *IDSS Commentary* (March 27, 2006).

16. "Beheading Video Reveals Zarqawi's Touch," *Afghanistan Watch* (January 6, 2006). Online at http://www.afghanistanwatch.org/newsletterarchive/listserv 1-6-06.htm.

17. "Child Be-Heading Uncensored," *Jawa Report* (May 24, 2007). Online at http://mypetjawa.mu.nu/archives/188003.php.

18. "Improvised Explosives. A Growing Menace in Afghanistan," Canadian Broadcast Channel, April 25, 2006.

19. Interview carried out with National Directorate of Security official in NDS headquarters, Kabul, April 2007.

20. Pamela Hess. "Taliban Regrouping in Southern Afghanistan," UPI, May 10, 2006.

21. Ibid.

22. For more on the Iraqi origins of Afghan suicide bombing see, Brian Glyn Williams, "Afghan Suicide Bombing," *Jane's Islamic Affairs Analyst* (August 13, 2007). Available under "Publications" at brianglynwilliams.com.

23. It should be noted that neither the Afghan mujahideen freedom fighters of the 1980s nor the pre–War on Terror Taliban used suicide bombing.

24. "Taliban Military Commander Mullah Dadallah: We Are in Contact With Iraqi Mujahideen, Osama bin Laden & Al-Zawahiri," *Middle East Media Research Institute. Special Dispatch Series* No. 1180 (June 2, 2006). Online at http://memri.org/bin/articles.cgi?Page=archives&Area=sd&ID=SP118006.

25. Syed Saleem Shahzad. "Taliban Resurgence in Afghanistan," *Le Monde Diplomatique* (September 2006).

26. Ron Moreau. "Terrorism: An Iraq-Afghan Alliance? The Taliban haven't quit, and some are getting help and inspiration from Iraq," *Newsweek*, September 18, 2005.

27. Syed Saleem Shahzad. "Osama Adds Weight to Afghan Resistance," *Asia Times*, September 11, 2004.

28. James Rupert. "20 Dead in Suicide Bomb at Mosque," *Peace Corps On-Line*, June 1, 2005. Online at http://peacecorpsonline.org/messages/ messages/467/2032507.html.

29. "Afghans Protest at Bomb Attacks," BBC.co.uk, January 18, 2006.

30. "Afghanistan: Are Militants Copying Iraqi Insurgents' Suicide Tactics?" Radio Free Europe/Radio Liberty, January 17, 2006.

31. There was also a suicide bombing in Urgun, Paktika (November 26, 2006) province aimed at a district police chief and Afghan special force commander that killed fifteen people. I have been unable to obtain specifics on the casualties, although most accounts claim that it was a mixture of civilians and militiamen.

32. Brian Glyn Williams. "Taliban Fedayeen. The World's Worst Suicide Bombers?" *Terrorism Monitor* (July 19, 2007).

33. Brian Glyn Williams. "Cheney Attack Reveals Taliban Suicide Bombing Patterns," *Terrorism Monitor* 5, no. 4 (February 27, 2007).

34. Others have noticed this trend. See for example, "Over 60 Percent of Suicide Bombers in Afghanistan are Physically Disabled," *The Mainichi Daily News*, October 28, 2008.

35. Daan Van Der Schriek. "New Terrorist Trends in Afghanistan," *Terrorism Monitor* 2, no. 22 (November 18, 2004). See also Carlotta Gall, "Taliban Step Up Afghan Bombings and Suicide Attacks," *New York Times*, October 21, 2006.

36. Soraya Sarhaddi Nelson. "Disabled Often Carry Out Afghan Suicide Missions," National Public Radio, *Morning Edition*, October 15, 2007.

37. Marc Sageman. *Understanding Terrorist Networks* (Pittsburgh: University of Pennsylvania Press, 2004). Sageman's excellent work focuses on the more elite Al Qaeda terrorist network.

38. Interview with Craig Harrison, Director of UN Security in Afghanistan, UNAMA Compound, Kabul, April 2007.

39. "Jihadist Dies from Accidental Discharge. Suicide Bomber Falls Down Stairs," Liveleak.com, January 24, 2008.

40. "Five Terrorists Die When Planting a Car Bomb in Afghanistan," *RIA Novosti* (Russia), January 2, 2008.

41. "Bombers in Afghanistan Usually Miss Targets," *St. Petersburg Times*, November 23, 2006.

42. B. Raman. "What's Cooking in the Jihadi Kitchen? Entry Pass for Heaven," *Terrorism Monitor* Paper no. 148 (March 11, 2006).

43. Mushtaq Yusufzai. "How Two Teens Were Recruited for Jihad," MSNBC. com, March 28, 2007.

44. "Afghan Suicide Bomber Kills Own Family," Associated Press, October 16, 2007.
45. Story relayed by Tom Gregg, director of UNAMA Mission, Gardez, May 2007.
46. "Afghan Suicide Bomber Kills Own Family," Associated Press, October 16, 2007.
47. "35 Killed in Kabul Suicide Bomb Attack," Associated Press, June 18, 2007.
48. According to some unsubstantiated reports, some of the victims may have died in panicked gunfire from guards who survived the explosion.
49. "Taliban's Bomb Expertise Grows as Regard for Civilians Cast Aside," *International Herald Tribune*, February 20, 2008.
50. "140 Afghans Killed in 2 Days of Bombings," Associated Press, February 18, 2007.
51. "Taliban leader says suicide army ready," UPI, March 1, 2007.

CHAPTER 10

CHINA AND CENTRAL ASIA

DEVELOPING RELATIONS
AND IMPACT ON DEMOCRACY

Morris Rossabi

CHINA AND CENTRAL ASIA: FROM SILK TO OIL, PRE-1990

From the second century, BCE, to the present, China has sought to ensure stability and security along its northwestern frontiers and has often used economic leverage, via commerce, to secure that objective.[1] It has also attempted to gain access to Central Asian products. Traditional Chinese dynasties and merchants principally desired horses, but contemporary China covets the area's abundant mineral and natural resources, including oil and natural gas. Pre-twentieth-century China also attempted to expand along its northwestern frontiers to create a buffer zone against the more powerful and possibly belligerent States in the so-called Western

Regions *(xiyu)*. Will the People's Republic of China (PRC) follow that pattern and try to use its economic relationship with the Central Asian countries to secure political leverage? The latest evidence suggests that it may, in fact, pursue such a policy, particularly on issues it considers to be vital.

In recent times—by the early twentieth century—Russia had annexed Western Central Asia and incorporated it into a so-called Western Turkestan, and China had established the province of Xinjiang in Eastern Central Asia. Control over the region remained when communism prevailed in the U.S.S.R. in 1917 and China in 1949.[2] However, the victories of communism in the two countries which controlled landlocked Central Asia did not result in stability, particularly after the onset of the Sino-Soviet dispute in 1957. Relations between the PRC and the Central Asian Soviet Republics of Kazakhstan, Kyrgyzstan, Tajikistan, Turkmenistan, and Uzbekistan soured, and neither had significant access to the other. Contacts between them often provoked crises. In 1962, after several years of repressive PRC policies during the radical Great Leap Forward era, at least sixty thousand Kazakhs and Uyghurs from Xinjiang fled and migrated to Soviet Central Asia, a great embarrassment for China.[3] The PRC then closed the border markets where the Central Asian and the non-Chinese and Chinese peoples of Xinjiang traded.

The onset of the Cultural Revolution in China in 1966 caused a further rupture with Central Asia. Radical policies in China, on the one hand, antagonized the Russians and their five Central Asian Soviets. On the other hand, they prompted unrest in Xinjiang from its non-Chinese population who were victims of the attacks on the religion, culture, and language of the Muslims and non-Chinese. As one specialist stated, the Red Guards "destroyed mosques, forced many religious leaders and ordinary Muslims to raise pigs, and frightened the various Turkic peoples into shedding their habitual clothes, adornments, scarves, and donning Mao suits."[4]

Chaotic conditions diminished as the Cultural Revolution wound down in the early 1970s, but relations between the Chinese and the non-Chinese populations in Xinjiang and between the PRC and the five Central Asian Soviet Republics did not improve. Hostilities flared up between the mostly Turkic peoples and the Chinese government in Xinjiang, and the Central Asian Soviets and the PRC unleashed propaganda barrages at each other. In the late 1970s, China and the Xinjiang Muslims condemned the U.S.S.R. for its intrusion in the Muslim land of Afghanistan while the Soviet leadership in both Russia and the Central Asian Soviets criticized the PRC for its radicalism and for its war with Vietnam. The continuing tensions between the U.S.S.R. and the PRC prevented contact between China and Central Asia. Trade in the region, which had been crucial to the Silk Roads, petered out.

The accession of Mikhail Gorbachev in 1985 and his realization that the U.S.S.R. needed new policies to survive ultimately led to change. Massive defense expenditures to resist the reputed U.S. military threat, economic mismanagement, and the population's restiveness with authoritarian government and with shortages of consumer goods, including housing, had created a crisis in the U.S.S.R, which Gorbachev sought to remedy through liberalization of the economy (*perestroika*) and a greater opportunity for freedom of expression (*glasnost*). The economic problems compelled a reevaluation of both domestic and foreign relations. Gorbachev recognized that the strained Sino-Soviet relationship necessitated the deployment of hundreds of thousands of soldiers, perhaps as many as four hundred thousand, on the border and tremendous military expenses. Believing that the time had come to ease tensions, he signaled to the Chinese that he sought peace by pledging the withdrawal of troops and by encouraging frontier trade. He tried as soon as possible to implement the pledges he had made and withdrew Soviet forces stationed along the Sino-Soviet borders from the Siberian-Northeast China frontier to the Central Asia-Xinjiang region. Within a couple of years, he also removed the approximately one hundred thousand troops based in Mongolia. All these reductions saved considerable sums for the increasingly overburdened Soviet economy and government while generating entente with the PRC.[5]

Such reconciliation between the U.S.S.R. and the PRC permitted the resumption of relations between China and Central Asia. As early as

1982, sporadic border trade had begun, but four years elapsed before the PRC formalized this commercial relationship. The pace of trade then accelerated. Total turnover, which had amounted to about $7 million in 1986, reached $464 million in 1992.[6] The simultaneous collapse of the U.S.S.R. proffered even more opportunities for the PRC and individual Chinese and non-Chinese entrepreneurs from Xinjiang. Chinese Muslims, known as Hui, as well as Uyghurs and other Turkic and Iranian groups and Chinese profited in this initial stage of commerce.[7]

CHINA'S OBJECTIVES IN CENTRAL ASIA AND DEMOCRACY

Post-1990, PRC interest in Central Asia has stemmed from a variety of concerns. Perhaps most visceral has been fear of a confrontation some time in the future with Russia. China viewed Central Asia as a buffer zone against a possibly resurgent Russia that attempted to dominate, or at least to have considerable leverage, in North and East Asia. Despite the collapse and break-up of the U.S.S.R. and the ensuing dissipation of the threat posed by one of the world's great powers, the PRC remained concerned. To be sure, the PRC recognized that the previous Soviet military threat had eroded, but a country that possessed the world's most sizable territory needed to be taken seriously.[8] On the one hand, the PRC needed to defuse tensions with Russia. On the other hand, its leaders had to attempt to create a buffer zone by securing leverage or at least influencing the Central Asian countries that separated them from Russia. Unlike some of the traditional Chinese dynasties, they could not annex territory in Central Asia, but they were eager to minimize tensions at whatever cost, even if it meant allying with and perhaps bolstering tyrannical rulers.

Another of the PRC's most pressing concerns has centered on its fear of ethnic separatist movements. Government leaders have worried that the non-Chinese peoples of Xinjiang would follow the model of the former Central Asian republics in seeking independence. They have tried to avert this threat and, in particular, to stem any Central Asian support for ethnic dissidents. In fact, Uyghur nationalists—along with the smaller number of Kazakh, Kyrgyz, and Tajik leaders in Xinjiang—who attempted to promote autonomy or independence believed that the newly established Central Asian countries would assist them. The PRC feared such fraternization between the mostly Turkic peoples of Central Asia and the Uyghur, Kazakh, and other Turkic dissidents in Xinjiang and was determined to avert the potential instability.

Still another PRC concern was the roles foreign countries might seek to play in Xinjiang and Central Asia. Russia was not the only State that had strategic and economic interests in the region. The PRC recognized that other countries might try to capitalize on the more open and fluid political environment after the U.S.S.R.'s demise. Turkey, which has ethnic, religious, and linguistic affinities with many of the regions' peoples, could attempt not only to promote a Pan-Turkic revival but also offer a different economic and political model, with perhaps a greater emphasis on parliamentary democracy. Iran, which shares the same language as the peoples of Tajikistan and several minorities in Xinjiang, could be an important trading partner for Central Asia and Xinjiang and China as well. Yet its fundamentalism could galvanize Xinjiang's Islamic leaders to foster an independence movement. The PRC needed to maintain cordial relations with Iran, but to limit contact between fervent Iranian Muslims and Tajiks, Uyghurs, and others in Xinjiang. Middle Eastern and South Asian countries could have relations with Central Asia and Xinjiang, but the PRC needed also to limit their relations with Turkic and Muslim peoples in China.[9]

Like the traditional Chinese dynasties, the PRC also sought goods from Central Asia. It coveted, in particular, mineral and natural resources. Central Asia has vast untapped natural resources. Kazakhstan has substantial quantities of oil, Turkmenistan has massive deposits of natural gas, and Uzbekistan has somewhat less gas and oil. China's economic growth dictated a search for natural gas and oil outside its borders. The Central Asian countries were among the closest of its neighbors with such resources. In turn, as the Chinese economy boomed, it required markets, including Central Asia, for its manufactured and consumer goods.

Such trade favored the PRC and smacked of a colonial relationship, offering the possibility of leverage over the Central Asian States. Like nineteenth-century imperialist countries, the PRC desired access to raw materials at relatively low prices while providing processed and manufactured products to Central Asia.[10] Although these commercial relations were valuable, the PRC, like the traditional Chinese dynasties, also attempted to use trade for vital political objectives. If it played significant roles in the Central Asian economies, it hoped to translate its economic clout into attaining its other goals. Its eagerness for stability and security was as, if not more, important than its commercial interests. Thus its policies resembled those of the traditional dynasties, which used China's economic power and commerce to secure their political objectives—averting raids and attacks from Central Asia. In the early 1990s, the PRC's political goals were delineation of its borders with Central Asia and control of ethnic dissidents in Xinjiang.

Its objectives certainly did not include promotion of democracy in Central Asia. Indeed, the Chinese leaders apparently had an easier time dealing with authoritarian rulers than with democratic States. Their own authoritarianism facilitated cooperation with dictatorial governments in Central Asia and served, to an extent, to bolster these regimes. The Central Asian States, which foreign and native elites had governed with scant restraints, were not accustomed to popular rule. The breakup of the U.S.S.R. had led to five independent countries in which strongmen took charge of the governments, and several imposed harsh autocratic rule. The PRC has had no compunction about dealing with dictatorial rulers in Turkmenistan, Uzbekistan, and other Central Asian lands and, in fact, has legitimized such governors when other countries have scarcely maintained relations with them.

SINO-CENTRAL ASIAN RELATIONS, 1991–2000

In 1991, with the collapse of the U.S.S.R., the PRC now confronted five countries in Central Asia, rather than just one, and needed to develop relations with each. It still hoped to maintain Central Asia as a buffer zone against a perhaps temporarily weakened Russia, which, the Chinese believed, could reemerge as a great power. Thus its first objective was to reduce tensions with the Central Asian countries by resolving problems. In 1992 it started by establishing formal diplomatic relations with the five Central Asian countries. The most prominent problem the PRC faced was delineation of the borders between itself and Kazakhstan, Kyrgyzstan, and Tajikistan, the three States with which it shared a common frontier. Kazakhstan alone had an approximately 1,500 kilometer border with the PRC.[11] As of 1992, differences persisted concerning the actual demarcation of the frontier territories. The PRC leadership perceived of a resolution of these boundary issues as vital for its national security and its domestic stability. After arduous negotiations in which the Kazakhs and the PRC finally reached an agreement, Li Peng, the Premier of the PRC, arrived personally in Almaty in April of 1994 to sign the treaty delineating the border.[12] Similarly, in July of 1996, President Jiang Zemin traveled to Bishkek to sign a treaty with Kyrgyzstan, which created a Joint Border Survey Commission to map out their border.[13] Tajikistan, which was wracked by a civil war for much of the 1990s, negotiated a border agreement with the PRC on August 13, 1999. Yet again, President Jiang, the highest-level PRC official, attended and signed the treaty in Dalian.[14] The most prominent PRC leaders continue to travel to the five Central Asian countries to devise new agreements.

Frontier issues were not limited to the delineation of the borders between the PRC and the three neighboring countries. China was also concerned about other cross-border problems, which it brought up almost as soon as the border demarcations had been concluded. Because Chinese leaders wanted to rein in frontier instability, the PRC pressed for cooperation to control arms and narcotics smuggling.[15] Criminal gangs operating along the frontiers also concerned the PRC. A few of the gangs took part in human trafficking, while others were, pure and simple, robbers. Although the PRC received some cooperation, violent incidents persisted. As late as 2003, armed robbers attacked and killed seventeen Chinese and Uyghur passengers and two drivers on a bus traveling from Xinjiang to Kyrgyzstan, a country that has a substantial pauper population.[16] Such incidents prompted the PRC to seek collaboration with the Kyrgyz government to ensure peace along their common borders. However, this sporadic violence did not subvert PRC-Kyrgyz relations.

Still another PRC concern was Islamic fundamentalism along its frontiers and the impact of such movements among its Muslim population in Xinjiang. PRC leaders feared that this religious fervor might spill over into Xinjiang, leading to religious dissidence. They also attempted to avert the possible influence of Pan-Turkism from Central Asia, which could lead to ethnic unrest in Xinjiang. According to Chinese officials, Uyghur so-called splittists could capitalize on religious extremism and ethnic nationalism to foment disturbances.

Resolution of boundary disputes and establishment of formal relations with the five Central Asian countries created a buffer zone against potential Russian expansionism but did not deal with possible Central Asian support for and fraternization with Xinjiang's Uyghurs, Kazakhs, Kyrgyz, and Tajiks who sought greater autonomy or perhaps independence. Sino-Russian tensions did recede: the number of Russian troops stationed along the frontier had diminished from about 400,000 in the early 1980s to approximately 119,000 by 2000, perhaps as well an indication of the parlous economic conditions facing the Russian government at that time.[17] However, Xinjiang had been periodically restive ever since the PRC's occupation of the region in 1949. The local population resented the migration of numerous Chinese over the next four decades. The economic power of the Production and Construction Corps (*Bingtuan*), a quasi-military, mostly Chinese force, in the region antagonized the Uyghurs, the Kazakhs, and other non-Chinese peoples.[18] A lengthy history of violence and other forms of protest by what James Scott has called "the weapons of the weak" had been troublesome for the entire tenure of PRC dominance.[19]

Faced with these circumstances, hundreds of thousands of Uyghurs and other, mostly Turkic, peoples had fled to near and distant lands, including Turkey and Germany.[20] In Munich, they had founded an Eastern Turkestan Cultural and Social Association, which appeared to be relatively non-political. However, activist movements, which demanded independence in a State of Uyghuristan, were also organized abroad. Their commitment to democracy, as with other diaspora Xinjiang movements, is uncertain. Whatever the diaspora's political commitments, the PRC was concerned about Uyghur and other Turkic refugees in Central Asia and possible contacts between them and Turkic intellectuals and nationalists in Xinjiang. Refugee Uyghur proximity to Xinjiang, in particular, worried Chinese leaders. In 1991, when Almaty hosted a meeting of the International Uyghur Union, the PRC's fears appeared to be borne out. The following year, the refugee community in Kashgar started to publish a Uyghur language newspaper, another alarming event for the PRC.[21]

Chinese leaders were already reeling from evidence of disturbances within Xinjiang. In April of 1990, the East Turkestan Islamic Party attacked government and security offices and killed at least six policemen on a bridge in Baren county in the Kyrgyz Autonomous District, a site about ten kilometers from Kashgar, one of the major cities in Xinjiang. The origins of the incident remain murky. One specialist attributes it to PRC efforts to impose birth limits on Turkic families; other scholars claim it sprang from a reputed government attempt to oust a mullah; and still others blame the unrest on government attempts to prevent construction of a mosque near the Kashgar airport.[22] Chinese troops crushed the outbreak, inflicting casualties in disputed numbers. Chinese accounts give a figure of sixteen Turkic peoples killed while other sources range from fifty to three thousand.[23] A wave of violence continued after the Baren incident. Assassinations and bombings plagued the authorities, culminating in outbreaks in 1995 in Khotan (during which, according to one account, "hundreds were killed")[24] and in 1997 in Ghulja (Yining) in a Kazakh region. The PRC responded to this violence with a Strike Hard Maximum Pressure Campaign, which led to the detainment and imprisonment of many Turkic peoples and the executions of a few. Rebiya Kader, a successful Turkic businesswoman, was ensnared in this campaign and jailed for so-called traitorous behavior.[25] Nonetheless, such a hard-line policy did not entirely control the unrest.

Because Uyghurs and other Turkic peoples in the Central Asian States, on occasion, fueled or contributed to the unrest, the PRC needed to devise policies that prompted these lands to prevent the Turkic groups from setting up bases for propaganda and proselytizing and to crack down on those advocating independence for Xinjiang. Continued lobbying by Chinese leaders was essential but insufficient. Pressure through regional alignments would be useful. Yet for its most important strategy, the PRC relied on the model developed by the traditional great dynasties. It employed economic leverage to influence the policies of Central Asian governments.

The PRC wished to obtain Central Asian natural resources and to provide, in return, processed and manufactured products, but simultaneously to use its commercial leverage to prod Central Asian governments to adopt different policies toward the Uyghur and other Turkic minorities and Xinjiang. To be sure, Chinese leaders wanted access to oil from Kazakhstan and natural gas from Turkmenistan. Moreover, they recognized that they could substitute for the U.S.S.R. in supplying consumer goods for the Central Asian countries. However, they were also aware of the difficulties concerning commerce. Because of the Soviet experience, many Central Asians were oriented toward Europe. It would require some effort to persuade them to shift their attention and interests to East Asia. Central Asian fears of China's growing power needed to be allayed. Kazakhstan, Kyrgyzstan, and Tajikistan, the three countries which shared borders with the PRC, regarded China's ascendancy with trepidation.

The Chinese also recognized that the Central Asian states lacked basic requirements of modern economies. Barter still characterized some of the region's trade. Its rudimentary banking systems impeded economic growth; its commercial laws were few, if not non-existent; roads, transport, and hotels were poor; and many entrepreneurs and merchants were poorly trained.[26] Despite such impediments, tens of thousands of Chinese, Hui, and Uyghur and other Turkic traders began to arrive in Central Asia in the early 1990s, and small-scale trade predominated.[27] No large-scale or highly sophisticated commerce developed. However, some of the Chinese and Turkic groups decided to settle in the Central Asian States, opening up shops or setting up stalls in bazaars and marrying local women. Such a migration may have been unsettling to the Central Asian governments, but they did not overtly object to the influx. The flurry of economic activity resulted in a doubling of trade from 1992 to 1997, reaching a total of $872 million.

Increasing trade offered the PRC greater leverage, which soon had repercussions. The Central Asian countries began to alter some of their policies to avoid alienating China. By the mid-1990s, they started to impose controls on the Uyghurs and other Turkic peoples within their borders. Despite their shared ethnicity and shared Islamic religion, they prevented the Turkic groups from taking any potential provocative actions against the PRC. They curbed the Uyghurs' propaganda proposing autonomy. As the president of Kazakhstan said, "If China stands against separatist movements, we in Kazakhstan will also stand against...separatist movements."[28] Kazakhstan and Kyrgyzstan banned Uyghurs from organizing pedagogical and military training sessions. All the Central Asian countries forbad demonstrations by Uyghur and other Turkic activists and even prevented them from any assemblies.[29] In 1996 the Central Asian States "signed protocols with China affirming that they would neither harbor nor support separatist groups."[30] All five leaders of these States were authoritarian and certainly did not respect democratic institutions. In addition to increasing trade with the PRC, a good relationship with authoritarian China would bolster their own positions.

China's growing power, particularly its increasing economic relationship with the Central Asian countries, led to a dramatic event in 1996. China and Russia convened a meeting with Kazakhstan, Kyrgyzstan, and Tajikistan in Shanghai. The two great powers shared common objectives in their meetings: both sought political stability and opposed religious fundamentalism and ethnic resurgence and wanted to crush terrorists. They brought these issues to the fore in the Shanghai meeting. Their joint economic and military power compelled the Central Asian governments to abide by Russian and Chinese initiatives concerning, in particular, ethnic and religious dissenters. Each successive year, the

Chinese and Russians secured greater Central Asian cooperation. Growing economic relations between the PRC and these neighboring States
prompted part of this development. Within three years, from 1997 to
2000, trade turnover spiraled from about $872,000,000 to approximately
$1,820,000,000.[31] Ensuing closer relations gradually paved the way for
Chinese goals. For example, in 1999, Kazakhstan detained and then
turned over three Uyghur so-called splittists (i.e., seekers of independence or greater autonomy) to the PRC authorities.[32] In general, from
the mid-1990s to 2000, the Central Asian countries clamped down on
Uyghur advocates of independence for Xinjiang.

TWENTY-FIRST CENTURY

Recognizing its successes in dealing with Central Asia and Xinjiang, the
PRC began the twenty-first century with a renewed emphasis on three
policies. First, it sought to cooperate with Russia in fostering political
stability along its borderlands in Central Asia, and its increasing commerce and its shared diplomatic interests with its Slavic neighbors could
be used to cement that relationship. Second, it promoted trade with Central Asia, partly to obtain vital energy supplies but also partly to gain
support for its political objectives in Xinjiang. Such goals would impede
democratic efforts in Central Asia because the authoritarian Chinese government collaborated with the similarly authoritarian and corrupt Central Asian governments. Third, the PRC attempted to develop policies
in Xinjiang to ingratiate itself with and to defuse tensions and so-called
splittism among the non-Chinese populations in the region, a carrot and
stick approach that it hoped would combat religious fundamentalism and
ethnic resurgence.

The PRC's first success was the negotiation of the Treaty of Good
Neighborly Relations, Friendship, and Cooperation. In July of 2001,
Vladimir Putin and Jiang Zemin, the respective heads of State, signed
the agreement, which laid a foundation for increased cooperation, particularly along the borderlands. The treaty, which was referred to as "the
most important Beijing-Moscow agreement since 1950,"[33] stated that

neither party would permit "the establishment on its territory of an organization or group which harms the sovereignty, security, and territorial
integrity of the other party."[34] It committed both sides to demilitarize
the frontiers and to avoid policies that would lead to military superiority
over the other. The Russians also agreed to train Chinese officers at their
military academies.

The treaty would serve not only to blunt minority groups from using
either China or Russia as bases for ethnic or religious movements on
each other's territory, but it also signaled closer ties between the two
countries. Although the two had different concerns and objectives and
surely did not wish to establish the world-wide alliance that prevailed
between them from 1950 to 1957, the treaty reflected a convergence of
interests in Central Asia and Xinjiang. Such shared interests resulted in
a mutual focus on their security relationships, leading to Russia's willingness and indeed eagerness to sell armaments to China. Over the past
eight years, the PRC has purchased billions of dollars worth of military
equipment from Russia. The sales have consisted of warplanes, ships,
and weapons systems.[35] However, the Russians have not provided the
most advanced weapons systems. Seeking to avoid alienating the PRC
through this rejection, they joined together with Chinese troops in a military exercise. In August of 2005, Chinese and Russian naval, air, and
ground forces reputedly trained against a possible terrorist attack, but
the large scale of the exercise hinted at a higher level of cooperation. The
United States' unilateralist initiatives under President George Bush also
stimulated Russo-Chinese collaboration. Concerns about U.S. intrusions
in Central Asia prodded them into developing alliances with the native
governments.

In June of 2001, Russia and China gathered together representatives
from Kazakhstan, Kyrgyzstan, and Tajikistan to found the Shanghai
Cooperation Organization (SCO). Uzbekistan, which had refrained from
earlier collaborations, now joined the SCO after an assassination attempt
on its Head of State Islam Karimov. Thus, of the Central Asian States,
only Turkmenistan and its Head of State Saparmyrat Niyazov, who proclaimed himself, in a cult of personality, as "Turkmenbashi" or Father

of the Turkmens, did not send representatives to the meeting. The SOC mandate emphasized security against terrorism, but the PRC had another objective in mind as well. It sought to use SOC as a means of reducing the threat represented by Uyghur and other Turkic activists seeking independence. As one specialist on Sino-Russian relations has noted, "China's rigid desire to promote the SCO appears to have been largely driven by a fear of the perils of ethnic separatism and the threat it posed to continued Chinese hegemony over politically restive Muslim ethnic groups in Xinjiang."[36] Within a short time, China capitalized on SCO to open an anti-terrorist center in Bishkek and to initiate military exercises with its Central Asian allies in this organization.

China and Russia appear to have perceived of the SCO as an antidote to NATO. As NATO expanded its membership to include Russia's Eastern European neighbors, Russia and China sought to attract the support of their Asian neighbors. With that kind of leverage, China could influence Central Asian policy concerning ethnic and religious resurgence. As a historian has written recently, "The SCO, together with the commercial ventures of mostly Chinese state firms, thus represented the greatest expansion of Chinese power beyond the Pamirs since the Tang period."[37] Such political power facilitated Chinese efforts against advocates of Uyghur and Turkic independence and human rights activists. As the Xinjiang scholar observed, "In return for good relations with the PRC, security cooperation, aid, and for Kazakhstan, lucrative oil deals, Central Asian governments sharply narrowed the scope of Uyghur activities in their countries.[38]

China's economic successes no doubt influenced the Central Asian countries. Its economic growth dictated a new form of organization. A more sophisticated organizational structure outstripped the itinerant Chinese and Uyghur traders, who earlier dominated economic relationships. Much larger economic units were required to handle the spurt in commerce. On the Chinese side, for example, the Production and Construction Corps played an ever-increasing economic role. Trade turnover between China and Central Asia increased from about $1.8 billion in 2000 to approximately $7.7 billion in 2005, an almost 400% jump in five years. Energy replaced consumer goods as the main item in trade. Transport of energy resources required the PRC to build pipelines, railroads, and roads. The opening of an Atasu-Alashankuo pipeline from Kazakhstan to China in 2005 meant that oil transmission could increase from 25,000 barrels a day to 200,000 barrels a day.[39] Trade turnover will thus grow dramatically from the 2005 official figures, the last reliable statistics available. Tajikistan and Kyrgyzstan, two relatively poor countries, enjoyed less trade with the PRC, although a newly opened road from China to Tajikistan may lead to greater commerce. A 2006 agreement between the PRC and the Uzbek state oil monopoly will doubtless generate more trade. Corrupt customs officials, bureaucratic delays, security threats from terrorism, cross-border crime and drug smuggling, and high tariffs added to high transport costs pose problems to growth of trade. However, the PRC, partly to gain access to natural resources and partly to ensure domestic stability in Xinjiang, appears determined to cope with these difficulties.

An even grander transport plan entails construction of a Eurasian land bridge that would complement the trade arriving from Europe by sea to southeast Chinese ports. Such an overland route would relieve some of the burdens imposed on China's harbors. This construction effort is long-range and will require cooperation with numerous other countries, some of which face considerable turmoil. Afghanistan and Pakistan, two main conduits for this land bridge, are currently unstable, impeding progress on this economically promising project.

The al-Qaeda attacks on New York City and Washington, D.C., on September 11, 2001, had a profound impact on China's relations with Central Asia and on its policies in Xinjiang. The U.S. planned to retaliate against al-Qaeda and its Taliban protectors and allies in Afghanistan, but it needed bases nearby from which to launch its air campaigns. Ignoring the SOC and thus denigrating its significance, U.S. leaders negotiated agreements to set up bases in Uzbekistan, Kyrgyzstan, and Tajikistan. Although the PRC looked askance at the prospect of air bases so close to its borders, it could not protest. After all, China had been complaining about Islamic terrorists for several decades, and the U.S. was attempting to erase that threat. Because the U.S. now adhered to the PRC's political policies, the Chinese leaders could not challenge the granting of bases to American airplanes and troops.

However, the PRC turned U.S. efforts to its advantage. It pressured the United States to label Uyghur "splittist" organizations as terrorist groups, and in August of 2002 U.S. Deputy Secretary of State Richard Armitage, seeking Chinese support for and at least acquiescence in the U.S.'s campaign in Afghanistan and in its projected invasion of Iraq, officially called the East Turkestan Islamic Movement (ETIM) a terrorist group.[40] It is true that ETIM leaders had met with Osama bin Laden and were implicated in bombings as well as in assassinations of both citizens and officials. Thus, the United States' listing of ETIM as a terrorist organization appears to have been accurate. However, the PRC went beyond condemnation of ETIM. Chinese leaders capitalized upon the fears following the attacks on the World Trade Center in New York and the Pentagon in the suburbs of Washington, D.C., to justify a crackdown on Uyghur separatists. Accusing "splittists" of more than two hundred terrorist acts and of killing more than a hundred people, the PRC perhaps exaggerated the terrorist threat. Chinese leaders played the "Uyghur card," describing the terrorists as part of a unified conspiracy with centralized leadership. One specialist challenges this view, observing that "a more nuanced assessment of the record of political violence in Xinjiang in the 1990s would not describe a unified movement, let alone blame a single organization."[41] Nonetheless, the PRC's depiction of Uyghur dissenters permitted it to denigrate advocates of human rights and democracy and to portray them as violent terrorists.

Thus Xinjiang was at the center of Sino-Central Asian relations. Much of the benefit of Central Asian trade would accrue to Xinjiang because it was the main transit point for such commerce. PRC leaders recognized its economic potential, if tensions with the Uyghurs and other non-Chinese peoples could be defused. They sought to develop policies that could contribute to that end, but some of these initiatives proved to be ambiguous: in practice, they did not necessarily assist the non-Chinese minorities.

The PRC's principal policy entailed an impetus to economic growth in Western China. Chinese leaders assumed that greater prosperity would help them win over the Uyghurs and other non-Chinese groups in Xinjiang. Yet a recent study reveals that even after fifteen years of this policy per capita income for Chinese in Xinjiang was higher than that for non-Chinese; that large State enterprises were sited mostly in Chinese areas, and that nearly all of the managers of these enterprises were Chinese; and that the State budget supported the extraction of mineral and natural resources and slighted spending on education and health.[42] In addition, the government's emphasis on expanding cotton cultivation and on virtually indiscriminate tapping of natural and mineral resources have generated desertification and shortages of water. Under these conditions, "the central and regional governments appear to be pursuing a classic policy of economic imperialism, or internal colonialism in the XUAR [Xinjiang Uyghur Autonomous Region]." Economic growth and greater investment, in and of themselves, may not quell Uyghur dissidence. Indeed, the July 2009 Uyghur demonstrations and riots in Urumchi, leading to the deaths of about two hundred people, confirm the continued animosity between the Uyghurs and the Chinese.

Once again seeking to ingratiate itself with the Uyghurs, the PRC has instituted an affirmative action policy, although it has not tolerated an affirmation of Uyghur culture. It has permitted Uyghur students to enter university with a lower score on entrance examinations. Yet from 2002 on, government instructions have emphasized the use of Chinese, not merely Uyghur, as the principal language of instruction in schools and universities.[43] These regulations also mandated bilingual education so that Uyghur students could have more career opportunities in a society based on fluency in the Chinese language, perhaps a laudable objective but one that undermines Uyghur identity. In other areas, the government has imposed strict restrictions on Islam and on religious dignitaries, including limitations on mosques. It has also censored literary works and music that could in any way stimulate Uyghur nationalism.[44]

The PRC's attempt to control Xinjiang and to deflect advocates of human rights and democracy spilled over into its relations with Central

Asia. To quell disturbances in Xinjiang and to minimize the aid non-Chinese minorities might secure from co-religionists in Central Asia, China used economic incentives and considerable political pressure to deflect neighboring governments from involvement with any Uyghur dissident groups. Through persuasion, cooperation, and the threat of possible sanctions, the PRC has managed to prevent Central Asia from serving as a base for Uyghurs and even from providing any diplomatic cover for the protection of ethnic resurgence among the non-Chinese minorities in China. Naturally, these PRC policies have necessitated active support for the Central Asian authoritarian governments. For example, China has not questioned or even requested an investigation of the Andijon incident of May 13, 2005, in Uzbekistan, when government forces shot and killed escaped prisoners and other demonstrators. Accusing them of criminal activities and of belonging to a terrorist organization known as the Islamic Movement of Uzbekistan, troops fired on the assembled demonstrators. The official government list of casualties amounted to 173 dead, but Human Rights Watch offers higher numbers, perhaps as many as one thousand.[45] Other accusations about Uzbek government policies of repression, including the use of torture and, in some cases, killing of prisoners, have appeared in the mass media and in U.S. Department of State reports, but the PRC has apparently not sought clarifications or explanations from the Uzbek authorities.[46] Neither did China challenge Saparmyrat Niyazov's oppressive rule in Turkmenistan. The PRC must have been aware of his bizarre cult of personality, which dominated the country from 1990 until his death on December 21, 2006, but Chinese officials scarcely commented on his autocratic ways. Indeed, the PRC's increasing trade turnover with and investment in some of the most authoritarian States and dictatorial governments legitimized, to a certain extent, these regimes. In sum, China's growing presence in Central Asia, as well as corruption among its various economic partners and governments, has tended to retard democracy and may, in the future, help to prop up authoritarian rulers.

In the immediate aftermath of the attacks of September 11, 2001, the United States sought to play a greater role in Central Asia and, at first, it succeeded, posing a potential challenge to the PRC and to Russia. As noted, it received permission to establish bases in Uzbekistan, Kyrgyzstan, and Tajikistan to prosecute its war against the Taliban in Afghanistan. After its initial resounding victories in Afghanistan, it remained in these bases, with the consent of the three Central Asian countries. At the same time, Chevron and other Western oil companies sought to negotiate with Azerbaijan and Kazakhstan, in particular, for access to petroleum and for construction of pipelines westward. These negotiations have been ongoing since the breakup of the U.S.S.R. and the establishment of the new countries in the Caucasus and Central Asia. The U.S. appeared to be competing successfully with Russia and China in Central Asia.

However, within a few years after the initial shock of September 11, 2001, the United States' position in Central Asia has eroded and the PRC has strengthened its relations with these States. The Uzbek ruler Islam Karimov, whom the United States had criticized for his suppression of the 2005 Andijon demonstrations and for his human rights violations, compelled the U.S. to close its air bases within his territory and has expelled numerous representatives of Western and U.S. NGOs from his lands. Kyrgyzstan and Tajikistan have renewed leases for the U.S. bases, but quite a number of Kyrgyz have demonstrated against the U.S. military presence. The termination or reduction of these U.S. bases has allayed the PRC's fears of a large U.S. military contingent near its borders while bolstering the SCO's security provisions. China has also outmaneuvered the Western and U.S. oil companies in securing access to Central Asia's energy resources. It has built a pipeline that stretches from Kazakhstan's rich Tengiz oil fields to Xinjiang. Moreover, the government of Kazakhstan has informed the Western oil companies that it wishes a higher percentage of the profits that would accrue from its oil reserves.

It is thus no accident that

> in the former Soviet Central Asian countries—the so-called Stans—China is the new heavyweight player, its manifest destiny pushing its Han pioneers while pulling defunct microstates like Kyrgyzstan and Tajikistan, as well as oil-rich Kazakhstan, into its orbit. The SCO gathers their Central Asian strongmen together

with China and Russia and may eventually become the NATO of the East.[47]

The PRC's growing influence does not portend well for democracy in Central Asia. Its own authoritarianism aside, China has, over the past fifteen years, been willing to collaborate with the region's most repressive and corrupt regimes in order to achieve its objectives. It has gained access to Central Asian natural and mineral resources and has exported considerable amounts of manufactured and consumer goods to the region. Its government has used economic leverage to persuade the Central Asian governments to prevent Turkic co-religionists from Xinjiang—who also often share their ethnicity and language—from using their territories as bases for efforts to foster greater autonomy and independence from China. It has been increasingly successful in competing with the United States and Russia for the allegiance of the Central Asian governments.

ENDNOTES

1. See Morris Rossabi, "Introduction," in *China among Equals*, ed. Morris Rossabi (Berkeley: University of California Press, 1983), 1–13.
2. Useful surveys of Russo-Chinese relations include: Mark Mancall, *Russia and China: Their Diplomatic Relations to 1728* (Cambridge, MA: Harvard University Press, 1971); S. C. M. Paine, *Imperial Rivals: China, Russia, and Their Disputed Frontier* (Armonk: M. E. Sharpe, 1996); and Alexander Lukin, *The Bear Watches the Dragon: Russia's Perceptions and the Evolution of Russian-Chinese Relations Since the Eighteenth Century* (Armonk: M. E. Sharpe, 2003).
3. George Moseley, *A Sino-Soviet Frontier: The Ili Kazakh Autonomous Chou* (Cambridge, MA: Harvard University Press, 1966), 107–109.
4. Gardner Bovingdon, "Heteronomy and Its Discontents: Minzu Regional Autonomy in Xinjiang," in *Governing China's Multiethnic Frontiers*, ed. Morris Rossabi (Seattle: University of Washington Press, 2004), 129.
5. Foreign Broadcast Information Service, *China*, October 23, 1986, D2; December 11, 1986, D1; July 20, 1987, D1.
6. Niklas Swanström, Nicklas Norling, and Zhang Li, "China," in *The New Silk Roads: Transport and Trade in Greater Central Asia*, ed. S. Frederick Starr (Washington, DC: Central Asia-Caucasus Institute and Silk Road Studies Program, 2007), 421.
7. Marika Vicziany and Guibin Zhang, "The Rise of the Private Sector in Xinjiang (Western China): Han and Uyghur Entrepreneurship" in coombs.anu. edu.au/SpecialProj/ASAA/biennial-conferecne/2004/Vicziany+Zhang-ASAA2004.pdf (accessed March 26, 2008).
8. Yitzhak Shichor, "The Great Wall of Steel" in *Xinjiang: China's Muslim Borderland*, ed. S. Frederick Starr (Armonk: M. E. Sharpe, 2004), 157.
9. Gregory Gleason, *The Central Asian States* (Boulder: Westview Press), pp. 146–50. For a study of Sino-Iranian relations, see John Garver, *China and Iran: Ancient Partners in a Post-Imperial World* (Seattle: University of Washington Press, 2006). Japan has had economic, but not political, interests in Central Asia.
10. Gleason, *Central Asian*, 145–146.
11. Tatiana Shaumien, "Foreign Policy Perspectives of the Central Asian States," in *Post-Soviet Central Asia*, ed. Touraj Atabaki and John O'Kane (London: I. B. Tauris & Co., Ltd., 1998), 70.

12. Guangcheng Xing, "China and Central Asia: Toward a New Relationship" in *Ethnic Challenges Beyond Borders*, ed. Yongjin Zhang and Rouben Azizian (New York: St. Martin's Press, 1998), 34, and Jeanne Wilson, *Strategic Partners: Russian-Chinese Relations in the Post-Soviet Era* (Armonk: M. E. Sharpe, 2004), 44.

13. "China, Kyrgyzstan Sign Joint Statement on Enhancing Co-op, Friendship," *China View* (August 15, 2007), http://www.news.xinhuanet.com/English/2007-08/15/content_6532960.htm (accessed September 6, 2007).

14. "China, Tajikistan to Seek Early Settlement of Border Issue," *People's Daily* (July 4, 2000), http://www.Peopledaily.com.cn/english/200007/04/eng20000704_44657.html (accessed July 25, 2004).

15. Roy Allison, "The Military and Political Security" in *Russia, the Caucasus, and Central Asia*, ed. Rajan Menon, Yuri Fedorov, and Ghia Nodia (Armonk: M. E. Sharpe, 1999), 38.

16. Michael Dillon, "Bus Attack Highlights Problems in Chinese-Kyrgyzstan Relations," *Caucasian Institute Analysis* (April 23, 2003), http://www.cacianalyst.org/?q=node/1090 (accessed May 5, 2003).

17. Wilson, *Strategic Partners*, 48.

18. David Bachman, "Making Xinjiang Safe for the Han? Contradictions and Ironies of Chinese Governance in China's Northwest" in *Governing China's Multiethnic Frontiers*, ed. Rossabi, 180; see Vicziany and Zhang, "Rise," for the *Bingtuan*'s economic dominance.

19. See James Scott, *Weapons of the Weak: Everyday Forms of Peasant Resistance* (New Haven, CT: Yale University Press, 1987).

20. Dru Gladney, "The Chinese Program of Development and Control, 1978–2001," in *Xinjiang*, ed. Starr, 114.

21. Kulbushan Warikoo, "Ethnic Religious Resurgence in Xinjaing," in *Post-Soviet*, ed. Atabaki and O'Kane, 275.

22. James Millward, *Eurasian Crossroads: A History of Xinjiang* (New York: Columbia University Press, 2007), 325–328; Justin Rudelson and William Jankowiak, "Acculturation and Resistance: Xinjiang Identities in Flux," in *Xinjiang*, ed. Starr, 316–317; and Warikoo, "Ethnic Religious," 277.

23. Millward, *Eurasian*, 327, and Rudelson and Jankowiak, "Acculturation," 316.

24. Rudelson and Jankowiak, "Acculturation," 317.

25. Numerous articles have been written about her case. See Vicziany and Zhang, "Rise."

26. Liu Qingjian, "Sino-Central Asian Trade and Economic Relations: Progress, Problems, and Prospects," in *Ethnic Challenges Beyond Borders*, ed. Zhang Yongjin and Rouben Azizian (New York: St. Martin's Press, 1998), 186–190.

27. Warikoo, "Ethnic," in *Post-Soviet*, ed. Atabaki and O'Kane; 280 cites a figure of 300,000 merchants reaching Central Asia.

28. Sean Roberts, "A Land of Borderlands: Implications of Xinjiang's Trans-Border Interactions," in *Xinjiang*, ed. Starr, 233.

29. Millward, *Eurasian*, 337.

30. Gladney, "Chinese Program," 109.

31. Swanström, Norling, and Li, "China," in *The New Silk Roads*, ed. Starr, 421.

32. Gladney, "Chinese Program," 109.

33. Shichor in Starr, *Xinjiang*, 154.

34. Wilson, *Strategic Partners*, 59.

35. Richard Weitz, "China and Russia Hand in Hand," *Global Asia* 2, no. 3 (Winter 2007): 53.

36. Wilson, *Strategic Partners*, 54.

37. Millward, *Eurasian*, 337.

38. Ibid.

39. Swanström, Norling, and Li, "China" in *The New Silk Roads*, ed. Starr, 396. For more on energy issues, see Mevlut Katik, "Kazakhstan Has 'Huge Plan' to Expand Energy Links with China: A EurasiaNet Interview with Foreign Minister of Kazakhstan Tokaev," *EurasiaNet*, March 13, 2006. Online at http://www.eurasianet.org/departments/recaps/articles/eav031306.shtml (accessed April 6, 2006).

40. Andrew Chang, "China Connection? Could a Distant Asian Province Become the Next Al Qaeda Safe Haven," ABC News, February 24, 2003. Online at http://www.coranet.radicalparty.org/pressreview/print.php?func=detail&par=4706 (accessed March 30, 2003).

41. Millward, *Eurasian*, 340.

42. Bachman, "Making Xinjiang Safe," in *Governing China's*, ed. Rossabi, 161–174.

43. Millward, *Eurasian*, 345.

44. See Bovingdon, "Heteronomy," in *Governing China's*, ed. Rossabi, 133–140, 144–147.

45. C. J. Chivers, "Rights Report Details Uzbek Crackdowns After Uprising in May," *The New York Times* (September 20, 2005); Robert McMahon, "Uzbekistan: Report Cites Evidence of Government 'Massacre' in Andijion,"

(June 7, 2005), www.rferl.org/featuresarticle/2005/6/53B/15C1E-995C-4339-819C-8090FBC94736.html (accessed June 20, 2005).

46. Jeffrey Thomas, "U. S. Lawmakers Propose Sanctions in Uzbekistan," Bureau of International Information Programs, U.S. Department of State, May 11, 2006. Online at www.usinfo.state.gov/sa/Archive/2006/May/11-331733.html (accessed July 6, 2007).

47. Parag Khanna, "Waving Goodbye to Hegemony," *New York Times Sunday Magazine* (January 27, 2008), 37.

BIBLIOGRAPHY

Aborisade, Oladimeji. *Politics in Nigeria*. New York: Longman, 2002.

Abou El Fadl, Khaled, Joshua Cohen, and Deborah Chasman. *Islam and the Challenge of Democracy*. Princeton, NJ: Princeton University Press, 2004.

Abou El Fadl, Khaled. *The Great Theft: Wrestling Islam from the Extremists*. New York: HarperOne, 2005.

Achcar, Gilbert. "Eleven Theses on the Resurgence of Islamic Fundamentalism." *International Marxist Review* 2, no. 3 (1987).

Ahmed, A. F. Salahuddin. "Bangladesh: History and Culture—An Overview." In *Bangladesh—National Culture and Heritage*, eds. A. F. Salahuddin Ahmed and Bazlul Mobin Chowdhury. Dhaka: Independent University, 2004.

Ahmad, Aziz. *An Intellectual History of Islam in India*. Edinburgh: Edinburgh University Press, 1969.

al-Azmeh, Aziz. *Secularism from a Different Perspective* (Arabic: *Al-ilmaniyah min manzour mukhtalef*). Beirut: Markaz Dirasat al-Wehda al-Arabiya, 1992.

al-Ghannouchi, Rachid. *Public Freedoms in the Islamic State*. Beirut: The Center for Arab Unity Studies, 1993.

Allen, Jack. *Randomness and Optimal Estimation in Data Sampling*. Rehoboth: American Research Press, 2002.

Allison, Roy. "The Military and Political Security." In *Russia, the Caucasus, and Central Asia*, eds. Rajan Menon, Yuri Fedorov, and Ghia Nodia. Armonk: M. E. Sharpe, 1999.

al-Mashat, Abdel Mon'em. "Egyptian Attitudes Toward the Peace Process: Views of an 'Alert Elite.'" *The Middle East Journal* 37 (1983).

Almond, G. A., S. Appleby, and E. Sivan. *Strong Religion: The Rise of Fundamentalisms Around the World*. Chicago: University of Chicago Press, 2003.

al-Qaradawi, Yusuf. *On the Fiqh of the Islamic State* (Arabic: *Min Fiqh al-Dawla Fil-Islam*). Cairo: Dar al-Shorouq, 2001.

———. *Secularist Extremism vs. Islam: Turkey and Tunisia*. Cairo: Dar al-Shorouq, 2001.

Anderson, Benedict. *Language and Power—Exploring Political Cultures in Indonesia*. Ithaca, NY: Cornell University Press, 1990.

Ansari, Iqbal. "Minorities and the Politics of Constitution-Making in India." In *Minority Identities and the Nation-State*, ed. D. L. Sheth and Gurpreet Mahajan. New Delhi: Oxford University Press, 1999.

———. *Political Representation of Muslims in India, 1952–2004*. New Delhi: Manak, 2006.

Armanios, F. "Islam: Sunnis and Shiites." *CRS Report* RS 21745.

Austin, Granville. *The Indian Constitution: Cornerstone of a Nation*. Oxford: Clarendon Press, 1966.

Babbie, Earl R. *The Practice of Social Research*. Belmont, CA: Thomson/Wadsworth, 2004.

Baghdadi, Ahmad. *Renovation of the Religious Thought* (in Arabic: *Tagdid Al-Fikr Al-Dini*). Damascus: Al Mada Publishing Company, 1999.

Bandopadhyay, Sekhar. "Transfer of Power and the Crises of Dalit Politics in India, 1945–47." *Modern Asian Studies* 34, no. 4 (2000): 893–942.

Barnett, Laura. "Afghanistan: The Rule of Law." Parliamentary Information and Research Service, PRB 07-17E, Library of Parliament of Canada, 2007.

Bawedan, Anies Rasyid. "Political Islam in Indonesia—Present and Future Trajectory." *Asian Survey* 44, no. 5 (2004).

Beblawi, Hazem, and Giacomo Luciani. *The Rentier State*. New York: Croom Helm, 1987.

Bellin, Eva. "Contingent Democrats: Industrialists, Labor, and Democratization in Late-Developing Countries." *World Politics* no. 52 (2000).

Bianci, Steven. *Libya: Current Issues and Historical Background*. New York: Nova Science Publishers, 2003.

Billings, Dwight B., and Shaunna L. Scott. "Religion and Political Legitimation." *Annual Review of Sociology* 20 (1994).

Bourqia, R., and Susan Gilson Miller. *In the Shadow of the Sultan: Culture, Power, and Politics in Morocco*. Cambridge, MA: Distributed for the Center for Middle Eastern Studies of Harvard University by Harvard University Press, 1999.

Bovingdon, Gardner. "Heteronomy and Its Discontents: Minzu Regional Autonomy in Xinjiang." In *Governing China's Multiethnic Frontiers*, ed. Morris Rossabi. Seattle: University of Washington Press, 2004.

Brace, Paul, and Barbara Hinckley. *Follow the Leader: Opinion Polls and the Modern Presidents*. New York: Basic Books, 1992.

Brass, Paul. *The Politics of India Since Independence*. Cambridge: Cambridge University Press, 1994.

———. *The Production of Hindu-Muslim Violence in Contemporary India*. Seattle: University of Washington Press, 2003.

Carson, Thomas. *Issues and Priorities for Bangladesh: The 2000 IFES National Survey*. IFES, November 2009.

Chandra, Kanchan. *Why Ethnic Parties Succeed: Patronage and Headcounts in India*. Cambridge: Cambridge University Press, 2004.

Chaudhri, Rashid Ahmad, Shamim Ahmad, and Ahmadiyya Muslim Association. *Persecution of Ahmadi Muslims and Their Response*. London: Press and Publication Desk, Ahmadiyya Muslim Association, 1989.

CIA World Factbook. Washington, D.C.: Central Intelligence Agency, 2007.

Cohen, Stephen Philip. *The Idea of Pakistan.* Washington, D.C.: Brookings Institution Press, 2004.

Crotty, William, ed. *Democratic Development and Political Terrorism/The Global Perspective.* Boston: Northeastern University Press, 2005.

Dahl, Robert. *Polyarchy.* New Haven, CT: Yale University Press, 1971.

Dahm, Bernhard. "Radikalisierung des Islam in Indonesien." In *Indonesia— The Presence of the Past,* ed. Eva Antje Missbach Streifeneder. Berlin: regiospectra.

Dawisha, Karen, and Bruce Parrott, eds. *Conflict, Cleavage, and Change in Central Asia and the Caucasus (Democratization and Authoritarianism in Post-Communist Societies).* New York: Cambridge University Press, 1997.

Dean, M. *Governmentality: Power and Rule in Modern Society.* London: Sage, 1999.

Denoeux, Guilain. "The Forgotten Swamp: Navigating Political Islam." *Middle East Policy* 9, no. 2 (2002).

Détienne, Marcel. *Les Ruses de l'intelligence.* Paris: Grasset, 1956.

Dionne, E. J. Jr., Jean Bethke Elshtain, and Kayla M. Drogosz, eds. *One Electorate under God? A Dialogue on Religion and American Politics.* Washington, DC: Brookings Institution Press, 2004.

El-Awa, Muhammad S. *On the Political System of the Islamic State.* Indianapolis: American Trust Publications, 1980.

Esposito, John L., John Voll, and Osman Bakar. *Asian Islam in the 21st Century.* New York: Oxford University Press, 2007.

Esposito, John L., and John Voll. *Islam and Democracy.* New York: Oxford University Press, 1996.

Fandy, Mamoun. *Saudi Arabia and the Politics of Dissent*. New York: St. Martin's Press, 1999.

Fealy, Greg. "Islamic Radicalism in Indonesia: The Faltering Revival?" Edited by ISEAS. *Southeast Asian Affairs*. Singapore: ISEAS, 2002.

————. "Islamisation and Politics in Southeast Asia: The Contrasting Cases of Malaysia and Indonesia." In *Islam in World Politics*, ed. Nelly Lahoud and Anthony H. Johns. London: Routledge, 2005.

Feldman, Noah. *After Jihad: America and the Struggle for Islamic Democracy*. New York: Farrar, Straus & Giroux, 2003.

Fernando, J. M. "The Making of the Malayan Constitution." *MBRAS Monographs* no. 31 (2002).

Fish, M. Steven. "Islam and Authoritarianism." *World Politics* 55 (2002).

Freedman, Amy L. "Economic Crises and Political Change: Indonesia, South Korea, and Malaysia." *Asian Affairs* 31, no. 4 (2005).

Garver, John. *China and Iran: Ancient Partners in a Post-Imperial World*. Seattle: University of Washington Press, 2006.

Gatsiounis, I. "Islam Hadhari in Malaysia." *Current Trends in Islamist Ideology* 3 (2006).

Gellner, Ernest. "Islam and Marxism." *International Affairs* (1991).

————. *Nations and Nationalism*. Oxford: Blackwell, 1983.

"German Intelligence Describes a 'New Quality' in Jihadi Threats." *Terrorism Monitor* 5, no. 7 (February 2008).

Gillespie, Richard, and Richard Youngs. *The European Union and Democracy Promotion: The Case of North Africa*. Portland: Frank Cass Publishers, 2002.

Gladney, Dru. "The Chinese Program of Development and Control, 1978–2001." In *Xinjiang: China's Muslim Borderland*, ed. S. Frederick Starr (Armonk: M. E. Sharpe, 2004).

Gleason, Gregory. *The Central Asian States.* Boulder: Westview Press, 1997. Goodin, Robert E. "Institutions and Their Design." In *The Theory of Institutional Design*, ed. R. E. Goodin. Cambridge: Cambridge University Press, 1996.

Hadenius, Axel. *Institutions and Democratic Citizenship.* New York: Oxford University Press, 2001.

Hadiz, Vedi R. "Reorganizing Political Power in Indonesia: A Reconsideration of So-called 'Democratic Transitions.'" *The Pacific Review* 16, no. 4 (2003).

Hafez, Mohammed M. *Why Muslims Rebel: Repression and Resistance in the Islamic World.* Boulder and London: Lynne Rienner, 2003.

Hafizullah Emadi. "Ethnic Groups and National Unity in Afghanistan." *Contemporary Review* 1 (January 2002).

Hamid, A. F. Abdul. "The Futuristic Thought of Ustaz Ashaari Muhammad of Malaysia." In *Blackwell Companion to Contemporary Islamic Thought*, ed. i. Abu-Rabi. Oxford: Blackwell Reference, 2009.

Hamilton-Hart, Natasha. "Terrorism in Southeast Asia: Expert Analysis, Myopia and Fantasy." *The Pacific Review* 18, no. 3 (2005).

Haqqani, Husain. *Pakistan: Between Mosque and Military.* Washington, DC: Carnegie Endowment for International Peace, 2005.

Harik, Iliya. "Opinion Leaders and the Mass Media in Rural Egypt." *The American Political Science Review* 65 (September 1971).

Hasan, Noorhaidi. *Islam, Militancy, and the Quest for Identity in Post-New Order Indonesia.* Ithaca, NY: Cornell University Press, 2006.

———. "The Salafi Movement in Indonesia: Transnational Dynamics and Local Development." *Comparative Studies of South Asia, Africa and the Middle East* 27, no. 1 (2007).

Hassan, M. H. "Islam Hadhari: Abdullah's Vision for Malaysia?" *IDSS Commentaries* no. 53 (2004).

Hassan, M. Kamal. "The Influence of Mawdudi's Thought on Muslims in Southeast Asia: A Brief Survey." *Muslim World* 93, no. 3/4 (2003).

Haykal, M. H. *The Life of Muhammad*. Indianapolis: NAIT, 1988.

Heath, M. R., and S. J. Bekker. *Identification of Opinion Leaders in Public Affairs, Educational Matters, and Family Planning in the Township of Atteridgeville*. Pretoria: Human Sciences Research Council, 1986.

Hefner, Robert W., ed. *Remaking Muslim Politics: Pluralism, Contestation, Democratization*. Princeton, NJ: Princeton University Press.

Hillman, Ben. "New Elections, Old Politics." *Far Eastern Economic Review* (January/ February 2006).

Horowitz, David. *Ethnic Groups in Conflict*. 2nd edition. Berkeley: University of California Press, 2000.

Huntington, Samuel P. *The Clash of Civilizations and the Remaking of World Order*. New York: Simon & Schuster, 1998.

———. "Democracy for the Long Haul." *Journal of Democracy* 7 (1996).

———. "Will More Countries Become Democratic?" *Political Science Quarterly* (1984).

Huq, Muhammad Enamul. *A History of Sufism in Bengal*. Dhaka: Asiatic Society, 1975.

Husain, S. Abid. *The Destiny of Indian Muslims*. Bombay: Asia Publishing House, 1965.

Ibrahim, Ferhad, and Gèulistan Gèurbey. *The Kurdish Conflict in Turkey: Obstacles and Chances for Peace and Democracy*. New York: St. Martin's Press, 2000.

"IED, A Weapon's Profile." *Defense Update/An International Online Defense Magazine* (2004).

Inglehart, Ronald, and Pippa Norris. "The True Clash of Civilization." *Foreign Policy* (March/April 2003): 63–70.

Inoguchi, Takashi, Edward Newman, and John Keane. *The Changing Nature of Democracy.* New York: United Nations University Press, 1998.

International Crisis Group (ICG). "Indonesia: Jemaah Islamiyah's Current Status." *Asia Briefing* no. 63, Jakarta/Brussels, 2007.

Jafri, A. B. S. *The Political Parties of Pakistan.* Karachi: Royal Book Co, 2002.

Jahan, Rounaq. *Bangladesh Politics.* Dhaka: University Press Limited, 2005.

Jalal, Ayesha. *The Sole Spokesman: Jinnah, the Muslim League and the Demand for Pakistan.* Cambridge: Cambridge University Press, 1985.

Jawed, Nasim. *Islam's Political Culture: Religion and Politics in Predivided Pakistan.* Austin: University of Texas, 1999.

Jayal, Niraja Gopal. *Representing India: Ethnic Diversity and the Governance of Public Institutions.* London: Palgrave, 2006.

Karatnycky, Adrian. "The 2001 Freedom House Survey: Muslim Countries and the Democracy Gap." *Journal of Democracy* 13 (2002).

Katzman, Kenneth. "Afghanistan: Government Formation and Performance." *CRS Report for Congress,* June 2007.

Kechichian, Joseph A., and Gustave E. von Grunebaum. *Iran, Iraq, and the Arab Gulf States.* New York: Palgrave, 2001.

Kedourie, Elie. *Democracy and Arab Political Culture.* Arlington: Washington Institute for Near East Policy, 1992.

Khalid, Adeeb. *Islam After Communism: Religion and Politics in Central Asia.* Berkeley: University of California Press, 2007.

Khalidi, Omar. "Muslim Ministers in the Union Cabinet: Half a Century of Distrust or Lack of Power." *Radiance* (February 11–17, 2001).

————. *Khaki and Ethnic Violence in India.* New Delhi: Three Essays Collective, 2003.

————. *Between Muslim Nationalists and Nationalist Muslims: Mawdudi's Thoughts on Indian Muslims.* New Delhi: IOS, 2004.

————. "Living as a Muslim in a Pluralistic Society and State: Theory and Experience." In *Muslims' Place in the American Public Square: Hopes, Fears and Aspirations,* ed. Zahid H. Bukhari et al. Walnut Creek, CA: Altamira Press, 2004.

————. "Politics of Official Language Status for Urdu in India." *Journal of South Asian and Middle Eastern Studies* 28, no. 3 (spring 2004).

————. *Muslims in Indian Economy.* New Delhi: Three Essays Collective, 2006.

————. "Entrepreneurs from Outside the Traditional Mercantile Communities: Muslims in India's Private Sector." *Journal of South Asian and Middle Eastern Studies* 21, no. 2 (winter 2008).

Khan, M. A. Muqtedar. "The Islamic States." In *Routledge Encyclopedia of Political Science,* ed. M. Hawkesworth and M. Kogan. London: Routledge Press, 2003.

Kortteinen, Timo. "Islamic Resurgence and the Ethnization of the Malaysian State: The Case of Lina Joy." *Journal of Social Issues in Southeast Asia* 23, no. 2 (2008).

Koss, Stephen."John Morley and the Communal Question." *Journal of Asian Studies* 3 (May 1967).

Kotzâe, H. J. *Transitional Politics in South Africa: Attitudes of Opinion-Leaders.* Stellenbosch: Centre for International and Comparative Politics, University of Stellenbosch, 1992.

Kramer, Martin. "Coming to Terms: Fundamentalists or Islamists?" *Middle East Quarterly* 10, no. 2 (2003).

Kronstadt and B. Vaugh. "Terrorism in South Asia." *CRS Report* RL32259.

Krosnick, Jon, and Shibley Telhami. "Public Attitudes Toward Israel: A Study of the Attentive and Issue Publics." *International Studies Quarterly* 39 (1995).

Kurzman, Charles, ed. *Liberal Islam: A Source Book*. New York: Oxford University Press, 1998.

Layachi, Azzedine. *State, Society & Democracy in Morocco: The Limits of Associative Life*. Washington, DC: Center for Contemporary Arab Studies, Edmund A. Walsh School of Foreign Service, Georgetown University, 1998.

Lee, H. P. "Constitutional Amendments in Malaysia." *Malaya Law Review* (1976).

Lehtonen, Risto, and Erkki Pahkinen. *Practical Methods for Design and Analysis of Complex Surveys*. Chichester, West Sussex, England and Hoboken, NJ: J. Wiley, 2004.

Lewis, Bernard. *Islam and the West*. New York: Oxford University Press, 1993.

———. "The West and the Middle East." *Foreign Affairs* 76 (1997).

———. *What Went Wrong: Western Impact and Middle Eastern Response*. New York: Oxford University Press, 2002.

Lindner, Bertil. "Bangladesh—A Cocoon of Terror." *Far Eastern Economic Review* (April 4, 2002).

Liphart, Arendt. *Democracy in Plural Societies: A Comparative Exploration*. New Haven, CT: Yale University Press, 1980.

Lukin, Alexander. *The Bear Watches the Dragon: Russia's Perceptions and the Evolution of Russian-Chinese Relations Since the Eighteenth Century*. Armonk: M.E. Sharpe, 2003.

Mahathir bin, Mohamad, and Makaruddin Hashim. *Politics, Democracy and the New Asia: Selected Speeches*. Subang Jaya, Selangor Darul Ehsan, Malaysia: Pelanduk Publications for the Prime Minister's Office of Malaysia, 2000.

Malley, Michael. "Indonesia: The Erosion of State Capacity." In *State Failure and State Weakness in a Time of Terror*, ed. Robert I. Rotberg. Washington, DC: Brookings Institution Press, 2003.

Mancall, Mark. *Russia and China: Their Diplomatic Relations to 1728.* Cambridge, MA: Harvard University Press, 1971.

Mark, C. "Islam: A Primer." *Congressional Research Service (CRS) Report* RS 21432.

Mawdudi, Sayyid Abulala. *Islamic Law and Constitution.* 9th edition. Translated and edited by Khurshid Ahmad. Lahore: Islamic Publications, 1986.

Mazrui, Ali. *Cultural Forces in World Politics.* Portsmouth, New Hampshire, UK: Heinemann, 1990.

McHenry, Donald, and Kai Bird. "Food Bungle in Bangladesh." *Foreign Policy* no. 72 (1977).

McMillan, Alistair. *Standing at the Margins: Representation and Electoral Reservation in India.* New Delhi: Oxford University Press, 2005.

Means, G. P. "The Role of Islam in the Political Development of Malaysia." *Comparative Politics* 1, no. 2 (1969).

Mendelssohn, Oliver, and Marika Vicziany. *The Untouchables.* Cambridge: Cambridge University Press, 1998.

Mili, Hayder, and Jacob Townsend. "Afghanistan's Drug Trade and How it Funds Taliban Operations." *Terrorism Monitor* 5, no. 9 (May 2007).

Miller, Judith. *God Has Ninety-Nine Names: Reporting from a Militant Middle East.* New York: Simon & Schuster, 1997.

Millward, James. *Eurasian Crossroads: A History of Xinjiang.* New York: Columbia University Press, 2007.

Moseley, George. *A Sino-Soviet Frontier: The Ili Kazakh Autonomous Chou.* Cambridge, MA: Harvard University Press, 1966.

Naipaul, V. S. *Among the Believers: An Islamic Journey*. New York: Knopf, 1981.

―――. *Beyond Belief: Islamic Excursions Among the Converted Peoples*. New York: Random House, 1998.

Nasr, Vali. "The Rise of 'Muslim Democracy." *Journal of Democracy* 16, no. 2 (2005).

Neo, J. Ling-Chien. "Malay Nationalism, Islamic Supremacy and the Constitutional Bargain in the Multi-Ethnic Composition of Malaysia." *International Journal on Minority and Group Rights* 13, no. 2 (2006).

Norris, Pippa, ed. *Critical Citizens: Global Support for Democratic Government*. New York: Oxford University Press, 1999.

Norris, Pippa, and Ronald Inglehart. "Islam and the West: Testing the 'Clash of Civilizations' Thesis." 2002. Forthcoming; available from the authors at pippa_norris@harvard.edu or www.pippanorris.com.

Nyman, Mikaela. "Democratising Indonesia—The Challenges of Civil Society in the Era of Reformasi." *NIAS Reports* 49 (2006).

Obeidi, Amal. *Political Culture in Libya*. Richmond, UK: Curzon, 2001.

O'Donnell, Guillermo, Philippe C. Schmitter, and Laurence Whitehead, eds. *Transitions from Authoritarian Rule—Prospects for Democracy*. Baltimore and London: Johns Hopkins University Press, 1986.

Paine, S. C. M. *Imperial Rivals: China, Russia, and Their Disputed Frontier*. Armonk: M. E. Sharpe, 1996.

Palan, V. T., and Y. T. Takeshita. "The Pattern of Fertility Among the Malay Chinese." In *Fertility Transition of the East Asian Populations*, ed. I. L. J. Cho and K. Kobayashi. Honolulu: University Press of Hawaii, 1979.

Paquette, Laure. *Building and Analyzing National Policy*. Lanham, MD: Lexington, 2002.

————. *Security in the Pacific Century*. New York: Nova, 2002.

————. *Strategy and Ethnic Conflict*. New York: Praeger, 2002.

Pew Research Center. *Views of a Changing World 2003*. Washington, DC: The Pew Research Center, 2003.

————. *Religion and Politics: Contention and Consensus*. Washington, DC: The Pew Research Center, 2003.

Pipes, Daniel. "There are no Moderates: Dealing with Fundamentalist Islam." *National Interest*, no. 41 (fall 1995).

————. *Slaves, Soldiers, and Islam: the Genesis of a Military System*. New Haven, CT: Yale University Press, 1988.

Porter, Donald. *Managing Politics and Islam in Indonesia*. London: RoutledgeCurzon, 2002.

Qingjian, Liu. "Sino-Central Asian Trade and Economic Relations: Progress, Problems, and Prospects." In *Ethnic Challenges Beyond Borders*, ed. Zhang Yongjin and Rouben Azizian. New York: St. Martin's Press, 1998.

Qodari, Muhammad. "Indonesia's Quest for Accountable Governance." *Journal of Democracy* 16, no. 2 (2005).

Qureshi, Zaheer Masood. "Electoral Strategy of a Minority Pressure Group: The Muslim Majlis-i Mushawarat." *Asian Survey* 8 (1968).

Rabasa, Angel M. *Political Islam in Southeast Asia—Moderates, Radicals, and Terrorists*. London: Routledge, 2003.

Rahim, R. A. Abd. "Traditionalism and Reformism Polemic in Malay-Muslim Religious Literature." *Islam and Christian-Muslim Relations* 17, no. 1 (2006).

Raman, B. "What's Cooking in the Jihadi Kitchen? Entry Pass for Heaven." *Terrorism Monitor* Paper no. 148 (2007).

Raza Khan, Mohamed. *What Price Freedom*. Madras, 1969.

Report on Indian Constitutional Reforms. London: HMSO, 1918.

Rieffel, Lex. "Indonesia's Quiet Revolution." *Foreign Affairs* 83, no. 5 (2004).

Roberts, Sean. "A Land of Borderlands: Implications of Xinjiang's Trans-Border Interactions." In *Xinjiang: China's Muslim Borderland*, ed. S. Frederick Starr. Armonk, NY: M. E. Sharpe, 2004.

Robinson, Francis. *Islam and Muslim History in South Asia.* New York: Oxford University Press, 2004.

Robinson, Richard. "Indonesia: Crisis, Oligarchy, and Reform." In *The Political Economy of Southeast Asia: Conflicts, Crises, and Change*, ed. Garry Rodan, Kevin Hewison, and Richard Robinson. Oxford: Oxford University Press, 2001.

Robinson, Richard, and Vedi R. Hadiz. *Reorganising Power in Indonesia: The Politics of Oligarchy in an Age of Markets.* London: Routledge, 2004.

Rossabi, Morris, ed. *China among Equals.* Berkeley: University of California Press, 1983.

Rudelson, Justin, and William Jankowiak. "Acculturation and Resistance: Xinjiang Identities in Flux." In *Xinjiang: China's Muslim Borderland*, ed. S. Frederick Starr. Armonk, NY: M. E. Sharpe, 2004.

Ruf, Werner, ed. *Islam and the West—Judgements, Prejudices, Political Perspectives.* Münster: LIT, 2002.

Sachedina, Abdulaziz. *The Islamic Roots of Democratic Pluralism.* New York: Oxford University Press, 2001.

Sageman, Marc. *Understanding Terrorist Networks.* Philadelphia: University of Pennsylvania Press, 2004.

Saktanber, Ay'se. *Living Islam: Women, Religion and the Politicization of Culture in Turkey.* London: I.B. Tauris, 2002.

Sampath, S. *Sampling Theory and Methods.* Boca Raton: CRC Press; Narosa Pub. House, 2001.

Sartori, Giovanni. *Democratic Theory*. Detroit: Wayne State University Press, 1962.

Scheuch, Erwin K. "Theoretical Implications of Comparative Survey Research: Why the Wheel of Cross-Cultural Methodology Keeps on Being Reinvented." *International Sociology* 4 (1989).

Schweitzer, Yoram, and Sari Goldstein Ferber. *Al Qaeda and the Internationalization of Suicide Terrorism*. Tel Aviv: The Jaffee Center for Strategic Studies Memorandum no. 78, November 2005.

Scott, James. *Weapons of the Weak: Everyday Forms of Peasant Resistance*. New Haven, CT: Yale University Press, 1987.

Senlis Group, Afghanistan. *Countering the Insurgency in Afghanistan: Losing Friends and Making Enemies*. London: MF Publishing, 2007.

Shahbuddin, Syed. The Origins of the Electoral System: Rules, Representation and Power-sharing in India's Democracy." In *India's Living Constitution: Ideas, Practices and Controversies*, ed. Zoya Hasan, 344–369. New Delhi: Permanent Black, 2002.

Shahzad, Syed Saleem. "Taliban Resurgence in Afghanistan." *Le Monde Diplomatique* (2006).

Shaumien, Tatiana. "Foreign Policy Perspectives of the Central Asian States." In *Post-Soviet Central Asia*, ed. Touraj Atabaki and John O'Kane. London: I. B. Tauris & Co., Ltd., 1998.

Shichor, Yitzhak. "The Great Wall of Steel." In *Xinjiang: China's Muslim Borderland*, ed. S. Frederick Starr. Armonk: M. E. Sharpe, 2004.

Siddiqui, A. H. *The Life of Muhammad*. Des Plaines, IL: Library of Islam, 1991.

Singh, Bilveer. "The Challenge of Militant Islam and Terrorism in Indonesia." *Australian Journal of International Affairs* 58, no. 1 (2004).

Slater, Dan. "Indonesia's Accountability Trap: Party Cartels and Presidential Power after Democratic Transition." *Indonesia* no. 78 (2004).

———. "The Ironies of Instability in Indonsia." *Social Analysis* 50, no. 1 (2006).

Smith, Benjamin. "If I Do These Things, They Will Throw Me Out: Economic Reform and the Collapse of Indonesia's New Order." *Journal of International Affairs* 1 (2003).

Smith, W. C. *Islam in Modern History.* Princeton, NJ: Princeton University Press, 1957.

Social, Economic and Educational Status of the Muslim Community of India: A Report. New Delhi: Prime Minister's High Level Committee, 2006.

Solomon, D. J. "Conducting Web-based Surveys." *Practical Assessment, Research & Evaluation* 7 (2001).

Spear, Percival. *A History of India, II.* New York: Penguin, 1965.

Stark, J. "Constructing an Islamic Model in Two Malaysian States: PAS Rule in Kelantan and Terengganu." *Sojourn: Journal of Social Issues in Southeast Asia* 19 (2004).

Stewart, Donna J. "The Greater Middle East and Reform in the Bush Administration's Ideological Imagination." *Geographical Review* 95, no. 3 (July 2005).

Suberu, Rotimi T. *Ethnic Minority Conflicts and Governance in Nigeria.* Ibadan, Nigeria: Spectrum: IFRA, 1996.

Subramaniam, S. "The Dual Narrative of 'Good Governance': Lessons for Understanding Political and Social Change in Malaysia and Singapore." *Contemporary Southeast Asia* 23 (2001).

Suleiman, Michael W. "Attitudes of the Arab Elite Toward Palestine and Israel." *The American Political Science Review* 67 (June 1973).

Surush, Abd al-Kar im, Mahmoud Sadri, and Ahmad Sadri. *Reason, Freedom, & Democracy in Islam: Essential Writings of Abdolkarim Soroush.* New York: Oxford University Press, 2000.

Swanström, Niklas, Nicklas Norling, and Zhang Li. "China." In *The New Silk Roads: Transport and Trade in Greater Central Asia*, ed. S. Frederick Starr. Washington, DC: Central Asia-Caucasus Institute and Silk Road Studies Program, 2007.

Taagepera, Rein. "Prospects for Democracy in Islamic Countries." In *Democratic Development and Political Terrorism/The Global Perspective*, ed. William Crotty. Boston: Northeastern University Press, 2005.

"Taliban Military Commander Mullah Dadallah: We are in Contact With Iraqi Mujahideen, Osama bin Laden & Al-Zawahiri." *Middle East Media Research Institute. Special Dispatch Series* no. 1180 (2006).

Tamimi, Azzam. *Rachid Ghannouchi: A Democrat Within Islamism*. New York: Oxford University Press, 2001.

Tessler, Mark. "Islam and Democracy in the Middle East: The Impact of Religious Orientations on Attitudes toward Democracy in Four Arab Countries." *Comparative Politics* 34 (2002): 337–354.

Thompson, M. R. "Whatever Happened to 'Asian Values'?" *Journal of Democracy* 12, no. 4 (2004).

de Tocqueville, Alexis. *Democracy in America*. New York: Penguin Putnam, 2001.

Ujo, A. A. *Understanding Political Parties in Nigeria*. Kaduna, Nigeria: Klamidas Books, 2000.

Ullah, Aman, and Robert V. Breunig. *Handbook of Applied Economic Statistics*, ed. Aman Ullah and David E. A. Giles. New York: Marcel Dekker, 1998.

Vakili, Vall. "Abdolkarim Soroush and Critical Discourse in Iran." In *Makers of Contemporary Islam*, ed. John L. Esposito and John O.Voll. Oxford: Oxford University Press, 2001.

Van Der Schriek, Daan. "New Terrorist Trends in Afghanistan." *Terrorism Monitor* 2, no. 22 (2004).

Van Klinken, Gerry. *Communal Violence and Democratization in Indonesia.* London: Routledge, 2007.

Varshney, Ashutosh. *Ethnic Conflict and Civil Society: Hindus and Muslims in India.* New Haven, CT: Yale University Press, 2002.

Vaugh, Bruce. "Islam in South and Southeast Asia." *CRS Report* (February 2005).

Von der Mehden, F. R.. "Islamic Resurgence in Malaysia." In *Islam and Development: Religion and Socio-Political Change*, ed. J. L. Esposito. Syracuse, NY: Syracuse University Press, 1980.

Wanandi, Jusuf. "Indonesia: A Failed State?" *The Washington Quarterly* 25, no. 3 (2002).

Wardak, Ali, Daud Saba, and Halima Kazem. *Afghanistan Human Development Report 2007, Centre for Policy and Human Development (CPHD).* Army Press: Islamabad, 2007.

Warikoo, Kulbushan, "Ethnic Religious Resurgence in Xinjaing." In *Post-Soviet Central Asia*, ed. Touraj Atabaki and John O'Kane. London: I. B. Tauris & Co., Ltd., 1998.

"Was Baitullah Mahsud Behind the Spanish Terror Operation?" *Terrorism Monitor* 5, no. 7 (February 2008).

Webber, Douglas. "A Consolidated Patrimonial Democracy? Democratization in Post-Suharto Indonesia." *Democratization* 13, no. 3 (2006).

Weber, M. *The Protestant Ethic and the Spirit of Capitalism.* 2nd ed. London: Routledge, 2001.

Weimann, Gabriel. "The Influentials: Back to the Concept of Opinion Leaders?" *The Public Opinion Quarterly* 55 (summer 1991): 267–279.

Weitz, Richard. "China and Russia Hand in Hand." *Global Asia* 2, no. 3 (winter 2007).

Wellbank, T. W., ed. "An Official View on Communal Electorates." In *The Partition of India: Causes and Consequences*. Boston: Heath, 1966.

Wilkinson, Steve. *Votes and Violence*. Cambridge: Cambridge University Press, 2004.

Williams, Brian Glyn. "Afghan Suicide Bombing." *Jane's Islamic Affairs Analyst* (2007). Available under "Publications" at brianglynwilliams. com.

———. "Cheney Attack Reveals Taliban Suicide Bombing Patterns." *Terrorism Monitor* 5, no. 4 (2007).

———. "The Failure of al Qaeda Basing Projects from Afghanistan to Iraq." In *Denial of Sanctuary. Understanding Terrorist Safe Havens*, ed. Michael Innes. London: Praeger, 2007.

———. "Taliban Fedayeen. The World's Worst Suicide Bombers?" *Terrorism Monitor* (2007).

———. "The Return of the Arabs. Al Qa'ida's Military Role in the Afghan Insurgency." *West Point Combating Terrorism Center Sentinel* 1, no. 3 (February 2008).

Wilson, Jeanne. *Strategic Partners: Russian-Chinese Relations in the Post-Soviet Era*. Armonk, NY: M. E. Sharpe, 2004.

Wingard-Nelson, Rebecca. *Data, Graphing, and Statistics*. Berkeley Heights, NJ: Enslow Publishers, 2004.

Wolpert, Stanley. *Morley and India, 1906–1910*. Berkeley: University of California Press, 1967.

World Bank. *World Development Report*. Washington, DC: World Bank, 2001.

Wright-Neville, David. "Dangerous Dynamics: Activists, Militants and Terrorists in Southeast Asia." *Pacific Review* 17, no. 1 (2004).

Xing, Guangcheng. "China and Central Asia: Toward a New Relationship." In *Ethnic Challenges Beyond Borders*, ed. Yongjin Zhang and Rouben Azizian. New York: St. Martin's Press, 1998.

Zachary, Abuza. "Militant Islam in Southeast Asia: Crucible of Terror." Boulder and London: Lynne Rienner, 2003.

Zaheer, Hasan. *The Separation of East Pakistan*. Karachi: Oxford University Press, 1994.

Zartman, I. William. *Political Elites in Arab North Africa: Morocco, Algeria, Tunisia, Libya, and Egypt*. New York: Longman, 1982.

Zogby, James J. *What Arabs Think: Values, Beliefs and Concerns*. New York: Zogby International, 2002.

LIST OF CONTRIBUTORS

Shiping Hua is professor of political science and director of the Center for Asian Democracy at the University of Louisville. He has published eight books in English, including *Scientism and Humanism: Two Cultures in Post-Mao China (1978–1989)* (SUNY Press, 1995) and *Chinese Utopianism: A Comparative Study of Reformist Thought in Japan, Russia and China (1898–1997)* (Stanford University Press-Wilson Center Press, 2009). He has also published two books in Chinese. His articles and presentations have appeared in popular media, such as *Wilson Quarterly*, *The New York Times*, and *The Voice of America*. Dr. Hua is the general editor of two book series: "Asia in the New Millennium," with University Press of Kentucky published annually in English and "Contemporary World's Classics: Political Science Series" (translations) with Renmin University Press published annually in Chinese. He is a guest professor of China's Peking University, Renmin University, and Nankai University. He was formerly president of the Association of Chinese Political Studies (2004–2006) and council chairman of United Societies of China Studies (2006–2009). Both were based in the United States. He was an Asian policy studies fellow at Woodrow Wilson Center for International Scholars-George Washington University during the 2004–2005 academic year.

Felix Heiduk is a research associate at Stiftung Wissenschaft und Politik (German Institute for International and Security Affairs) in Berlin, Germany, where he works mainly on Southeast Asian politics. His main focus is on transition processes, civil wars, the rise of Islam, and Islamic militancy in the region, as well as nontraditional security issues. Prior to his work at Stiftung Wissenschaft und Politik, he studied political science at Free University Berlin. He is currently finishing his PhD thesis on the Acehconflict/Indonesia. In 2005 he spent four months in Indonesia as a visiting fellow at the Centre for Strategic and International Studies in Jakarta in order to conduct field research for his PhD thesis. In 2006 Felix Heiduk worked as a consultant for the Friedrich-Ebert Foundation in Aceh/Indonesia. Since 2005 Felix Heiduk has also been teaching Southeast Asian Politics at Free University Berlin.

Touqir Hussain is an adjunct professor at Georgetown University. He is a former senior diplomat from Pakistan, having served as Ambassador to Japan (1998–2003), Spain (1993–1995), and Brazil (1990–1993). He also held senior positions in the Pakistani Foreign Office, including that of Additional Foreign Secretary heading the bureaus of the Middle East, the Americas, and Europe.

From 1996 to 1998, he was Diplomatic Adviser to the Prime Minister. Since moving to the U.S., Ambassador Hussain has worked at the U.S. Institute of Peace and the George Washington University, conducting research on Islam, democracy, and extremism. He has written for American and Pakistani newspapers on these topics and security issues involving South Asia.

Tariq Karim is a former Bangladeshi diplomat with over three decades of experience. Among key assignments he held at headquarters were Additional Foreign Secretary (1995–1997) with responsibility for the South Asian region, Director General for United Nations and Economic Affairs (1982–1984), and Director of Personnel (1973–1974). He served in Bangladesh Missions abroad, notably as Ambassador to the United States, and earlier as High Commissioner to South Africa (with concurrent accreditation to Botswana, Lesotho, Namibia, and Swaziland, and consular jurisdiction over Zambia and Zimbabwe), Ambassador to Iran (with concurrent accreditation to Lebanon, and Deputy Chief of Mission in Beijing and New Delhi. He opted for early retirement from the Bangladesh Foreign Service in 1998 in order to return to academia. He joined the University of Maryland (1999–2000) initially as a Ford Fellow in the capacity of Distinguished International Executive in Residence. He is now a doctoral candidate (ABD) in the Department of Government and Politics at the University of Maryland. State fragility, civil society, democratic transition, human rights and rule of law, governance issues in South Asia; and political Islam and globalization issues are among his primary areas of academic interest. While pursuing graduate studies, with his expertise in the structure of government institutions, diplomacy and negotiation, and contemporary Islam, he was Senior Advisor at the IRIS Center of the University of Maryland in 2002–2005. He is currently Bangladesh's High Commissioner to India.

Omar Khalidi is a librarian for the Aga Khan Program at the Massachusetts Institute of Technology and independent scholar. He was educated in India, Britain, and the United States. He received his PhD from the University of Wales. His research interests include the sociology of politics, upward and downward economic mobility of ethnic groups, nationalism, and diaspora. He is the author of *Muslims in Indian Economy* (2006), *Khaki and Ethnic Violence in India* (2003), and other works.

Laure Paquette is professor of political science at Lakehead University in Thunder Bay, Ontario, Canada. Dr. Paquette has been invited to speak in over 25 countries. She has held a number of fellowships (NATO, Japan Foundation, Canadian International Institute for Peace and Security, Chiang Ching-Kuo Foundation,

CIHR/CHRSF). Dr. Paquette has published 12 books, including *Strategic Activism* and *Political Strategy and Tactics.*

Morris Rossabi is professor of Chinese and inner Asian history at the City University of New York and author of *Khubilai Khan* (1988), *Voyager from Xanadu* (1992), and *China and Inner Asia* (1975). His latest book, *Modern Mongolia: From Khans to Commissars to Capitalists* (University of California Press, 2005) focuses on developments in Mongolia since the collapse of communism in 1990. Dr. Rossabi earned his PhD from Columbia University.

Naveed S. Sheikh teaches International Relations in the School of Politics, International Relations, and Philosophy (SPIRE) at Keele University in the United Kingdom. Educated in the United Kingdom, at the universities of Buckingham, Durham, and Cambridge, he has held research appointments at Harvard University, the Rajiv Gandhi Foundation (New Delhi), Hosei University (Tokyo), the University of Notre Dame, and the University of Louisville. His research interests include identity in security studies, the evolution of Muslim radicalism, and the international politics of Islam. He is the author of *The New Politics of Islam: Pan-Islamic Foreign Policy in a World of State* (Routledge) and *Saudi State, Wahhabi World: The Globalization of Muslim Radicalism* (Praeger). He is also the editor of the journal published by Routledge, *Totalitarian Movements and Political Religions.*

Brian Glyn Williams is assistant professor of Islamic history at the University of Massachusetts, Dartmouth. Prior to this appointment, he was professor of Middle Eastern history at the University of London. He is the author of *The Crimean Tatars, The Diaspora Experience and the Forging of a Nation*, and numerous articles on Islam and the Middle East. Dr. Williams has spent considerable time in the Islamic world and his field research includes time spent with nomads descended from the Mongols in Kazakhstan, interviews with Kosovo Liberation Army commanders in Kosovo and Macedonia, travels in the Middle East from Turkey to Egypt, time spent in pre-war Bosnia, and most recently, he has lived with a powerful anti-Taliban warlord in northern Afghanistan where he interviewed Taliban prisoners. He has given speeches at Harvard University, the London School of Economics, the Naval War Academy, and Britain's premiere foreign policy think tank, the International Institute for Strategic Studies. Dr Williams currently writes on issues related to Al Qaeda terrorism for the Washington DC-based Jamestown Foundation's widely respected journal, the *Terrorism Monitor* and has served as a terrorism advisor for Britain's Scotland Yard.

Moataz Fattah is associate professor of political science at Central Michigan University, USA, and Cairo University, Egypt. Dr. Fattah is the author of three books, two published in Arabic and one English-language book, *Democratic Values in the Muslim World* (Lynn Reinner, 2006). He has published several articles and book chapters in both Arabic and English. Dr. Fattah earned his PhD from Western Michigan University.

Muqtadar Khan is associate professor in the Department of Political Science and International Relations at the University of Delaware and the rirector of Islamic Studies. He is the author of *American Muslims: Bridging Faith and Freedom* (Amana, 2002), *Jihad for Jerusalem: Identity and Strategy in International Relations* (Praeger, 2004), *Islamic Democratic Discourse* (Lexington Books, 2006), and *Debating Moderate Islam* (University of Utah Press, 2007).

INDEX